CREDIT UNIONS

CREDIT UNIONS:
A MOVEMENT BECOMES
AN INDUSTRY

Olin S. Pugh
F. Jerry Ingram

UNIVERSITY OF SOUTH CAROLINA

Reston Publishing Company, Inc.
A Prentice-Hall Company
Reston, Virginia

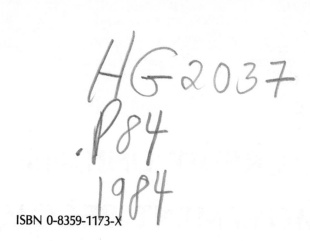

ISBN 0-8359-1173-X

Printed in the United States of America

Preface

This book attempts to fill a significant gap in the literature on credit unions. While there were several general studies of the credit union movement in the 1960s and early 1970s, there are no recent studies on the industry as it exists today. The current status of the credit union industry is such that it merits consideration and understanding both within and outside the industry. Credit unions now possess the capability of becoming a formidable competitive force in the savings and consumer credit sectors of the financial marketplace. While credit unions are becoming a factor in the payment and credit mechanism of the nation, they are not well understood and appreciated in many sectors. Their unique history is not well recognized. As the industry evolves as a modern financial intermediary mechanism, it is desirable to have a fairly comprehensive treatment of its recent trends available to the interested public.

Many individuals made important contributions to this study. Research and advisory assistance was rendered by several professional staff members of both the National Credit Union Administration and the Credit Union National Association. The overall support of the College of Business Administration of the University of South Carolina was outstanding as was the assistance of several graduate assistants. The typing and manuscript assistance of Anne Davis and Kay Elledge has been noteworthy at all times.

Anyone familiar with the credit union industry has to be impressed by the devotion and dedication of many thousands of volunteers who made the industry possible. While the role of the volunteer may not be as obvious in the industry at the present as it was in the past, we dedicate this work to the volunteers and sponsoring agencies which nurtured a fledgling movement into an organized and effective industry.

Olin S. Pugh
F. Jerry Ingram
Columbia, South Carolina

Contents

Automated Teller Machines
Issues and Problems Confronting Credit Unions as
    They Come of Age in the 1980s
Credit Unions in the National Financial
    Marketplace
Interest Rate Considerations
Recent Credit Union Developments
Regulatory and General Changes in 1981-1982
Structural and Competitive Problems
Prospective Structural Changes
Credit Union Industry Prospects

A Movement Becomes An Industry

EARLY HISTORY OF THE MOVEMENT

A (federal) credit union is presently defined as "a cooperative association organized. . . . for the purpose of promoting thrift among its members and creating a source of credit for provident or productive purposes."[1] This definition is reflective of the views held by the founders of the credit union movement in the nineteenth century. The modern credit union remains a member-owned, member-controlled nonprofit organization striving to meet the regular financial needs of its members. Credit unionism grew out of the recognized needs of lower income groups at a time when neither an established outlet for small savings nor personal credit facilities were readily available to the masses.

Roots

The roots of the cooperative credit movement lie in the more general cooperative movements in Germany during the 1840s. Cooperative credit societies represented a blending of humanitarian and religious concerns over the financial fate of the working classes, including both urban and rural groups. The "common bond" approach

[1] National Credit Union Administration, *The Federal Credit Union Act as Amended to March 31, 1980,* Washington, 1980.

to membership in the credit societies was emphasized as a means of maintaining a feeling of mutual responsibility.

Credit cooperatives were established in Germany in the mid-nineteenth century by Schulze-Delitzsch and Raiffeisen on a democratic basis. The movement developed rather slowly but did spread geographically.[2] Alphonse Desjardins established the first cooperative bank in Quebec Province in 1900 and his influence was extended to the United States a few years later. The major force in moving the cooperative credit concept to the United States was the interest and financial support of Mr. Edward Filene, a wealthy Boston merchant. Filene's interest in the cooperative credit movement grew out of his extensive travels throughout the world in 1907. He observed cooperative banking as a means of improving the economic lot of the poor and working classes in other nations. Filene encouraged Pierre Jay, Commissioner of Banking for Massachusetts, to support cooperative credit societies. Jay brought Desjardins from Canada to support the Massachusetts Credit Union Act of 1909. In the same year, Desjardins helped to organize the first legally chartered cooperative credit society in the United States in Manchester, New Hampshire. Massachusetts enacted the first complete credit union act in 1909. Filene saw the credit societies as an encouragement to provide personal thrift and a source of helpful loans to working groups.

The Movement Organizes

In spite of the philanthropic and humanitarian motives involved in the credit union movement little was accomplished for a number of years. The Russell Sage Foundation provided some financial support in New York and elsewhere but the movement still languished. By 1919 Filene believed that a sufficient number of credit unions had been organized in Massachusetts, New York, and North Carolina to justify an organized move at the national level in the

---

[2] For the most detailed discussion of the formative years of the credit unionism see J. Carroll Moody and Gilbert C. Fite, *The Credit Union Movement,* University of Nebraska Press, Lincoln, 1971. Also see National Credit Union Administration, *Chartering and Organizing Manual for Federal Credit,* Washington, March 1980.

name of a National Committee on People's Banks. The financial and industrial trends of the 1920's provided a more favorable environment for the development of credit societies. A more industrialized nation with developing consumer goods industries resulted in more savings by workers as well as greater demands for consumer credit. Mutual savings banks and Morris Plan banks were being developed during the same period of development.

The Massachusetts Credit Union Association employed Roy F. Bergengren as managing director in 1920 with the understanding that his major role was to be a promoter of the credit union movement. Filene provided much of the financial support required to operate a Credit Union National Extension Bureau managed by Bergengren. Through this Bureau, Bergengren promoted enabling legislation authorizing credit unions in many states and assisted in the organization of individual credit unions. Filene also had established the Twentieth Century Fund which became the primary financing agency for the credit union extension work by Bergengren. Although considerable effort was devoted to the establishment of credit unions among small farmers in the South, little was accomplished. Filene did not believe that rural credit unions were feasible and this phase of the extension work was reduced. Nevertheless, overall progress had occurred in the credit union movement. By 1930, thirty-two states had enacted credit union legislation and 1,100 individual credit unions had been organized.[3]

The New Deal

The economic depression of the 1930s gave additional impetus to the cooperative movement in general and to credit unionism in particular. Political support for credit unions emerged in the Congress, and in 1932 the Congress authorized credit unions for the District of Columbia as well as included credit unions among those institutions eligible to borrow from the Reconstruction Finance Corporation. More general federal legislation was enacted in the form of the Federal Credit Union Act of June 26, 1934. This Act was designed "to promote thrift and provide credit for provident

[3] Moody and Fite, p. 126.

and productive purposes" through the chartering, supervision and examination of Federal credit unions. Bergengren considered this act as the "greatest single step forward in the history of the credit union movement."[4]

When the Federal Credit Union Act was passed in 1934, 38 states had enacted credit union laws and almost 2,500 credit unions were in operation. Five state leagues of credit unions were also in operation. The zealous efforts of Bergengren and Filene had shown significant results to which the Congress contributed immeasurably in the 1934 Act. With this as a springboard for action, Bergengren and Filene held a national meeting of credit union delegates in Colorado in 1934 which led to the development of the Credit Union National Association (CUNA). The further development of state leagues to affiliate with CUNA became a basic objective. National headquarters of CUNA were opened in Madison, Wisconsin in 1935. By the end of 1935 there were 3,372 operating credit unions with $50 million of assets and by 1939 there were 7,964 associations with $194 million of assets.[5] As Federal charters grew, states were stimulated to take a greater interest in the credit union movement. Further support for the movement came in 1937 when President Roosevelt joined with the Congress in enacting legislation prohibiting the taxation of federal credit unions except on the basis of real or personal properties.

Despite what appears as a remarkable growth rate the credit union remained a very small part of the financial community in 1941 with only $322 million in assets. World War II brought a marked slowdown in the movement. Consumer credit restrictions, shortages of goods, and an emphasis upon war financing resulted in a slowdown of credit unionism. The number of active credit unions actually declined during the war years. It was not until 1950 that the movement surpassed its prewar position in number of credit unions operating, that is 9,891 in 1941 and 10,591 in 1950. The number of credit union members ranged around the 3 to 4 million levels during these years.

The Federal Credit Union Program was transferred from the Farm Credit Administration to the Federal Deposit Insurance Corporation in April 1942. The relationships of CUNA with the FCA had become

[4] Moody and Fite, p. 166.
[5] Moody and Fite, p. 359.

strained but there was scant improvement in the relationship with the FDIC. In June 1948, the Credit Union Section was transformed into the Bureau of Federal Credit Unions assigned to the Social Security Administration. CUNA officials were restive over the fees charged by the federal agencies as well as the latent fear that CUNA's influence in the movement might be challenged by the federal agency. One outlet for CUNA's idealistic zeal had become the development of credit unions throughout the world. The World Extension Division of CUNA maintained the original philosophy of the credit union movement which had begun to erode on the domestic front as the need for "business-like" procedures became more obvious to the leaders of credit unionism.

RECENT GROWTH PATTERNS

Credit unions had to await the growth of worker incomes and the consumer credit industry in general before the movement could develop into a role of significance in the economy. As consumer income and consumer credit exploded in the late 1950s, 1960s and early 1970s, the credit union movement developed accordingly. Further Congressional and regulatory support together with the growth of saving through financial intermediaries contributed to the rapid pace of credit unionism in recent decades.

The number of credit unions in the United States grew from 10,591 with 4.6 million members in 1950, to 20,047 with 12.0 million members in 1960. Total assets jumped from $1 billion in 1950 to $5.6 billion in 1960. Such an impressive growth record was the result of overall economic growth and the active promotional efforts of CUNA, the CUNA Mutual Insurance Society, and state credit union leagues. This was the decade of tremendous growth in the number of active credit unions. It remained for the following decades to permit the overall growth of the average size of credit unions and to project many of them into coping with national money and capital market conditions.

During most of the decade of the 1960s the number of active credit unions remained in the 21,000 to 23,000 range. In the United

States, credit union membership increased from 12 million in 1960 to 22.8 million in 1970. While membership was growing 89 percent in the decade, total assets jumped from $5.6 billion to $17.9 billion, or 218 percent. The 1960s was the decade when the credit union movement began to shift its emphasis from organizing new societies to developing those already chartered.

The passage of federal legislation establishing the National Credit Union Administration in 1970 was another milestone in the development of credit unionism. This new federal supervisory agency and the accompanying program of federal insurance for savings added tremendously to the stability of the movement and contributed to the financial growth of the movement. Credit union membership grew from 22.8 million in 1970 to 46 million in 1980, with total assets rising from $17.9 billion to $73.2 billion in 1980 (Tables 1-1 and 1-2). Thus the rapid pace of growth of the movement was maintained throughout most of the 1970s.

From a movement originating with a spirit of cooperative idealism by the 1970s credit union leaders had to confront the fact that the nature of the movement had changed greatly and that they were serving members with different patterns of employment and needs. Adequate savings could not be derived from the lower income groups and the very poor were not good credit risks. The ultimate effect was that the credit union movement developed more of a middle-income orientation than one devoted to lower-income groups. Thus, the decade of the 1970s highlighted the fact that while there were those in the movement stressing the cooperative and idealistic aspects of credit unionism the main thrust of management became one of establishing sound management practices designed to stabilize the individual units while permitting steady growth. The money market conditions of 1978-1980 heightened these tensions within the industry and they are still being worked out in the 1980s. One of the more obvious conflicts surrounds the degree to which saver interests may have been subjugated to borrower interests in credit union management.

From a Consumer Movement to a National Market Force

Credit unions in the United States now have 47 million members and $85 billion in assets. What has been thought of as a small cooperative credit movement operating with volunteer committee mem-

Table 1-1   Growth in Member Savings and Total Assets of State and Federal Chartered Credit Unions, Selected Years, 1933-1980 (in millions)

	State Chartered		Federal Chartered		Total	
Year	Savings	Assets	Savings	Assets	Savings	Assets
1933	29.5	35.5	–	–	23.5	35.5
1936	59.4	73.6	8.5	9.1	67.9	82.7
1939	126.0	145.8	43.3	47.8	169.3	193.6
1942	193.1	221.1	109.8	119.6	302.9	340.7
1945	242.7	281.5	140.6	153.1	383.3	435.1
1949	445.4	510.7	285.0	316.4	730.4	827.1
1951	622.1	693.6	457.4	504.7	1,079.5	1,198.3
1954	1,109.2	1,237.2	931.4	1,033.2	2,040.6	2,270.4
1957	1,792.4	2,021.1	1,589.1	1,788.8	3,381.5	3,809.9
1960	2,637.0	2,988.5	2,344.3	2,669.7	4,981.3	5,658.2
1961	2,966.4	3,353.9	2,673.5	3,028.3	5,639.9	6,782.1
1962	3,311.5	3,758.2	3,020.3	3,429.8	6,331.8	7,188.0
1963	3,711.5	4,213.1	3,452.6	3,916.5	7,164.1	8,129.6
1964	4,207.7	4,800.0	4,017.4	4,559.4	8,225.1	9,359.4
1965	4,682.4	5,385.2	4,538.5	5,165.8	9,220.9	10,551.0
1966	5,127.3	5,937.8	4,944.0	5,668.9	10,071.3	11,606.7
1967	5,682.4	6,658.2	5,420.6	6,208.2	11,030.0	12,866.4
1968	6,326.3	7,310.1	5,986.2	6,902.2	12,312.5	14,212.3
1969	7,026.9	8,123.9	6,713.4	7,793.6	13,740.3	15,917.5
1970	7,857.5	9,088.8	7,628.8	8,860.6	15,486.3	17,949.4
1971	9,167.2	10,568.5	9,191.2	10,553.7	18,358.4	21,122.2
1972	10,669.8	12,274.9	10,956.0	12,513.6	21,625.8	24,788.5
1973	11,913.9	13,806.2	12,597.6	14,568.7	24,511.5	28,374.9
1974	13,147.7	15,233.0	14,370.7	16,714.7	27,518.4	31,947.7
1975	15,521.5	17,804.3	17,529.8	20,208.5	33,051.3	38,012.8
1976	17,967.9	20,640.0	21,130.3	24,395.9	39,098.2	45,035.9
1977	20,939.9	24,191.1	25,576.0	29,563.7	46,515.9	53,754.8
1978	23,715.5	27,587.9	29,802.5	34,760.1	53,518.0	62,347.9
1979	25,628.0	29,523.8	31,831.4	36,467.8	57,459.3	65,991.7
1980	29,480.0	33,143.0	32,263.3	40,091.8	61,743.3	73,234.8

Sources: National Credit Union Administration, *Annual Report for 1980,* and *1980 Annual Report on State Chartered Credit Unions.*

bers has evolved into a significant financial industry. This chapter attempts to set forth the recent history of credit unions in the United States.

As indicated earlier, credit unions are nonprofit cooperatives designed to provide basic financial services to their members. Such an association sells shares and makes loans available to a membership which is presumed to have a common bond of employment, or other economic or neighborhood interest. The common bond of interest has been interpreted less rigorously in recent years, thereby opening

Table 1-2   Development of State-Chartered and Federal-Chartered

Year	Active State Credit Unions	Active Federal Credit Unions	Total Active Credit Unions
1929	974	–	974
1933	2,016	–	2,016
1936	3,490	1,751	5,241
1939	4,782	3,182	7,964
1942	5,662	4,105	9,767
1945	4,923	3,760	8,683
1949	5,427	4,497	9,924
1951	5,881	5,398	11,279
1954	7,814	7,227	15,041
1957	9,463	8,735	18,198
1960	10,243	9,905	20,148
1961	10,341	10,271	20,612
1962	10,418	10,632	21,050
1963	10,427	10,955	21,382
1964	10,536	11,278	21,814
1965	10,617	11,543	22,160
1966	10,743	11,941	22,684
1967	10,858	12,210	23,068
1968	10,817	12,584	23,401
1969	10,855	12,921	23,776
1970	10,701	12,977	23,678
1971	10,553	12,717	23,270
1972	10,362	12,708	23,070
1973	10,217	12,688	22,905
1974	10,108	12,748	22,856
1975	9,874	12,737	22,611
1976	9,781	12,757	22,538
1977	9,580	12,750	22,330
1978	9,443	12,759	22,202
1979	9,274	12,738	22,012
1980	9,025	12,440	21,465

Sources: Derived from National Credit Union Administration, and Bureau of Federal Credit Unions, State Chartered

up membership to many individuals who would not have been eligible in a previous generation.

Until 1921, the credit union movement was confined to the urban working class groups of New England. The organizations largely involved the workers in the industrial plants. By 1934, credit union laws had been adopted by most states. Congress enacted the Federal Credit Union Act which enabled credit unions to be established in any state. In large measure, the credit union movement was an out-

Credit Unions, and Number of Members, Selected Years, 1929-1980

Number of Members in State Charters (000)	Number of Members in Federal Charters (000)	Total Membership (000)
264.9	–	264.9
359.6	–	359.6
854.5	315.9	1,170.4
1,459.4	849.8	2,309.2
1,797.1	1,347.5	3,144.6
1,626.4	1,216.5	2,842.9
2,271.1	1,819.6	4,090.7
2,732.5	2,463.9	5,169.4
3,756.8	3,598.8	7,355.6
4,963.8	4,897.7	9,861.5
5,971.8	6,087.4	12,059.2
6,335.8	6,542.6	12,878.4
6,745.3	7,007.6	13,752.9
7,079.6	7,499.7	14,579.3
7,530.5	8,092.0	15,622.5
8,115.2	8,640.6	16,755.8
8,650.7	9,271.9	17,922.6
9,188.9	9,873.8	19,062.7
9,720.3	10,508.5	20,228.8
10,326.5	11,301.8	21,628.3
10,852.5	11,966.2	22,818.7
11,381.7	12,702.1	24,083.8
12,118.0	13,572.3	25,690.3
12,886.1	14,665.9	27,552.0
13,580.8	15,870.4	29,451.2
14,196.4	17,066.4	31,262.8
15,129.5	18,623.8	33,753.3
16,375.4	20,426.7	36,802.1
17,460.7	23,259.3	40,720.0
18,409.5	24,789.6	43,111.0
19,234.7	26,829.4	46,014.1

Credit Unions Annual Reports, various years, and N.C.U.A. Annual Report, 1980.

growth of depression in the United States and elsewhere and was designed to provide credit to the working classes at reasonable rates. World Was II halted the growth of credit unions and a renewed impetus was not realized until the late 1940s. It was not until the last two decades or so that the industry began a growth pattern that has culminated in its present position which is now attracting so much attention in the financial community.

Credit unions are now providing federally-insured savings and share

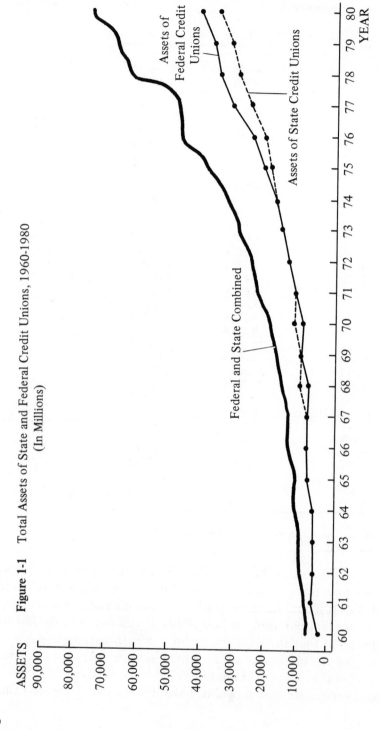

Figure 1-1 Total Assets of State and Federal Credit Unions, 1960-1980 (In Millions)

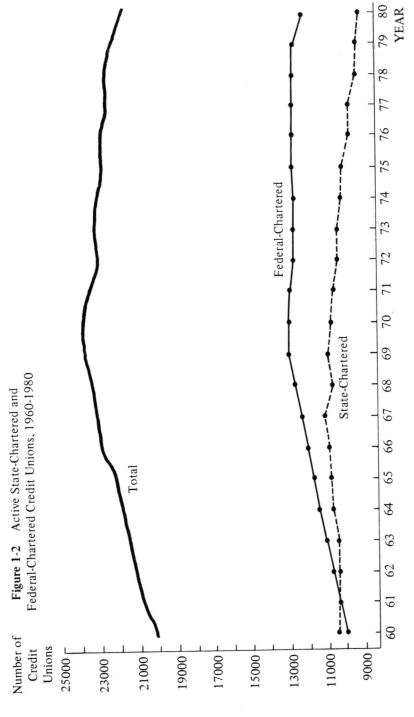

Figure 1-2 Active State-Chartered and Federal-Chartered Credit Unions, 1960-1980

draft services, issuing credit cards in certain locales, permitting pay-roll withholdings for both savings and loan repayments, and providing highly competitive rates on savings instruments and consumer loans. With lower administrative costs and no tax liability, the typical credit union can provide credit services and reward its savers at rates which are more attractive than established financial depository institutions.

Number of Active Credit Unions

Table 1-3 documents the growth of credit unions from 1936 (earliest meaningful and reliable data) through 1980. As shown in the table, credit unions were established at an impressive rate from 1936 to 1945 (65.7 percent).

However, credit unions had to await the growth of worker incomes and the widespread development of consumer credit before they could take on a role of significance in the economy. But with rising levels of consumer income and consumer credit in the 1950s and 1960s combined with the popularity of saving through financial

Table 1-3 Credit Union Growth, in Numbers and Percentage Change, Selected Years 1936-1980

Year	Active State Credit Unions	Active Federal Credit Unions	Total Active Credit Unions
1936	3,490	1,751	5,241
1945	4,923	3,760	8,683
1965	10,617	11,543	22,160
1970	10,701	12,977	23,678
1975	9,874	12,737	22,611
1980	9,025	12,440	21,465
Percentage Change Over Selected Periods			
1936-1945	41.1%	114.7%	65.7%
1945-1965	115.7	207.0	155.2
1965-1970	0.8	12.4	6.9
1970-1975	− 7.7	− 1.8	− 4.5
1975-1980	− 8.6	− 2.3	− 5.1
1970-1980	− 15.7	− 4.1	− 9.3

Source: Derived from National Credit Union Administration and Bureau of Federal Credit Unions, *Annual Reports.*

intermediaries, credit unions grew very rapidly (155.2 percent from 1945 to 1965). In the 1960s and 1970s, the overall support of the Congress and federal regulatory authorities have also been contributing factors to their growth. The number of active credit unions in the United States remained in the 21,000 to 23,000 range during the decade of the 1960s and reached its zenith in 1969. Since then, the number of credit unions has declined slightly (-9.3 percent from 1970 to 1980).

Membership

Perhaps more important than the number of credit unions is the number of members. Table 1-4 details the growth in credit union membership from 1936 to 1980. Again, the percentage increases were very impressive during the periods 1936-1945 and 1945-1965 (142.9 percent and 489.4 percent, respectively). This rather hectic pace diminished from the mid-1960s to the mid-1970s but has been on the upswing since that time. In fact, credit union membership more than doubled during the 1970s.

Table 1-4   Growth in Credit Union Membership in Numbers and Percentage Change, Selected Years, 1936-1980

Year	Number of Members in State Charters	Number of Members in Federal Charters	Total Membership
	(000)	(000)	(000)
1936	854.5	315.9	1,170.4
1945	1,626.4	1,216.5	2,842.9
1965	8,115.2	8,640.6	16,755.8
1970	10,852.5	11,966.2	22,818.7
1975	14,196.4	17,066.4	31,262.8
1980	19,234.7	26,829.4	46,064.1
Percentage Change Over Selected Periods			
1936-1945	90.3%	285.1%	142.9%
1945-1965	398.9	610.3	489.4
1965-1970	33.7	38.5	36.2
1970-1975	30.8	42.6	37.0
1975-1980	35.5	57.2	47.3
1970-1980	77.2	124.2	101.9

Source: Derived from NCUA and Bureau of Federal Credit Unions, *Annual Reports.*

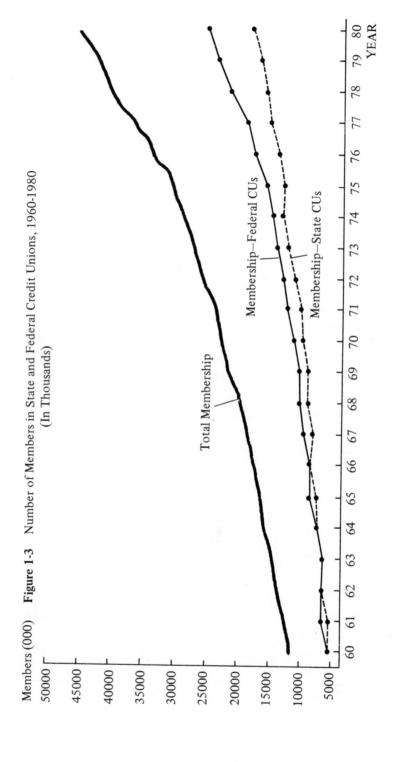

Members (000)

Figure 1-3   Number of Members in State and Federal Credit Unions, 1960-1980
(In Thousands)

Total Membership

Membership—Federal CUs

Membership—State CUs

YEAR

14

Total Assets and Total Savings

Not only has membership in credit unions registered constant growth, but the members were depositing ever increasing amounts. Tables 1-5 and 1-6 demonstrate the growing importance of credit union deposits in terms of both total assets and total savings. While roughly the same general patterns of growth can be observed in Tables 1-4, 1-5 and 1-6, assets and savings clearly grew proportionately faster than membership. This reflects both the growing affluence of credit union members and their confidence in (and satisfaction with) their credit union.

State Vs Federal Credit Unions

Tables 1-3 through 1-6 also allow an assessment of the relative importance of state vs federal credit unions over the period. First, note in Table 1-3 that the growth in the number of federal credit unions is consistently larger (or the decline smaller) in each time segment tabulated. This same federal dominance also prevails in terms of membership, assets and deposits as shown in Tables 1-4, 1-5 and 1-6, respectively.

Credit Union Growth by Common Bond

Unfortunately, historical data on the development of the credit union movement by common bond grouping is rather sketchy. Consequently, this aspect of credit union growth can best be tracked since the mid-1960s for federal credit unions. Table 1-7 indicates that, in terms of the number of credit unions, the only dynamism registered from 1966-1980 was among residential (or community) common bond credit unions. This sector more than doubled over the period while occupational and associational groups were essentially flat. Some of the increase in residential common bonds can be attributed to the federal government's active encouragement of credit union development in urban poverty neighborhoods. However, current data on life of CUs by common bond clearly suggest that most charters were occupational during years of rapid growth.

Table 1-5 Growth in Total Assets of State and Federal Chartered Credit Unions, Selected Years, 1936-1980

Year	State Chartered	Federal Chartered	Total Assets
	(000,000)	(000,000)	(000,000)
1936	$ 73.6	$ 9.1	$ 82.7
1945	281.5	153.1	435.1
1965	5,385.2	5,165.8	10,551.0
1970	9,088.8	8,860.6	17,949.4
1975	17,804.3	20,208.5	38,012.8
1980	33,143.0	40,091.8	73,234.8

Percentage Change Over Selected Periods

1936-1945	282.5%	1,582.4%	426.1%
1945-1965	1,813.0	3,274.1	2,324.9
1965-1970	68.8	71.5	70.1
1970-1975	95.9	128.1	111.8
1975-1980	86.2	98.4	92.7
1970-1980	264.7	352.5	308.0

Source: NCUA, *Annual Reports* and *Annual Reports for State Chartered Credit Unions.*

Table 1-6 Growth in Member Savings in State and Federal Chartered Credit Unions, Selected Years, 1936-1980

Year	State Chartered Savings	Federal Chartered Savings	Total Member Savings
	(000,000)	(000,000)	(000,000)
1936	$ 59.4	$ 8.5	$ 67.9
1945	242.7	140.6	383.3
1965	4,682.4	4,538.5	9,220.9
1970	7,858.5	7,628.8	15,486.3
1975	15,521.5	17,529.8	33,051.3
1980	29,480.0	32,263.3	61,263.3

Percentage Change Over Selected Periods

1936-1945	308.6%	1,554.1%	464.5%
1945-1965	1,829.3	3,127.9	2,305.7
1965-1970	67.8	68.1	67.9
1970-1975	97.5	129.8	113.4
1975-1980	89.9	84.0	86.8
1970-1980	275.2	322.9	298.7

Source: NCUA, *Annual Reports* and *Annual Reports for State Chartered Credit Unions.*

Table 1-7 Federal Credit Unions by Common Bond Groupings (1966-80)

Year	Occupational	Associational	Residential	Total
1966	9,840	1,848	253	11,941
1967	9,999	1,930	281	12,210
1968	10,219	1,999	366	12,584
1969	10,452	2,010	459	12,921
1970	10,508	1,974	495	12,977
1971	10,378	1,867	472	12,717
1972	10,374	1,857	477	12,708
1973	10,367	1,838	483	12,688
1974	10,391	1,861	496	12,748
1975	10,378	1,898	491	12,737
1976	10,354	1,899	504	12,757
1977	10,344	1,891	515	12,750
1978	10,293	1,934	532	12,759
1979	10,229	1,968	541	12,738
1980	9,991	1,918	531	12,440

Percentage Growth Over Selected Periods

1966-1970	6.8%	6.8%	95.6%	8.7%
1970-1973	−1.3	−6.9	− 2.4	−2.2
1973-1975	0.1	3.2	1.7	0.4
1975-1980	−3.7	1.1	8.1	−2.3
1966-1980	1.5	3.8	109.9	4.2
1970-1980	−4.9	−2.8	7.3	− 4.1

Source: NCUA, *Annual Reports.*

Table 1-8 also details the membership distribution shifts in federal credit unions over the 1966-1980 period. While associational credit unions maintain their share of membership, the residential common bond group doubled its relative proportion at the expense of the occupational group.   Moreover, as indicated in Table 1-9, the distribution of total assets also shifted during the period. The residential group tripled its share, the associational group increased its share from 7.0 percent in 1966 to 10.5 percent in 1980 and the occupational group dropped from 91.8 percent to 85.9 percent during the period.

However, these shifts did not result in a significant change in the occupational group's dominance of the industry in absolute terms. Note in Table 1-10 that in 1980 occupational credit unions held over $31.1 billion of federal chartered assets of $36.3 billion in savings deposits compared to $3.9 billion for associational credit unions and only $1.3 billion for the residential group.

Table 1-8   Membership in Federal Credit Unions by Percentage
And by Common Bond Grouping (1966-1980)

Year	Occupational	Associational	Residential	Total
1966	82.4%	15.5%	2.1%	100.0%
1967	81.9	15.8	2.3	100.0
1968	81.2	15.9	2.9	100.0
1969	80.9	15.6	3.5	100.0
1970	81.0	15.2	3.8	100.0
1971	81.6	14.7	3.7	100.0
1972	81.6	14.6	3.8	100.0
1973	81.7	14.5	3.8	100.0
1974	81.5	14.6	3.9	100.0
1975	81.2	14.9	3.9	100.0
1976	81.2	14.9	3.9	100.0
1977	81.1	14.8	4.1	100.0
1978	80.7	15.1	4.2	100.0
1979	80.3	15.5	4.2	100.0
1980	80.3%	15.4%	4.3%	100.0%

Source: NCUA, *Annual Reports.*

Table 1-9   Distribution of Federal Credit Unions
Total Assets by Common Bond Groupings

Year	Occupational	Associational	Residential
1966	91.8%	7.0%	1.2%
1967	91.9	6.8	1.3
1968	92.0	6.6	1.4
1969	92.1	6.3	1.6
1970	92.2	6.0	1.8
1971	92.5	5.6	1.9
1972	92.7	5.4	1.9
1973	92.5	5.2	2.3
1974	92.1	5.5	2.4
1975	92.3	5.3	2.4
1976	91.6	5.8	2.6
1977	90.7	6.5	2.8
1978	90.5	6.7	2.8
1979	89.4	7.5	3.1
1980	85.9%	10.5%	3.6%

Source: NCUA *Annual Reports.*

Table 1-10   Amount of Share Accounts in Federal Credit Unions,
By Common Bond Groupings (in thousands)

Year	Occupational	%	Associational	%	Residential	%	Total
1966	$ 4,539,579	91.8%	$ 32,850	6.9%	$ 61,603	1.3%	$ 4,944,033
1967	4,982,495	91.9	368,258	6.8	69,910	1.3	5,420,663
1968	5,510,865	92.1	394,245	6.6	81,071	1.3	5,986,181
1969	6,187,986	92.2	420,163	6.3	105,237	1.5	6,713,385
1970	7,070,265	92.3	454,407	6.0	134,132	1.7	7,628,805
1971	8,510,792	92.6	509,540	5.5	170,850	1.9	9,191,182
1972	10,172,249	92.8	576,634	5.3	207,124	1.9	10,956,077
1973	11,666,450	92.6	650,679	5.2	280,479	2.2	12,597,607
1974	13,260,596	92.3	770,880	5.4	339,268	2.3	14,370,744
1975	16,215,796	92.5	901,384	5.1	412,643	2.4	17,529,823
1976	19,402,380	91.8	1,196,390	5.7	531,522	2.5	21,130,293
1977	23,292,261	91.1	1,587,940	6.2	695,816	2.7	25,576,017
1978	27,031,764	90.7	1,917,171	6.4	853,568	2.9	29,802,504
1979	28,374,773	89.1	2,456,054	7.7	1,000,573	3.2	31,831,400
1980	31,048,059	85.6	3,911,264	10.8	1,304,020	3.6	36,263,343

Source: NCUA *Annual Reports.*

Asset Size Distribution

All Credit Unions

Data on credit union assets and number of operating institutions reveal that credit unions have grown in size of operating unit, both in assets and in membership. Table 1-11 reviews recent changes (1965-1980) in the asset size distribution of operating credit unions (both state and federal). The table clearly indicates that the trend is toward even larger credit unions. In 1965, credit unions with more than $5,000,000 in assets accounted for only 27.5 percent of total credit union assets. By 1980, this group held 77.2 percent of all credit union assets while the proportion held by the smaller asset size categories ($250,000 and less) had diminished from over 11 percent in 1965 to only 1 percent in 1980. The data indicates that the very small credit union plays a rapidly diminishing role in the industry.

Table 1-12 makes an interesting point. The actual to potential credit union member ratio varies substantially with asset size. Only 1 in 4 potential members elect to join the smaller credit unions but

Table 1-11 Percentage Distribution of All Operating Credit Unions
By Asset Size, Selected Years, 1965-1980

All Credit Unions (In thousands of dollars)	1965	1970	1975	1978	1979	1980
Less than $100						
Number	45.9	37.9	23.3	16.2	14.8	13.7
Percentage of total assets	3.7	2.1	.7	.3	.3	.2
100.0–249.9						
Number	21.5	21.4	20.3	17.9	17.2	17.3
Percentage of total assets	7.4	4.7	2.1	1.1	1.0	.7
250.0–499.9						
Number	12.9	14.4	16.3	16.2	16.4	15.9
Percentage of total assets	9.6	6.8	3.5	2.2	2.0	1.7
500.0–999.9						
Number	9.3	11.0	14.2	15.5	15.7	15.5
Percentage of total assets	13.7	10.2	6.1	4.0	3.7	3.2
1,000.0–1,999.9						
Number	5.6	7.4	10.7	12.8	13.1	13.4
Percentage of total assets	16.1	13.7	9.1	6.7	6.4	5.6
2,000.0–4,999.9						
Number	3.5	5.2	8.5	10.8	11.6	12.1
Percentage of total assets	22.0	20.9	16.0	12.3	12.1	11.1
5,000.0–and over						
Number	1.3	2.7	6.7	10.5	11.2	12.1
Percentage of total assets	27.5	41.6	62.5	73.4	74.5	77.2
Percentage of total assets	100.0%	100.0%	100.0%	100.0%	100.0%	100.0%

Source: NCUA, *Annual Reports of State-Chartered Credit Unions.*

40-60 percent of the potential members opt to join the larger (and better established) credit unions. More ominously, the table also indicates some erosion of the membership ratio in all asset size categories during the decade of the 1970s.

State vs. Federal

The asset size distribution trends noted above also hold true when state and federal credit union data are analyzed separately. Table 1-13 shows that the typical state and federal credit union grew substantially in asset size from 1965 to 1980. However, the table does demonstrate that a larger percentage of federal credit unions moved into the $5,000,000 + category over the period.

Table 1-12 Federal Credit Union Membership Trends by Asset Size, 1971-1980

Asset Size Category	1971	1975	1979	1980
Less than $250,000				
Actual members	1,738,951	1,412,995	1,076,229	1,018,783
Potential members	6,353,851	5,508,221	4,737,682	3,974,659
Actual to potential ratio	27.4	25.7	22.7	25.6
$250,000–$999,999				
Actual members	2,517,025	2,596,384	2,681,255	2,600,130
Potential members	4,396,429	5,193,252	6,149,425	5,966,274
Actual to potential ratio	57.3	50.0	43.6	43.6
$1,000,000–$4,999,999				
Actual members	4,159,840	4,688,116	5,781,300	5,653,661
Potential members	6,114,103	7,637,001	10,363,035	10,566,890
Actual to potential ratio	68.0	61.4	55.8	53.5
$5,000,000–$19,999,999				
Actual members	3,048,664	4,395,539	6,530,006	6,200,062
Potential members	4,151,555	6,593,862	10,349,713	9,923,864
Actual to potential ratio	73.4	66.7	63.1	62.5
$20,000,000 or more				
Actual members	1,237,655	4,013,394	8,720,857	9,046,451
Potential members	2,047,346	5,313,765	12,223,719	15,666,172
Actual to potential ratio	60.5	75.5	71.3	57.7
Total				
Actual members	12,702,135	17,106,428	24,789,647	24,519,087
Potential members	23,063,274	30,246,101	43,823,574	46,097,859
Actual to potential ratio	55.1	56.6	56.6	53.2

Source: Calculated from NCUA data in *Annual Reports.*

Reserves

The reserves, a part of the accumulated capital of credit unions, has also grown substantially in recent years. Table 1-14 indicates well over a four-fold increase in the total dollar reserves of federal credit unions from 1966 to 1980. The table also reveals that credit unions of all common bond types enjoyed marked increases in reserves of the same period but with the residential group accumulating reserves more rapidly.

On the other hand, Table 1-15, shows a noticeable decline in reserves as a percentage of total assets. The ratio for all federal unions declined during the 1966-1980 time period from 6.0 percent to 3.7 percent. Similar deterioration can be noted in all three common

Table 1-13 Percentage Distribution of State and Federal Credit Unions by Asset Size, December 1970, 1975, and 1980 (in thousands)

Year	Total	Less than $100	$100.0–249.9	$250.0–499.9	$500.0–999.9	$1,000.0–1,999.9	$2,000.0–4,999.9	$5,000.0 and over
1970								
State credit unions operating	100.0	36.4	22.0	14.0	11.3	7.7	5.4	3.2
Percentage of total assets of state credit unions	100.0	1.9%	4.3%	5.9%	9.4%	12.6%	19.2%	46.7%
Federal credit unions operating	100.0	39.2	20.8	14.7	10.7	7.2	5.1	2.3
Percentage of total assets of federal credit unions	100.0	2.3	5.0	7.7	11.0	15.0	22.7	36.3
All operating credit unions	100.0	37.9	21.4	14.4	11.0	7.4	5.2	2.7
Percentage of total assets of all credit unions	100.0	2.1	4.7	6.8	10.2	13.7	20.9	41.6
1975								
State credit unions operating	100.0	22.9	20.4	16.1	14.1	10.7	8.7	7.1
Percentage of total assets of state credit unions	100.0	.7	2.0	3.3	5.7	8.7	15.8	63.9
Federal credit unions	100.0	23.7	20.3	16.4	14.3	10.6	8.3	6.4
Percentage of total assets of federal credit unions	100.0	.7	2.1	3.7	6.4	9.5	16.2	61.3
All operating credit unions	100.0	23.3	20.3	16.3	14.2	10.7	8.5	6.7
Total assets of all credit unions	100.0	.7	2.1	3.5	6.1	9.1	16.0	62.5
1980								
State credit unions operating	100.0	12.8	17.6	15.3	15.2	13.7	12.3	13.2
Percentage of total assets of state credit unions	100.0	.2	.9	1.5	3.0	5.4	10.5	78.5
Federal credit unions operating	100.0	14.3	17.2	16.3	15.7	13.2	12.0	11.3
Percentage of total assets of federal credit unions	100.0	.2	.9	1.8	3.5	5.8	11.7	76.1
All credit unions	100.0	13.7	17.3	15.9	15.5	13.4	12.1	12.1
Percentage of total assets of all credit unions	100.0	.2%	.9%	1.7%	3.2%	5.6%	11.1%	77.2%

Source: NCUA, *Annual Reports of State Chartered Credit Unions.*

Table 1-14   Amount of Reserves of Federal Credit Unions
By Common Bond Grouping ($ millions)

Year	Occupational	Associational	Residential	Total
1966	$ 312,388	$22,533	$ 3,958	$ 338,879
1967	359,297	25,331	4,845	389,473
1968	413,444	28,148	5,765	447,357
1969	474,879	31,053	7,896	513,828
1970	540,010	34,541	10,369	584,920
1971	597,222	37,121	12,580	646,923
1972	670,070	40,305	14,733	725,108
1973	752,990	43,954	19,117	816,061
1974	841,391	49,089	22,656	913,137
1975	949,391	54,634	25,907	1,029,932
1976	1,087,944	60,649	31,881	1,180,475
1977	1,218,594	67,776	38,284	1,324,655
1978	1,261,003	65,763	38,646	1,365,414
1979	1,320,694	72,565	45,901	1,439,160
1980	$1,357,163	$80,730	$62,699	$1,490,593

Source: NCUA *Annual Reports.*
*Reserves include Regular Reserves and Other Reserves. Other Reserves include reserves for contingencies, supplemental reserves, and special reserves for losses.

Table 1-15   Reserves* as a Percent of Total of Total Assets of
Federal Credit Unions by Common Bond Groupings

Year	Occupational	Associational	Residential	Total
1966	6.0%	5.7%	5.7%	6.0%
1967	6.3	6.0	6.1	6.3
1968	6.5	6.2	6.2	6.5
1969	6.6	6.3	6.4	6.6
1970	6.6	6.5	6.6	6.6
1971	6.1	6.3	6.3	6.1
1972	5.8	6.0	6.1	5.8
1973	5.6	5.8	5.8	5.6
1974	5.5	5.4	5.6	5.5
1975	5.1	5.1	5.3	5.1
1976	4.9	4.3	5.1	4.8
1977	4.5	3.5	4.6	4.5
1978	4.0	2.8	3.9	3.9
1979	4.1	2.7	4.1	4.0
1980	3.9%	1.9%	3.7%	3.7%

Source: NCUA *Annual Reports.*
*Reserves include Regular Reserves and Other Reserves. Other Reserves include reserves for contingencies, supplemental reserves, and special reserves for losses.

bond groupings, but the associational groups decline (5.7 percent to 1.9 percent) is particularly sharp. This situation has prompted widespread concern regarding the capital adequacy of the industry and this matter is currently under careful study by the NCUA and others.

OTHER MEASURES OF CREDIT UNION GROWTH

Credit unions operated for many years as small organizations staffed largely by volunteers as members of operating committees. The average size of credit unions in the United States in 1950 was about $100,000 in assets. By 1965 average assets per credit union were $477,000, and by 1978 the average size was $2.8 million and in 1980, $3.4 million. The median size credit union is much less, however, standing at only $575,000 in 1978 and about $750,000 in 1980.

The Navy Federal Credit Union in Washington reported assets of $866 million in 1980 and was the largest credit union. Some 54 credit unions had assets above $100 million each at year end 1980. A recent estimate of the National Credit Union Administration notes that some 16,200 of the 21,500 credit unions in the nation have assets below $2 million. Indeed, there are still 10,000 credit unions with assets below $500,000 each which remain outside the mainstream of the industry.

Employment in credit unions remains relatively low but the pace of growth is impressive. Full-time employment grew from 20,582 in 1965 to 73,500 in 1979, or 257 percent. There are still significant contributions of time and effort by part-time employees and volunteers. The Credit Union National Association reported in 1980 that there were 26,540 part-time employees and 145,500 volunteers actively involved in the industry. While the role of the volunteers in the actual operations of the larger credit unions is no doubt nominal in many cases, they still provide many of the essential services in the smaller associations. The many active volunteers are of considerable value both in terms of their contributions to the management process as well as spokesmen in the political arena for the basic spirit of a cooperative credit system.

The close correlation in the growth of average savings balances per member and average dollar loans outstanding is apparent from the data in Table 1-16. Average savings per member grew from $563 in

1965 to $1,497 in 1980, while loans outstanding per member advanced from $496 to $1,118. Savings balances and loan balances cover a wide range in size from a few dollars to $20,000 or more. Many members have no loans outstanding and use the credit union as a savings institution. Other members have a purely nominal savings relationship while using the credit union as a source of borrowing.

Automobile loans comprise the largest single category of credit union lending activity. In 1975, car loans amounted to 45 percent of total credit union loans; in 1980, car loans were 47 percent of credit union loans outstanding. The industry estimates that it financed 21.5 percent of U.S. car loans in 1978 and 18.2 percent in 1980

Members borrow for many diverse reasons, most of which are labeled as consumer credit. But, the credit union industry is now extending first mortgage loans and promises to become a competitor in the mortgage industry as well. First mortgage loans outstanding amounted to $4.1 billion in 1979, or some 8 percent of total credit union loans. Credit unions with assets above $2 million are now authorized to make mortgage loans to members.[6]

Expansion of Credit Union Services

The small credit union operating in an office space donated by an employer and managed by volunteers serving in behalf of their fellow employees is rapidly disappearing. Although there are still credit unions operating in this manner they have little impact upon the national market. Much of the above material should have demonstrated that the institutionalization of credit unions into an industry posture has resulted in the development of local institutions providing a rather broad range of services which will no doubt be extended still further.

Credit unions no longer operate under very restrictive size and maturity limitations on their loans. No member can borrow more than 10 percent of total share capital but this is not a real barrier to lending. Credit unions can now extend long-term mortgage loans as well as all of the traditional types of consumer loans.

Perhaps the largest single force impacting upon credit union

[6] Charles P. Edmonds, III and Robert B. Rogow, "Credit Unions Move Into the Home Mortgage Market," *Real Estate Review,* Summer 1979, pp. 31-34.

Table 1-16 Selected Measures of Financial Strength
And Employment Size in Credit Unions, 1965-1980

	1965	1970	1975	1978	1980
Average size (total assets) of credit unions	$477,000	$758,000	$1,689,000	$2,855,000	$3,412,464
Average savings per member	$ 563	$ 678	1,054	$ 1,296	$ 1,427
Average dollar loans outstanding per member	$ 496	$ 619	$ 906	$ 1,257	$ 1,063
Full time employees	20,582	26,159	40,725	58,821	73,560

Source: Compiled and calculated from data in various Credit Union National Association *Yearbooks.*

activity in the present generation is the development of electronic funds transfer services in all phases of the financial community. As banks and savings institutions brought more and more of these services to the public, credit unions began to seek powers which would allow them to compete effectively. As the public became more sensitive to interest yields on savings and the possibilities of using savings balances as a part of their working cash balances to meet routine household needs, credit union leaders became very restless in their historic role in the economy. With the aid of many supporters in the Congress, the industry was authorized to issue share drafts against savings shares, to install automatic teller machines, to issue bank and other credit cards, and to plan for the provision of trust services. They may also borrow money through central loan facilities and issue money market certificates and establish individual retirement accounts. All of this means that the credit union industry is moving quite rapidly into new areas of personal financial services and that it is becoming a financial intermediary of significance in the economy. However, their small size may significantly impede them in this endeavor.

A Central Liquidity Fund was provided by the Congress in 1978 and is now operational. The original concept of the legislation was to establish a type of central bank, or lender of last resort for the credit union industry as a means of preventing a liquidity crisis. An earlier United States Central Cooperative was established in 1974, composed of state-level central credit unions, for about the same purpose. The Central Loan Facility now has some operating experience and rules have been issued providing for liquidity reserves.

The National Credit Union Administration issued final rules in September 1979 establishing a 5 percent liquidity reserve requirement for all federally-insured credit unions with assets of $2 million or more, or those which operate a share draft program. The liquidity reserve is to be determined monthly and will consist of cash, deposit accounts with maturities of 1 year or less, federal and agency securities, and other instruments. The reserves which have been accumulated out of earnings over the years, amounting to about 4.5 percent of total savings, are not held for liquidity purposes. Such operating reserves do provide a cushion against losses and reduce the costs of funds available since no dividend or interest payments must be made on that portion of the organization's liabilities. However, these reserve requirements have never really been a binding constraint for most credit unions and may soon be eliminated.

The share-draft (a type of check) controversy continued until 1980, though some 1,700 credit unions were issuing them in the Spring of 1979. A United States Court of Appeals held in April 1979 that the National Credit Union Administration had exceeded its authority in impowering share drafts and that the practice would have to cease by January 1980 unless Congress acted to authorize the practice by then. The Monetary Control Act of 1980 specifically authorized the share draft program as well as giving credit unions other powers and freedom from regulation.

Share drafts are used by savers to pay their bills in the same way as a bank check and they are processed and transferred through the banking system in much the same way. In order to have better entreé into the financial system and clearing processes, credit union groups have purchased banks in various parts of the country, and they have access to the Automated Clearing House system used by the banks and other savings associations.

The Credit Union National Association has recently begun to release material referring to a credit union financial system in words such as these:

> Advances in the art of technology, along with expanded legal powers, have paved the way for many innovative financial services. Credit union members have both expected and demanded that these services be made available to them ...
>
> Basically, the national credit union financial system is a coordinated and interrelated network of credit unions and their service

organizations. The system augments the ability of credit unions to provide financial services to their members and to maintain and enhance their competitive position in the financial services market-place.[7]

These are not the words of a timid and struggling cooperative movement seeking to provide a simple plan for savings and a source of small personal loans. Rather, they reflect a thrust of ideas and action designed to provide a complete system of household financial services. Who are these members seeking such a range of services? They are, of course, a fair cross section of the working households of the nation. The 47 million members in the country do represent a significant segment of the population. It must be realized, however, that many households hold multiple memberships and that many are not active at any point in time. From a consumer panel survey of mostly middle-income households in South Carolina in late 1976, it was determined that 60 percent had savings accounts in banks, 60 percent had accounts in savings and loan associations, and 43 percent had at least one spouse as a credit union member.[8] While these percentages overstate the membership for the total population, they do indicate the extent of the credit union industry. However, there was no significant increase in credit union usage reported in a 1980 follow-up study of the same panel.

Credit union services are generally expanding at a noteworthy pace. Table 1-17 documents the many services available in 1981-82 by the (asset) size of credit unions.

As the operational definition of the "common bond" of membership has been expanded through time, the potential for additional membership remains large. There are now credit unions for such diverse groups as the hairdressers in Connecticut, the owners of Arabian horses, and Alaska U. S. A., which has locations throughout Alaska and a "service center" in Denver, Colorado.

Credit unions are now beginning to branch rather extensively. Federal credit unions find it very easy to branch at the present. If the branching movement continues to accelerate, the industry is

---

[7] CUNA, "News Background," May 1, 1979.

[8] F. J. Ingram and O. S. Pugh, *Financial Services: Household Attitudes and Practices,* Bureau of Business and Economic Research, University of South Carolina, 1977.

Table 1-17 Services by Asset Size, 1982

	1-250,000	250,001-500,000	500,001-1,000,000	1,000,001-2,500,000	2,500,001-5,000,000	5,000,001-10,000,000	10,000,001-25,000,000	25,000,001-50,000,000	50,000,001 & over	Total All CUs
IRA/Keogh	2.8%	12.1%	22.3%	43.5%	65.1%	80.3%	89.3%	90.4%	87.1%	36.6%
DD-Federal recur payment	5.6	8.7	18.8	38.2	59.0	77.2	90.1	92.8	93.9	34.3
DD-Corporate payroll	12.6	16.4	20.0	29.1	39.2	47.3	60.3	62.7	75.5	28.1
Payroll deduction	78.8	84.0	88.0	91.6	93.0	93.9	97.4	97.1	90.2	88.0
Money orders	2.2	4.5	8.9	17.8	29.2	47.0	56.1	68.4	57.1	18.6
Travelers checks	2.9	7.2	15.1	30.0	50.7	66.6	80.4	84.2	79.8	28.5
Financial counseling	23.0	33.6	42.2	56.1	68.8	72.1	74.3	77.0	67.5	48.0
Share drafts	1.1	2.3	6.6	19.9	42.6	62.9	80.0	83.7	84.7	22.9
ATMs	—	0.1	0.3	0.7	1.6	5.0	15.2	27.8	37.4	2.9
Membership										
Once a member, always a member	70.0	79.7	85.5	89.7	88.4	92.1	92.3	92.8	83.4	83.6
Includes family members	77.0	86.7	90.0	92.2	93.4	96.4	95.7	92.8	86.5	88.6
Select employee groups	17.6	21.4	25.0	26.1	31.3	31.8	37.2	36.4	32.5	25.4
Share Certificates										
MMC	2.4	8.4	17.0	35.3	54.4	66.1	73.1	83.7	74.2	29.9
Cert. of indebtedness	0.8	1.1	1.7	3.9	5.5	7.4	10.5	8.1	9.8	3.5
Other certificates	8.7	20.4	29.4	42.3	51.3	60.6	69.4	74.6	79.1	35.3

Source: Credit Union National Association, *Credit Union Report, 1982.*

Table 1-18   State-by-State Credit Union Statistical Information, 1982

	No. CUs	State Charter	Federal Charter	Members	Members/ Population	Savings ($000)	Loans ($000)	Reserves ($000)	Assets ($000)	Share* Drafts ($000)
Alabama	287	112	175	702,778	17.8%	1,394,721	795,533	67,689	1,535,434	82,341
Alaska	24	–	24	313,136	71.5	626,396	474,481	22,593	719,431	102,612
Arizona	135	65	70	691,498	24.2	1,012,290	682,324	42,323	1,106,692	63,067
Arkansas	145	45	100	148,770	6.5	179,924	115,164	13,867	204,127	3,975
California	1,349	421	928	5,951,927	24.1	10,880,816	7,451,414	517,960	12,108,221	791,976
Colorado	293	133	160	786,577	25.8	1,562,434	932,529	66,976	1,722,346	81,181
Connecticut	429	159	270	755,780	24.0	1,062,438	754,520	47,594	1,176,810	38,829
Deleware	70	–	70	113,824	18.9	164,286	112,645	9,850	180,672	5,978
D.C.	134	–	134	473,452	75.3	761,762	498,177	26,028	826,628	195,498
Florida	536	226	310	1,950,486	18.7	3,288,128	2,169,419	151,617	3,635,748	304,577
Georgia	442	169	273	888,466	12.2	1,448,669	1,002,544	52,664	1,601,051	35,995
Hawaii	150	4	146	400,667	40.3	880,383	603,893	45,218	968,765	17,125
Illinois	1,294	931	363	1,896,666	16.6	3,437,621	2,145,641	208,349	3,764,520	154,976
Indiana	527	101	426	1,189,282	21.7	2,234,596	1,173,272	83,681	2,430,333	111,711
Iowa	342	333	9	520,176	17.9	778,629	495,933	77,218	863,566	41,462
Kansas	230	179	51	510,437	21.2	767,758	484,092	38,997	828,490	22,827
Kentucky	240	104	136	387,393	10.6	518,361	334,063	36,285	583,102	22,381
Louisiana	465	96	369	648,902	14.9	855,663	660,372	42,236	948,967	25,127
Maine	147	23	124	340,760	30.0	513,578	300,922	24,207	560,697	23,031
Maryland	218	24	194	916,817	21.5	1,589,586	1,022,637	73,292	1,740,186	64,783
Massachusetts	597	295	302	1,603,732	27.7	3,167,869	2,049,527	106,872	3,511,740	78,308
Michigan	826	531	295	2,839,763	31.2	4,150,788	2,841,598	212,034	4,650,597	282,915
Minnesota	306	253	53	750,731	18.2	1,334,760	834,724	61,931	1,457,474	100,387
Mississippi	222	64	158	355,759	10.9	326,176	252,700	14,661	373,408	13,554

Missouri	360	329	31	658,213	13.3	1,203,214	666,859	49,665	1,292,711	N.A.
Montana	123	26	97	202,449	25.3	356,671	232,808	14,922	398,594	22,242
Nebraska	145	64	81	279,761	17.6	389,403	245,627	18,988	423,381	14,176
Nevada	56	13	43	205,803	23.4	383,258	279,967	14,496	415,546	22,656
New Hampshire	64	37	27	224,867	23.6	305,186	222,552	16,642	333,390	21,271
New Jersey	633	53	580	828,991	11.1	1,236,010	749,025	50,302	1,363,749	35,362
New Mexico	96	41	55	276,285	20.3	497,858	307,464	19,714	545,111	36,210
New York	1,156	84	1,073	2,209,045	12.5	3,867,274	2,436,198	196,994	4,270,281	177,488
North Carolina	337	210	127	717,563	14.1	1,639,772	936,401	62,756	1,816,467	70,277
North Dakota	91	65	26	128,000	20.5	326,963	164,059	13,193	348,678	34,392
Ohio	1,212	601	611	1,991,654	18.5	2,770,303	1,898,020	145,776	3,077,480	118,040
Oklahoma	159	51	108	589,961	18.6	1,254,573	765,421	49,400	1,347,682	100,913
Oregon	197	34	163	661,114	25.0	1,094,317	739,798	45,111	1,199,906	72,850
Pennsylvania	1,534	196	1,338	1,876,699	15.8	2,744,846	1,844,544	108,764	3,040,553	80,682
Puerto Rico	244	232	12	494,274	15.2	578,653	578,653	24,073	744,251	N.A.
Rhode Island	96	76	20	355,681	37.1	828,534	528,636	61,873	910,566	1,304
South Carolina	174	37	137	462,037	14.4	691,575	469,215	33,762	758,334	37,885
South Dakota	92	–	92	112,769	16.3	181,312	102,455	6,097	195,900	13,656
Tennessee	510	338	172	873,665	18.8	1,575,554	1,044,599	69,407	1,747,394	46,306
Texas	1,282	485	797	3,397,185	22.2	6,313,886	3,979,797	226,744	6,934,923	342,454
Utah	260	196	64	614,489	39.5	981,898	668,287	62,661	1,076,166	38,777
Vermont	74	68	6	94,359	18.3	114,021	93,294	5,769	127,227	N.A.
Virginia	401	133	268	1,768,172	32.2	3,159,065	2,161,929	150,531	3,491,916	152,485
Washington	328	172	156	1,087,488	25.6	1,994,991	1,262,373	58,534	2,214,136	121,005
West Virginia	214	29	185	206,186	10.6	326,727	222,609	20,339	374,053	9,978
Wisconsin	592	588	4	1,190,402	25.0	1,203,015	957,755	120,632	1,953,336	152,837
Wyoming	56	–	56	92,670	18.5	126,033	91,371	6,681	139,779	9,810

Source: Credit Union National Association, *Credit Union Report, 1982.*

likely to have increases in its operating costs as well as a partial loss of support as a neighborhood or common-bond association.

Finally, credit unions have spread their influence across the country. Table 1-18 provides detailed and graphic proof that credit unions are indeed a national industry.

Credit Union Associations

From the onset of credit unit promotion under the auspices of Filene and Bergengren in the early 1900s, several credit union leagues were established to promote the chartering of credit unions and to assist in the operations of state chartered credit unions.

Credit Union National Association

With the passage of the Federal Credit Union Act in 1934, Filene and Bergengren called a national conference of state level credit union representatives to develop what became known as the Credit Union National Association. This national service organization was located in Madison, Wisconsin and became a vocal spokesman for the movement at the national level. Many services are provided to credit unions in the form of various insurance programs, promotion and management literature, research and management assistance, centralized purchasing of certain materials, and public relations. CUNA has evolved into a very complex structure of affiliated service divisions and organizations and remains the unified spokesman for both the national and state chartered associations.

The State Leagues

State level credit union leagues now operate in all states and they are members of CUNA. Major responsibilities of state leagues include legislative representation, education, organization of new credit unions, and public relations. League fieldmen traveled their states providing consulting type management and financial services as well as meeting with groups to facilitate the chartering of new credit unions. After some time and with the growth of the movement, state leagues began to provide many specialized services to the individual associations in the form of accounting and financial services and printing and management supplies directly or through affiliated corporations.

National Association of Federal Credit Unions

The National Association of Federal Credit Unions (NAFCU) is an important lobbying and communications arm for member federal credit unions. NAFCU's primary activity is representing the interests of its member and, by extension, the industry to the federal government.

SUMMARY: CREDIT UNION INDUSTRY GROWTH AND PROSPECTS IN PERSPECTIVE

What are some of the reasons for the extraordinary growth experienced by credit unions over the last 30 years or so? If we summarize these reasons we have a better perspective for looking at the future course of development. The underlying motivation of the credit union movement was to establish mutual or cooperative associations of workers or others with a common bond, to provide an outlet for orderly savings and a source of small loans. In the main, these associations were for lower and middle-income groups who did not feel that the existing financial institutions desired to take small savings deposits and extend small loans at reasonable rates. Men of goodwill were willing to sponsor the movement nationally and employers joined in with their support as a means of providing a worthwhile service to their employees. The government was willing to allow such associations to operate without taxation, and indeed at a later date to provide insurance for the savings accounts. Cooperative associations have been favored for many years in this country and the more recent trend of consumerism tends to maintain their position.

Throughout the years, the principal advantage to the credit union movement has been the direct and indirect contribution of employers or other associational groups. Most credit unions were given office space, payroll withholdings for both regular savings and installment collections, assistance in organization and development, and encouragement to committees to do a good job for their fellow members. In other words, a large part of the organizational and management expenses of smaller credit unions were in large measure donated by employers and volunteers from the group.

Credit unions have also had the advantage of not being subjected to the rather stringent interest rate limitations of Regulation Q which have kept interest payments on savings accounts in banks and savings and loan associations to rather low levels. The result has been that credit unions have generally declared a dividend rate on savings above the rates paid by either the banks or the savings and loan industry. The higher rate, typically 6 or 7 percent in recent years, has made the credit union more attractive as a savings repository.

Since credit unions have generally had the cost advantages of subsidized quarters, minimal operating and personnel costs, and freedom from taxation, they have been able to keep their loan rates below market rates for similar credit. Their expanding role in consumer credit provides evidence of their relative attractiveness as a credit supplier. Throughout the years, credit unions were able to provide new car loans at around an 8-9 percent annual percentage rate and small individual loans at around 11-12 percent. These rates were distinctly lower than finance company rates and somewhat below rates charged by banks for similar credits. The provision of free credit life insurance for borrowed funds as well as life insurance on savings shares has also made credit unions more attractive to members. Much of this translates into saying that credit unions have enjoyed distinct cost advantages which they have shared with their membership.

The rapid growth in dollar activity and the dramatic expansion of the range of services proposed for credit unions will result in a lessening of their cost advantages. One of the principal reasons for this is the fact that the expanded activities of many associations are now placing them into the nation's money and capital markets on a month-to-month basis. As noted in the reference to the development of a credit union financial system, the credit union industry must now compete with aggressive institutions seeking the short-term savings of the public, both as regular savings accounts and as money market certificates. As credit unions "mature" and as they begin to serve members with higher income levels, they find that they must pay competitive rates to people doing business with more than one type of institution and pay national rates when they have to borrow to meet their member needs. Just as importantly, the disposition of credit union credit committees to approve almost all loan applications adds to the problem. Thus, the real issue may be reduced to the fact that modern credit unions may no longer be able to project the image of the small "self-help" association existing to assist the small saver and the small borrower.

Since Regulation Q is likely to be phased out for other depository institutions in the near future, credit unions are likely to lose some of their advantage in paying higher rates on savings accounts than other savings intermediaries. This may slow down their growth rate in savings accumulation, and, if so, will certainly make it more difficult to have sufficient loanable funds within the limits of traditional charges devised by the industry.

Problems of liquidity management have surfaced in the credit union industry in recent years and are almost certain to become more common-place in the future. With the issuance of credit cards, share drafts, and automated teller machines, credit unions can no longer calculate that savings will remain for a considerable length of time. Cash drainage will become a more serious problem and credit unions will have to position themselves to meet these losses. The Central Liquidity Fund will be of some value in this respect, but it will impose a burden upon management, and ultimately upon the membership. Loan losses are also likely to rise as the industry provides more liquidity to its members and as the industry deals with groups which are less cohesive than in the past. Increased mobility of the work force and household residence will also contribute to higher loss ratios.

The credit union movement, or industry, has always been hampered by the lack of experienced management. While volunteerism may be cost effective in some respects it is not the way to obtain trained and experienced management personnel capable of planning and implementation of policies to meet the challenges of the expanded range of services which the public and the Congress seem to expect. If the industry is to grow effectively, and if it is to provide the services which are now being planned, credit unions must attract more management talent and train many of those now involved in the industry. And this educational effort cannot be limited to the full-time managers of the associations. Key board and committee members must also be made sensitive to the requirements of an industry which has moved into a position of significance in the national marketplace.

A rapidly growing credit union industry will at some point attract the active attention of legislative groups seeking new sources of tax revenue. Just as the mutual savings and loan industry was brought under parts of the income tax code in 1969, credit unions cannot expect to be insulated forever from some form of taxation. Even so, they are likely to maintain a distinct tax advantage over both commercial banks and finance companies.

All of this might lead one to believe that the future of credit unions as an industry is not very bright. But such is not the case. Credit unions have the tremendous advantage of being popular in most political circles and enjoying the support of most employers and other associational groups. Credit unions will grow because they are in the center of household finance, both as a means of routine savings and as a source of credit and because of their relative convenience. Households have turned to institutional forms of savings over the years and the 20,000 credit unions place them in contact with many of the households. In addition, consumer credit has been a growth sector of the economy and this is the area in which credit unions have their natural advantage.

Movements toward share drafts, credit cards, automated payments and the rest will keep the industry in touch with the younger elements of society. If the industry proceeds cautiously and obtains adequate managerial talents to provide such services, it will grow as a result. The existing network of banking and clearing relationships will make such things feasible. Other financial institutions will be forced to devote more attention to credit unions as highly effective competitors for the consumer's savings and as a supplier of the consumer's dollar needs in daily life.

Organization of Credit Unions and Industry Structure

INTRODUCTION

As indicated in Chapter 1, both the organizational characteristics of credit unions and credit union organizations have been major factors in the evolution of the movement. This chapter delves more deeply into these matters in order to promote enhanced understanding of the uniqueness of credit unions and the credit union industry.

CHARTERING AND COMMON BOND REQUIREMENTS

The organization and chartering of a credit union has always been a relatively simple process. Local groups have been assisted by credit union representatives from the days of Bergengren. State credit union leagues and the National Credit Union Administration provide extensive advisory services and assistance to small groups which are interested in the establishment of a credit union. Federal law requires that at least seven people serve as the organizing group for a new organization with a specific location, territory, and field membership. A determination of the economic feasibility of the proposed credit union is required. Recent federal guidelines require that 200 employees be available as members for an occupational group, 300 potential members for an associational group, and a population of

1,000 for a community charter.[1] The relative ease with which charters have been obtained in the past is attested to by the large number which have been chartered in recent decades in comparison with banks and other savings associations. All but three states provide state charters for credit unions at the present time.

Credit unions are controlled by their members with each member having a single vote regardless of size of accounts. Each member must subscribe to at least one share to become a member of the association. Further savings are in the form of additional share purchases in the traditional mode of operation and savers are compensated through dividends declared on shares. Certificate holders and other investment instruments issued by credit unions do receive a fixed rate of interest (technically, dividends because they are not guaranteed) as a result of recent developments in the industry. As mutual associations with a common bond of interest, the management of credit unions is in the hands of members except for special functions delegated to management personnel retained to perform daily duties. Thus, much of the management work remains uncompensated except among the larger associations.

COMMON BOND PRACTICES

The common bond of membership is the most distinguishing feature of the modern credit union industry. There are many other mutual financial institutions which do not have a common bond of membership requirement. Without a common bond requirement there is little to set the modern credit union apart from other mutual groups. Modern common bond relationships follow occupational, associational, and community or residential lines on any common basis of membership or activity. In the formative years of the movement many associations followed occupational and agricultural community lines. Common bond definitions have become more open-ended over the years with a consequent reduction in the intensity or degree of com-

[1] NCUA, *Chartering and Organizing Manual for Federal Credit Unions,* Washington, 1980, pp. 1-2.

mon interest. While this does make possible a more diverse membership over wider geographic areas, it does expose the industry to criticism that the industry has departed from its original purpose.

In the formative years of the credit union movement in the United States concerted efforts were made to organize local farmers and agricultural workers with little success. Industrial growth caused the credit union leadership to concentrate upon groups along occupational lines in industrial and service areas. Government workers were also heavily involved in the United States movement but membership along religious lines was much less frequent than in Canada or Europe. In 1958, for example, church associational credit unions comprised 5.6 percent of U. S. credit unions, in sharp contrast with the 26.1 percent of Canadian credit unions.[2]

Table 2-1 shows the common bond relationships for U. S. credit unions for the 1958-1980 period. Associational groups declined in relative importance over recent years, falling from 17.9 percent of all credit unions in 1958 to 16.2 percent in 1980. Associational memberships have been constituted from religious, fraternal, professional, labor unions, and other associational groups. Some of these groupings may be altered in the future as efforts are made to consolidate various groups with a common employer into a single credit union. Residential groupings have remained a fairly constant percentage of all credit unions in recent years, constituting roughly 4 percent of credit unions. The community to be served must be clearly delineated before a charter can be received. There is now the reality that some employ-

Table 2-1   Credit Unions in the U. S. by Common Bond Groupings, Selected Years, 1958-1980

Classification	1958	1968	1973	1978	1979	1980
Associational[1]	17.89%	17.39%	16.63%	13.61%	17.39%	16.17%
Occupational	59.19	57.59	56.47	57.35	54.98	55.84
Educational Services	5.79	6.98	7.68	9.63	8.18	8.52
Government Employees[2]	13.67	14.65	15.33	15.77	15.55	15.18
Residential	3.46	3.39	3.89	3.64	3.90	4.29
	100.00%	100.00%	100.00%	100.00%	100.00%	100.00%

Source: C.U.N.A., *Annual Yearbooks.*
[1] Church, Labor Union, Co-op, Fraternal, Professional, and Trade Association.
[2] Employees' National, State, County, and Local Governments.

[2] Credit Union National Association, *Yearbook, 1959,* Madison, Wisconsin, pp. 8-9.

ment-based credit unions are being converted to community-based credit unions as plants are closed or relocated, or other employment groups reduced.

Credit unions based upon common bond employment other than educational and governmental have maintained their relative importance through the years, ranging around 54 to 59 percent of all credit unions. Manufacturing employment constitutes the principal part of the occupational groupings, amounting to about 32-34 percent of the total. On the other hand, credit unions based upon government employment and educational employment have grown rather rapidly. The most rapid growth occurred among the educational service groups as they constituted 5.8 percent of all credit unions in 1958 and 8.5 percent in 1980. Credit unions for government employees rose from 13.7 percent in 1958 to 15.2 in 1980.

Since the common bond concept delineates the credit union industry from other mutual financial institutions and helps to safeguard the tax exempt status of credit unions, the modern credit union leadership must concern itself with the changing employment, associational, and residential patterns of the nation. Although the common bond requirements have been interpreted rather generously over the years, they still serve to limit the geographical areas and eligible membership available to individual credit unions. These limitations may well become one of the more sensitive issues confronting the modern credit union industry.

MEMBERSHIP REQUIREMENTS AND RIGHTS

Credit union membership may include groups having a common bond of occupation, association or interest, or to groups with a well-defined neighborhood, community, or rural district. This Federal Credit Union Act definition of membership is also representative of state credit union requirements for membership. Common practice also includes the fact that members of the immediate family of the credit union member may also be members of the credit union. Individual members who leave the field of membership are often permitted to retain membership, although practices vary greatly from state to state and from association to association. The federal act is silent on this issue.

The Federal Credit Union Act and the statutory requirements of many states require that each member shall pay a uniform entrance fee if required by the board of the association. This fee is often only one dollar although it may be greater from time to time. One duty of the board of directors of the credit union is to act upon applications for membership under such conditions as are prescribed by its by-laws. The one-person one-vote doctrine prevails in the industry since members with multiple shares are not permitted to exercise multiple voting rights.

BOARDS AND OFFICERS

Federal and most state laws require that a credit union be managed by a board of not fewer than five (5) directors elected from the membership. The board of directors exercises general control of the business affairs, funds, and records of the credit union. Federal credit union boards meet monthly and as necessary, a practice which is followed by most state credit unions. Board members (except treasurers) receive no compensation and they must elect several executive officers from their fellow board members. The board has the power to act upon membership applications and credit applications, to determine interest rate policies, and to exercise general supervision over all functional areas of each association. Each board must elect a president, a vice-president, a secretary, and a treasurer who shall constitute the executive committee of the credit union. The secretary-treasurer positions may be held by the same person. No executive officer (again, except the treasurer) may be compensated for services rendered.

The credit committee is either elected from the membership at the annual members meeting or, in certain instances, may be appointed by the board of directors. This committee is designated as the primary lending authority within the credit union and may itself appoint one or more loan officers to perform many of the regular duties of the committee.

The board of directors of each association appoints a supervisory committee of at least three persons, one of whom may be a member of the board. The supervisory committee's primary function is to scrutinize the fiscal and management policies of the credit union through regular audit and other examination procedures. The committee reports to the board of directors and to the membership. Members are not compensated for their services.

Other committees, such as an investment committee, may be appointed from time to time by the board. The board has to determine compensation for the clerical and management assistance required for the proper administration of each association. Federal statutes still prohibit payment for services to any board member other than the treasurer. A few states do allow other board members to be compensated for personal services. This tradition and practice, coming from the earlier belief that credit union management services ought to be regarded as philanthropic in nature, may tend to inhibit the growth of professional management techniques in the evolving credit union industry of the nation.

THE STATE LEAGUES AND THE CREDIT UNION NATIONAL ASSOCIATION

As indicated earlier, no discussion of the organizational development of the credit union from a consumer movement to what can be properly called an industry would be complete without emphasizing the role of the Credit Union National Association (CUNA) and the state credit unions leagues which have played such strategic roles in the development process. Indeed, most observers would agree that (along with the surprisingly supportive regulatory agencies as discussed in Chapter III) CUNA and the state leagues have provided much of the impetus for the growth, expansion and increasing sophistication of credit unions.

Credit unions early recognized the many disadvantages inherent in their small average size and accompanying dependence on volunteer and part-time employees. Particularly in the early years of the movement, the only source of real strength appeared to be in numbers. The Massachusetts Credit Union Association (MCUA) was consequently established in 1917 in order to "disseminate information in respect to the benefits of credit unions . . . .; to organize and assist in the organization of credit unions; to make loans to credit unions at a rate not exceeding 6 percent per annum and generally to promote and assist credit unions.[3] MCUA was the first state credit union *league,* as well as being a *central* credit union.

The State Leagues

Today every state in the country has a credit union league. These are nonprofit, cooperative organizations of individual credit unions and are fully financed by member dues. The leagues serve as trade lobbies in the various state legislatures (the feeling being that credit unions need to organize in order to counteract the political influence of banks and finance companies); they provide comprehensive financial advice and help organize new credit unions; they operate printing and purchasing cooperatives for supplies and equipment used by their members; and, finally, the leagues serve as clearinghouses for information of interest to individual institutions. Figure 2-1 illustrates the organizational structure of a typical state league.

One particular type of financial advice is an interlending service, offered by many leagues in conjunction with their state central credit union. The centrals are chartered to serve local credit unions and certain types of individuals who are ineligible for membership under other bonds of association. (Credit union officers, for example, were until recently proscribed from borrowing from their own organizations.) The centrals lend their own funds to member unions (as did MCUA), as well as providing a clearinghouse function for member interlending—a sort of combination of the Federal funds market and (highly informal) Federal Reserve System for credit unions. The corporate central functions are discussed again in Chapter VII.

Credit Union National Association

Most state leagues seek membership in the Credit Union National Association (CUNA). Founded in 1934, CUNA has emerged as the leading

---

[3] From the Massachusetts act chartering MCUA, quoted in Moody and Fite, *op. cit.,* p. 70.

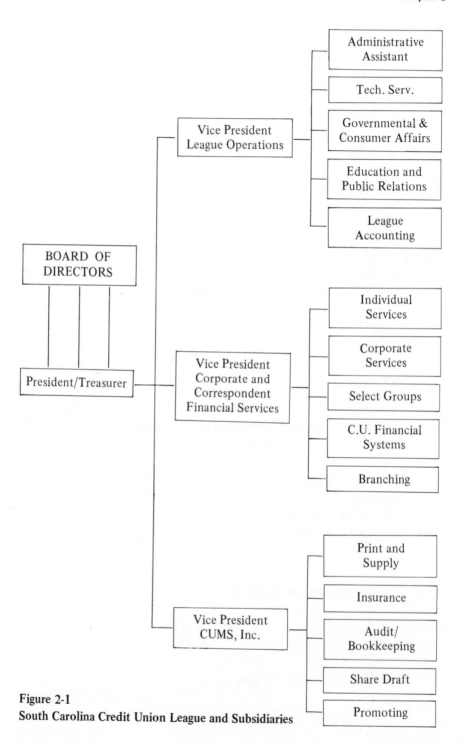

Figure 2-1
South Carolina Credit Union League and Subsidiaries

force of the credit union movement in the United States. Just as state leagues represent an effort to overcome selected diseconomies of small scale at the level of a single institution, CUNA does so for an even greater range of activities.

The CUNA Mutual Insurance Society (CUNAMIS) was founded in September 1935 in order to provide saver and borrower life insurance to credit union members. Previously there had been several state-level insurance firms serving credit unions, but CUNAMIS was the first entrant into the field capable of effectively competing with other national loan insurers. (Bergengren claimed that the new CUNAMIS competition promptly led the other insurance firms to lower their premiums drastically.) By 1971, CUNA Mutual had grown to be the nation's thirteenth largest writer of life insurance policies, with $17.2 billion in effect.

In 1966, CUNA undertook the formation of the ICU Services Corporation as a means of providing credit unions access to ever-more complicated segments of the capital markets. ICU oversees interlending among credit unions at a national level. Even more novel and far-reaching, however, are its several government security programs. These are designed to provide a repository for credit union surplus funds, including overnight money. It has also been suggested that ICU borrow in the capital markets and re-lend such funds to individual credit unions. ICU is thus a potential substitute for the Central Liquidity Facility.

Still another example of CUNA's attempts to reap economies of scale is to be found in the CUNADATA Corporation, which has incorporated (in Wisconsin) by CUNA, CUNA Mutual, and several state leagues. CUNADATA is intended to develop "a complete, unified computer accounting system for U. S. credit unions."[4] By mid-1972 CUNADATA had produced the software and operating procedures necessary to make computerized accounting available to every credit union in the country. There has been a great deal of discussion in trade papers concerning the ability of credit unions to compete effectively in the new competitive era. Many other service capabilities have been added in recent years. Figures 2-2 and 2-3 provide an overview of both the organizational structure and range of services offered by CUNA. All in all, state credit union leagues and CUNA (and NAFCU) operations are an integral part of the credit union industry.

---

[4] Moody and Fite, *op. cit.,* p. 350.

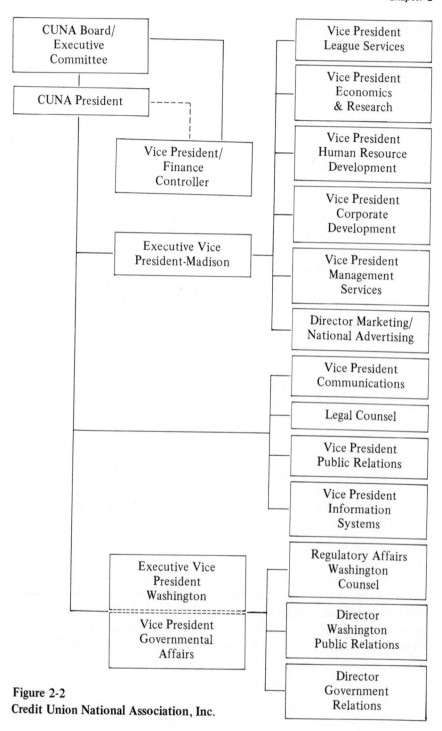

Figure 2-2
Credit Union National Association, Inc.

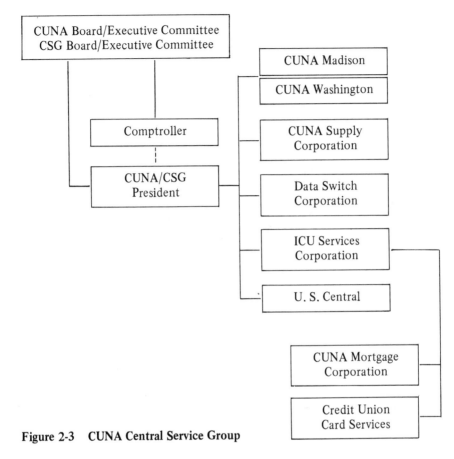

Figure 2-3   CUNA Central Service Group

SUMMARY

The influence of credit union organizational characteristics and credit union organization on the rapid growth of credit union industry in the United States is analyzed in this chapter. From a struggling philanthropic movement in the early 1900s the modern credit union industry has evolved into a significant segment of the financial system. The cooperative and nonprofit aspect of the movement has been maintained but the necessity for professional management assistance is becoming widely recognized. The nation's financial markets are now so well integrated that cooperative savings and borrowing efforts can no longer be isolated from national market forces. The unique organizational makeup of credit unions and the catalytic role of credit union trade associations are given particular emphasis in the discussion.

Credit Union Regulations

INTRODUCTION

It is generally accepted that a depository financial institution operates under as many governmental constraints as any firm in the private economy. The credit union regulatory authorities at both the state and federal level have played and will continue to play critical roles in the evolution of the industry even in the "deregulated" 1980s and beyond. This chapter attempts to provide an overview of credit union regulation along with a closer look at specific aspects of the regulatory environment in which credit unions must operate.

Additionally, the trend toward less strenuously regulated financial markets (particularly the provisions of the landmark Depository Institution Deregulation and Monetary Control Act of 1980) is examined in some detail. Thus, the material in this chapter serves as a natural springboard for the discussion of the summary outlook for the credit union industry which follows in Chapter VII.

AN OVERVIEW OF CREDIT UNION REGULATION IN THE UNITED STATES[1]

Regulation and control of financial institutions is currently the responsibility of a number of disparate agencies. The resulting Balkani-

[1] See *CUNA's Comparative State Credit Union Laws* for details of the various state legislation regarding credit unions.

zation is based on institutional form (for example, the Federal Reserve Board of Governors for banks and the Federal Home Loan Bank Board for savings and loans, etc.), chartering agency (state vs. federal) and particular functions (for example, deposit insurance agencies are often administratively separate from other regulators). This situation has been criticized on grounds that it generally results in a wasteful duplication of facilities and resources, as well as an undesirable "competition" among alternative regulators for the favor of institutions.

Since 1966 the growing similarity of the depository intermediaries has led to an attempt at coordinated efforts among regulatory authorities. Historically, joint determination of the various Regulation Q type ceilings in order to maintain an explicit bank-nonbank interest rate differential is the most noteworthy example of this thrust. Moreover, restrictions governing thrift institution liability instruments have been steadily loosened to prevent commercial banks from achieving a competitive advantage. The adoption of reforms liberalizing the asset and liability powers of all depository intermediaries has created a need for even greater coordination among regulators.

Chartering

Credit unions can generally be chartered under either federal or state law. Just five states (Alaska, Deleware, Nevada, South Dakota, and Wyoming) do not provide for state chartered institutions. The powers and regulation of credit unions vary considerably depending on the chartering agency.

The power to charter at the state level is generally vested in the office of the state's bank regulator who also examines and supervises credit unions. Corresponding federal powers have been delegated to a series of agencies since 1934. Initially, control was given to the Farm Credit Administration; between 1942 and 1948 it was a branch of the Federal Deposit Insurance Corporation; from then until 1953 the Federal Security Agency was responsible for Federal credit unions. This agency was liquidated in 1953 and the credit union functions were transferred to the Bureau of Federal Credit Unions in the Department of Health, Education and Welfare. Only in 1970 did Congress deem credit unions sufficiently important to justify their own independent regulatory body. Effective March 10, 1970, the National

Credit Union Administration (NCUA) was created to assume all the powers and responsibilities of the Bureau of Federal Credit Unions. NCUA now charters, examines, supervises and insures all Federal credit unions.

Bonds of Association

Federal law requires that "credit union membership shall be limited to groups having a common bond of occupation or association, or to groups within a well-defined geographic area. Membership is available to those individuals who share the common bond, as well as their immediate families. It is important to note the legal emphasis on the common bond; in particular, the residential bond of association is required to be well-defined. Some authorities assert that the spirit of Congressional intent with respect to residential (or community) credit unions seems to emphasize bonds of association that are primarily rural and it was assumed that farmer cooperatives, already organized to buy and sell their products jointly, would wish to provide consumer credit as well.

State statutes generally provide for the same three types of common bonds organization, although there are certain exceptions. Occupational ties and those based on associations through religious, fraternal, and labor groups are virtually universal but there is some inconsistency with respect to the chartering of community-based institutions. Virginia and Indiana, for example, allow for no residential credit unions while Maryland limits them to rural areas.

Taxation

This is the area of most bitter contention between credit union proponents and those representing other financial intermediaries. No federal credit union may be taxed on its income or financial assets by any level of government. Real property is, however, fully taxable.

The provisions of the several state laws in this regard vary greatly. Mississippi and North Dakota conform to the federal legislation. Many other states tax credit unions essentially in the same fashion as they do mutual savings banks or savings and loan associations. Several states tax their credit unions' income in the same manner as that of other corporations.

Dividends

Dividend payments (or interest) on credit union savings differ from other depository intermediaries in two respects. First, their maximum allowable rates have generally been higher than the Regulation Q type ceilings imposed on other institutions. State provisions have varied from a low ceiling of 4 percent per year in New Hampshire to no limit at all in several other states. The most common ceiling in earlier years was 6 percent but these ceilings are being relaxed very rapidly.

A second distinction is based on the means employed by various intermediaries to compute their dividend and interest payments. In recent years commercial banks, mutual savings banks and savings and loan associations have steadily shortened their compounding period, thus raising the effective interest rate paid on depositor savings. Day of deposit to day of withdrawal and even instantaneous compounding are now quite common. State chartered credit unions are largely blocked from pursuing this course because they are usually prohibited from paying dividends on shares that are held for less than one month. (An exception is that grace days—usually between 5 and 15—are allowed at the beginning of each month.) Heretofore this restriction has not proven burdensome to credit unions in competing for funds since they have had a sizable rate ceiling advantage. The dilution or elimination of Regulation Q constrains will, however, change this.

Loans

The primary assets of all credit unions are loans to members. Both the federal and state laws specifically emphasize that the terms and charges on such loans are expected to be reasonable. The rate is to be inclusive of all charges incidental to the making of the loan contract. Consequently, credit unions routinely include the cost of borrower life and disability insurance in their stated loans rates. Most other consumer lenders add this cost as a special surcharge, which usually amounts to approximately ½ percent per year.

Another important area of regulation concerns the maturity of loans issued. Until recently federal credit union loans were limited to 10 years. State laws are generally silent on this subject, leaving the issue to be dealt with by an individual institution's by-laws. The effect of such rules and by-laws has been to confine credit union lending primarily to short-maturity personal loans. In particular, the mortgage component of credit union loan portfolios has been quite small, although growing. Not only have the loan maturity limitations of various acts and by-laws not encouraged 20- or 30-year loans, but many credit unions are reluctant to tie up the savings of so many members in a single loan. It is felt that these funds can be better used in the form of several smaller loans. Thus, credit unions will generally eschew the opportunity to make mortgage loans—at least until they learn to access the secondary mortgage market.

Finally, there are limits on the permissible size of a single loan. Unsecured loan limits are typically on the order of $1,000 to $2,500 (varying by state), and secured personal loans usually may not exceed 10 percent of capital.

Investments

Credit unions usually prefer to have a portfolio containing only personal loans made to its members, however; such a close balance of funds demanded and supplied rarely occurs. Rather, it is common for a credit union to have excess shares available for investment. Restraints on allowable credit union investments are considerably more confining than those applicable to other intermediaries. Particular regulations in this area vary widely, but the most common outlets for such funds are government securities (federal, state, and some municipal), savings and loan deposits, deposits in insured banks, loans to other credit unions, and the purchase of the credit union's own shares.

Shares and Deposits

Credit union shares are analogous to a corporation's equity capital in that there can be no guarantee of interest payment or repayment of principal. If a credit union's loans were to be 100 percent in default, the members would (technically) have only a residual claim against it. Depositors at other institutions, on the other hand, can be guaranteed a specific interest rate in advance of the dividend period and possess a primary claim on assets in the event of default. Traditionally, credit unions issued only one type of liability—the share account. In order to become a member, one had to purchase at least one share (whose par value was generally five dollars). A basic tenet of the movement is that all members have equal voice in deciding credit union affairs— "one-man, one-vote." More recently, credit unions have been empowered to issue certificates of deposits and NOW accounts (share drafts) comparable to those available at competing institutions.

A major feature of credit union deposits that distinguishes them from those of other intermediaries is the life insurance coverage that is extended to members in proportion to their shares. Generally, members receive coverage under a group policy carried by the credit union with the CUNA Mutual Insurance Society, the extent of coverage varying with a member's age and the size of his account. As mentioned above, it is estimated that the cost of such insurance, which is an expense for the credit union, is equivalent to an extra ½ percent annual dividend payable on the account.

Share Insurance

It was not until quite recently that credit unions were given a federal share insurance program similar to those provided by the Federal Deposit Insurance Corporation and the Federal Savings and Loan Insurance Corporation. Amendments to the Federal Credit Union Act in October 1970 created the National Credit Union Share Insurance Fund under the control of the Administrator of the NCUA. All federal credit unions are required to join the insurance fund, while any state institution may apply for protection under the plan.

At the state level there are several insurance funds that pre-date that of the NCUA. Moreover, it has not been uncommon in the history of the credit union movement for a liquidating institution's sponsoring organization voluntarily to provide the resources to return 100 percent on member shares. This has occurred most frequently among occupational credit unions.

Reserves

Federal law initially required that 20 percent of net earnings (before the declaration of any dividend) be set aside as reserves in order to protect members' equity. Such accumulation was required to continue until total reserves equaled 10 percent of shareholdings. In addition, many credit unions hold sizable special reserves for losses, supplemental reserves, and undivided earnings. These mandatory bad debt reserves have long been criticized as being far in excess of historic credit union loss experience, thus having the effect of transferring income from today's shareholders to tomorrow's. In 1970 the law was changed to require the accumulation of reserves only up to 10 percent of the credit union's total risk assets. State laws are generally structured in the same fashion as the old federal law—with a required annual addition to reserves (based on net annual income) and a mandatory minimum level of total reserves (usually based on total assets or shares).

Credit unions are also empowered to borrow from any source up to some specified percentage of their capital and surplus. In the federal legislation this limit is 50 percent; state norms vary between 25 and 50 percent.

CREDIT UNION REGULATORS

Introduction

As indicated in the preceding discussion, government regulation of credit unions is similar to government regulation of banks, mutual savings banks and savings and loan associations. In the dual chartering system, state-chartered credit unions are chartered, examined and supervised by the states and federally-chartered credit unions are chartered, examined and supervised by the National Credit Union Administration, a federal government agency. In the same manner as banks chartered by the federal government are required to use "natinal" or "N. A." (National Association) in their names and savings and loan associations "federal," credit unions chartered by the National Credit Union Administration use "federal" in their names. State-chartered credit unions are prohibited from using the word "federal" in their titles.

In addition to a similar method of supervision, credit unions historically shared with other depository financial intermediaries the substantial burden of an extensive and increasing amount of government regulation at the state and federal level. Indeed, the credit union burden may be heavier than that borne by other depositories because: (1) a disproportionate percentage of recent regulatory initiatives have dealt with consumer credit and (2) the resources that credit unions can devote to complying with the regulations are relatively smaller than the resources available to most commercial banks, savings and loan associations and mutual savings banks.

The similarities of government regulation among financial institutions must not be allowed to mask some notable differences in the case of credit unions. These differences are found in the relationship among the state supervisory agencies, the National Credit Union Administration and the share insurance programs at the state and federal level.

The following discussion of credit union regulation will include a review of supervisory structure at both the state and federal levels, the various share insurance programs and the expansion of government regulation beyond the traditional areas (chartering, examining, and supervising).

State Credit Union Regulation

State Supervisory Agencies

In the vast majority of states with credit union laws, the agency responsible for commercial bank supervision is also responsible for credit union supervision. In most such states, credit unions are under the direct jurisdiction of the banking supervisor or a department of financial institutions which includes banks and other thrift institutions. Several of these states designate a specific individual as the credit union supervisor. In other states, supervision is delegated to a division of corporations or securities, a department of commerce or some similar agency with jurisdiction over business regulation. However, four states (Kansas, Texas, Wisconsin and Nevada) have a separate credit union department or agency. It should also be noted that there has been an effort by the credit union industry to establish separate credit union agencies in each state. In 1974, CUNA issued a revised Model Credit Union Act containing a provision for an independent credit union agency to supervise credit unions in each state and has since prepared a Model Credit Union Agency Act.

Several factors have contributed to the effort for independent credit union agencies at the state level. Generally, there is a feeling that bank supervisors are not sympathetic to credit union goals and tend to oppose expansion of credit union powers without good reason. Additionally, many credit union leaders feel that an independent agency imparts status to the credit union industry—the creation of an independent agency amounts to public validation of credit unions. The state supervisory authority charters, examines and supervises the state-chartered credit unions within the state.

Chartering

As detailed in Chapter 1, the number of state credit union charters issued by state credit union supervisors has recently been noticeably less than the number of federal credit union charters issued. This decline when coupled with an increase in liquidations has resulted in a steady diminution in the number of operating state-chartered credit unions. As of the end of 1980 there were 9,025 state credit unions compared with 10,679 in 1970, a decline of 15.5 percent. Qualitatively, many states have taken a different attitude regarding credit union field of membership than does NCUA. For instance, there are more state credit unions with residential common bonds and several states permit state credit unions to include in their field of membership quite disparate groups of employees.

A few states have what might be thought of as a gestation provision in their laws. Under these rules, established credit unions are permitted to accept small groups of employees of a common employer located within a certain distance. Once the group of employees increases to a specified size or their total share balances exceed a specified amount, the group must organize its own credit union. This mechanism provides credit union accessibility to those who would otherwise be denied it simply because they work for a small business, and reduces the liquidation rate among embryonic credit unions.

Examinations

As might be expected, the examination practices of the various states differ considerably. In those states where credit unions and banks are under the same supervisory agency, the bank examiners also examine credit unions although in some cases a specific number of examiners is designated to specialize in credit union examinations. A considerable number of states accept an audit by an approved external auditor in lieu of an examination by the supervisory agency, but this is some-times limted to smaller credit unions. This delegation of the examina-tion function is not without some merit. With the host of securities law and the rulings of the Financial Accounting Standards Board and similar bodies, the line that distinguishes audits from examinations is now practically nonexistent.

State credit unions pay examination fees to defray expenses related to the credit union activities of the state supervisory agency. Usually, these monies go into the state's general fund and, thus, it is difficult to determine whether or not credit union supervision at the state level pays its own way.   .

State Share Insurance

Before the establishment of the National Credit Union Share Insur-ance Fund in 1970, the majority of states relied on stabilization funds which were financed by dues. The degree of success experienced by these funds varied from state to state. Many state leagues continue to operate stabilization funds even though their need is being dimin-ished by share insurance programs.

The National Credit Union Share Insurance Fund induced those state credit unions that were fearful of federal regulatory encroach-ment to devise programs for more effective state-operated share in-surance program. More effective insurance programs have been estab-lished in several states since 1970. These insurance corporations are not agencies of the state government, but most are examined and supervised by the same agency that supervises credit unions. Currently, states require credit unions to insure their accounts. Of these, some require state credit unions to be insured by the National Credit Union Share Insurance Fund, others require federal insurance or insurance by a state-approved insurance plan while still others require state credit unions to be insured by a state insurance program.

None of these share insurance organizations can draw on the funds or credit of the state in which they are chartered or on any other government entity. Consequently, several of the state share insurance organizations are reinsured under contracts with private insurers. Most of these insurance organizations belong to the National Share and Deposit Guaranty Corporation, a trade association. This organization arranges the reinsurance contracts, promotes the organization of insurance funds at the state level and eventually hopes to provide financial and managerial services to its members.

National Credit Union Administration

The federal agency responsible for chartering, supervising, examining and insuring federal credit unions is the National Credit Union Administration. NCUA also insures the accounts of those state credit unions that opt for (or that are required by state law) to become federally insured. NCUA is an independent agency financed by fees and assessments paid by the credit unions under its jurisdiction, an arrangement comparable to that of the national banks and the Comptroller of the Currency. A schematic diagram of NCUA's organizational structure is provided in Figure 3-1.

Structure

The NCUA is currently directed by a three-member Board. Board members (chairman and two members) are appointed by the president with the advice and consent of the Senate for specified terms.

NCUA differs organizationally from other federal financial institutions regulators in that the chartering, supervisory, examining and insurance functions are vested in the one agency. There is no separate entity for insurance such as the Federal Deposit Insurance Corporation or the Federal Savings and Loan Insurance Corporation. Rather, share insurance for credit unions is provided through the Share Insurance Fund, a separate fund administered by the Board of NCUA.

Divisions

Prior to 1983 the NCUA was divided into eight separate functional divisions and six regional offices. An examination of the functions of

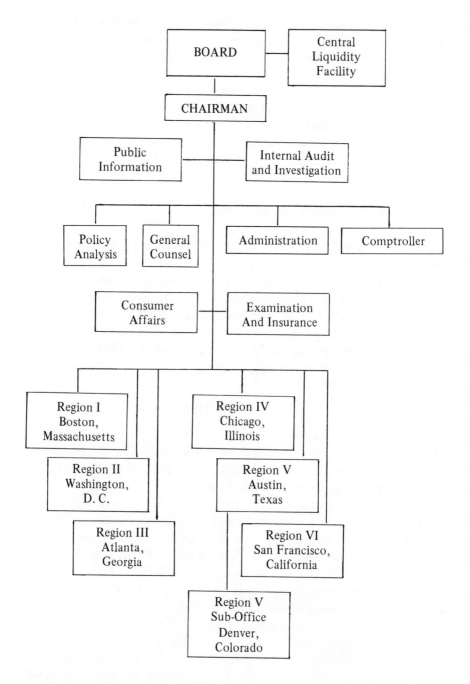

Figure 3-1   NCUA Organization Chart

these divisions gives an insight into the responsibilities of the NCUA:

1. Administration,
2. Examination and Insurance,
3. Consumer Affairs,
4. General Counsel,
5. Policy Analysis and Research,
6. Internal Audit and Investigation,
7. Comptroller,
8. Public Information.

In 1982 the NCUA acted to reverse a five-year trend of increasing numbers of personnel in the Washington office and to reallocate positions and personnel in the field. The eight functional divisions were reorganized into two offices: The Office of Programs, and the Office of Services. This facilitated a reduction of personnel in the Washington office from 207 in fiscal year 1981 to 135 in fiscal year 1982.

The Office of Administration. This division plans, directs, and administers the activities of NCUA in the areas of management analysis, personnel management, manpower utilization, internal security, procurement, property management and general office services, including publications and printing. Further, it files a group tax return on behalf of all federal credit unions with the Internal Revenue Service. It is responsible for financial management activities including the preparation and control of financial plans, fiscal accounting, budgets, management of the Operating and Share Insurance Funds, investments, assets acquired from liquidating credit unions and the operation of loan management and share payout functions.

The Office of Examination and Insurance. This office is the basic operational office since it performs the functions for which NCUA exists. It develops standards and procedures and conducts examinations of federal credit unions, establishes accounting standards and forms, supervises problem credit unions, directs the share insurance program for federal and state-chartered credit unions, handles chartering, merger, conversion and liquidation activities, reviews reports of examinations of federally-insured, state-chartered credit unions to determine insurability and provides assistance to insolvent insured credit unions.

The Office of Consumer Affairs. Consumer credit legislation vests the Board with the responsiblitily for administering such laws for federal credit unions. To meet this responsibility, a Consumer Affairs Division was established within the Office of Examination and Insurance to handle customer complaints and to oversee compliance with consumer laws and regulations.

NCUA's separate consumer compliance examination program became operational in July 1980. Under this program, specially trained consumer examiners provide guidance to credit union officials to assist them in complying with consumer laws. Although this enforcement function is mandated by law, the program's approach is a positive one which stresses helping officials to develop corrective actions when violations are encountered. It also emphasizes educating officials in the requirements of consumer laws.

In 1982 the consumer exam program was integrated into the regular examination program. The agency had found few violations of consumer laws, and the great majority of those were technical in nature. The agency believes that its responsibility for consumer compliance could best be served through an educational approach in the form of seminars, and a review of all major consumer compliance areas during each exam.

NCUA's enforcement program includes examination of Federal credit unions for compliance with the Truth in Lending Act, the Equal Credit Opportunity Act and other consumer laws, investigation of member complaints and education of credit union officials, staff and members.

The Office of General Counsel. As the legal arm of NCUA, the Office of General Counsel renders legal advice, handles litigation and drafts and reviews legislation and regulations. It performs all liasion functions with the Office of the Federal Register and serves as NCUA's claims officer.

The Office of Policy Analysis and Research. This is the research division of NCUA and, as such, serves as the central repository for financial and statistical data on federal and state credit unions. It conducts research and studies, and publishes research reports and the Annual Reports of the NCUA. It is also responsible for planning, data management and statistical analysis.

The Office of Internal Audit and Investigation. As the internal control function, this office performs operational audits in the field offices to determine the effectiveness of examiner and regional staff policies and procedures in implementing the Federal Credit Union Act and in adhering to Civil Service Commission policies concerning personnel management, equal employment opportunity and delegations of authority.

Office of the Comptroller. All the financial management functions of the NCUA are assigned to this office. Thus, the Comptroller is in effect the chief accountant and treasurer of the NCUA.

The Public Information Office. This division handles all requests for information and publishes and distributes materials on federal credit unions including the *NCUA Quarterly*.

Regional Offices. The six regional offices of NCUA are the operational bases for the field examination staff and the entry points for applications for chartering and insurance. These offices also handle on-site liquidation activities and conduct reviews of examination reports. Each office is headed by a regional administrator. In fiscal year 1982 regional staff was reduced by 25 positions, but field examiners were at the highest level of staffing in five years, comprising 57% of the agency workforce. In fiscal year 1983 a total of 72 new examiner positions have been authorized which will bring the examiner force to nearly 400. At that time nearly 80% of the agency's staff will be in the regional offices.

Chartering

Chartering activities at the NCUA are more voluminous than chartering activities for national banks in the Office of the Comptroller of the Currency or for federal savings and loan associations in the Federal Home Loan Bank Board. As discussed earlier, the entry barriers for credit union charters differ from the barriers for other depository institutions and are probably less difficult to overcome. Perhaps more importantly, NCUA itself differs from the other financial institution supervisory agencies in that it actually helps to organize federal credit unions.

Relationship with the Industry

The fact that employees of NCUA actually help organize federal credit unions emphasizes the unique relationship between NCUA and the credit union industry it regulates. Since its beginnings as the Credit Union Section of the Farm Credit Administration, NCUA has organized not just federal credit unions, but also state credit unions. As a matter of practice, state credit unions were organized in states where the credit union laws were more favorable. The first director of the Section, who came from the credit union movement, adopted a policy that no one would be hired as an "examiner" unless he had already organized more than six credit unions.

This same attitude still exists in the NCUA and in the industry. The provision in the Federal Credit Union Act requiring appointees to the National Credit Union Board to be people with "tested credit union experience" is a reflection of the attitude; so are NCUA's Organizer's Recognition Program, which awards certificates to those who organize federal credit unions; Thrift Honor Awards which go to credit unions with active thrift education and counseling programs; and Milestone Awards for credit unions which have been in operation longer than 25 years.

How long this close relationship can survive in an administrative law environment characterized by public disclosure and accountability and displeasure with cozy industry/agency arrangements remains to be seen, of course.

Probable Survival

Over the years, NCUA has given a great deal of attention to the probability of survival of a federal credit union. The probable survival rate, of course, may prove useful in deciding whether to insure a charter. At the time the charter is issued, the chances of survival are 3 in 5. During the first ten years of operation, the probability of survival increases rapidly and after 16 years survival is almost certain.

Data on the probability of success based on the type of common bond has been compiled also. Table 3-1 shows that the probability of success ranges from 86 percent for telephone employee credit unions to 22 percent for personal service membership groups. As might be expected, credit unions with occupational common bonds have a higher survival rate than those with an association or residential common bond.

Table 3-1 Probability of Success of Federal Credit Unions, by Type of Membership

Type of Membership	Survival Rate	Type of Membership	Survival Rate
Total	59.7		
Associational groups, total	51.1	Transportation, communications,	
Cooperatives	40.8	and utilities	63.7
Fraternal and professional	46.4	Railroad transportation	59.7
Religious	58.4	Bus transportation	54.8
Labor unions	46.7	Motor freight transportation[2]	55.1
Other associational groups	58.7	Air transportation	49.3
Occupational groups, total	62.1	Other transportation	48.8
Agriculture	*78.7	Communications	*79.7
Mining	66.7	Telephone	*86.1
Contract construction	53.7	Utilities	*75.9
Manufacturing	57.3	Wholesale and retail trade	51.5
Food and kindred products	48.8	Finance, insurance, and real estate	62.2
Textile mill products and		Services	70.4
apparel	43.1	Hotels and other lodging places	25.4
Lumber and wood products	43.8	Personal services	22.2
Paper and allied products	*68.7	Misc. business services	66.4
Printing and publishing	64.8	Medical and other health	*83.5
Chemicals and allied products	*73.5	Hospitals	*84.7
Petroleum refining	53.6	Educational services	*75.9
Rubber and plastics products	61.8	Elem. and secondary	*76.3
Leather and leather products	44.2	Colleges and universities	*75.8
Stone, clay, and glass products	*70.2	Other services	54.8
Primary metal industries	63.5	Government	71.8
Fabricated metal products	51.9	Federal government	64.4
Machinery, incl. electrical	59.6	Civilian	66.4
Transportation equipment	51.1	Military	60.0
Motor vehicles and equip-		State and other government	*80.4
ment	54.9	Other occupational groups	63.9
Aircraft and parts	44.9	Residential groups, total	48.1
Instruments[1]	55.7	Urban community	47.2
Other manufacturing	60.7	Rural community	48.7

*Significantly high survival rates.

[1] Professional, scientific, and controlling instruments, photographic and optical goods; watches and clocks.

[2] Including warehousing.

Note: Survival rates are based on the experience of all Federal credit unions chartered from 1934 to December 31, 1974.

Source: National Credit Union Administration Research Report No. 9, July 1975, as cited in Melvin and Davis, *op. cit.,* p. 57.

Examinations

Generally, the literature on bank examinations concludes that in addition to the primary goal of preventing failures there are several important secondary purposes for examination:

1. to maintain the solvency and liquidity of the institution,
2. to police adherence to the banking laws;
3. to discover poor management or dishonesty; and
4. to protect small depositors.

Credit unions are examined for many of the same reasons. Naturally the overriding purpose for examining credit unions is to prevent failures, not primarily because of the impact a failure might have on the local economy, but rather because of the impact the failure would have on the credit union members. Especially before the adoption of federal share insurance in 1971, examinations of credit unions were vital to the protection of the members' savings. NCUA examines each federal credit union once a year. The cost of these examinations are financed by fees charged to the credit unions.

Supervision

Supervisory activities of financial institution regulatory agencies are focused on preventing and correcting operating problems. Through the issuance of regulations limiting or controlling certain practices or activities, the regulations attempt to prevent problems from developing. The remedial aspect of regulatory supervising generally arises as a result of discoveries made during the examination. NCUA performs both supervisory activities for federally related credit unions.

The Board has many supervisory tools available. The Federal Credit Union Act allows them to suspend or revoke charters or even to place a federal credit union in involuntary liquidation if the credit union is insolvent or has violated the provisions of the Federal Credit Union Act, its bylaws or any NCUA regulations. Additional powers are provided under the share insurance provisions of the Federal Credit Act including the power to:

1. issue cease and desist orders,
2. suspend or remove officers and directors.
3. require additional reserves, and
4. terminate insurance.

Salvage

The salvage remedies used by NCUA are similar to those used by FDIC or FSLIC in that the Board may make loans to an insured credit union, purchase its assets, or establish accounts in the credit union in order to assist in avoiding liquidation. They may also guarantee the purchase of assets by any buyer and encourage a merger with another credit union. If these efforts fail, the Board may declare the credit union in involuntary liquidation and designate a liquidating agent.

Liquidations

Liquidations of credit unions should not be compared with the failure of banks or savings and loan associations. Bank failures make headlines; liquidated credit unions generally slip into oblivion with little fanfare because they are an everyday part of credit union supervision. During 1980, 265 federal credit unions were liquidated. Of these, 236 or 89 percent were involuntary. The remaining entered liquidation voluntary via a decision of their respective boards of directors. Since 1934, a total of 8,907 federal credit unions have been liquidated (as of 1980). The very nature of credit unions (as discussed in earlier chapters) makes the rate of liquidations quite unremarkable. Most credit union liquidations occur in the early years of operation. Consequently, a relatively small amount of deposits are involved. Of the federal credit unions which liquidated in 1980, 72 percent had total shareholdings of less than $108,000 and 45 percent had less than $25,000. Only six had more than $500,000 in shares.

Financing of Regulatory Activities

All the chartering, examining and supervisory functions of NCUA are financed by fees and assessments paid by federal credit unions and from charges to the Share Insurance Fund. There is no Congressional authorization for expenditures since the NCUA is not appropriated funds through the Congressional budget process. However, in keeping with the increased pressure for accountability, NCUA is now "on budget" and subject to the Office of Management and Budget guidelines.

Share Insurance Fund

Until 1970, the share accounts in federal credit unions were generally uninsured. At that time legislation was passed that established a National Credit Union Share Insurance Fund within the National Credit Union Administration. The law required all federal credit unions to become insured and allowed the Administrator (replaced by the Board in 1978) to extend coverage to willing state-chartered credit unions that met the criteria established in the law.

For many years CUNA and other credit union associations (particularly those related to the state-chartered credit unions) opposed efforts to create a federal share insurance program on grounds that it would increase government regulation and weaken the dual chartering system. However, since share insurance was established, savings in Federal credit unions have grown vigorously. The NCUA attributes much of this growth to the fact that the insurance stimulated an increase in the number of large accounts held in credit unions. This assertion is supported by the fact that at year-end 1970, the total amount of shares held in accounts larger than $5,000 was $2.1 billion (28 percent of the total) compared to $6.1 billion (42 percent of the total) at year-end 1974. This 185 percent increase in larger denomination share accounts is contrasted with a 51 percent increase in accounts smaller than $5,000 during the same time period.

Although the share insurance legislation gives state-chartered credit unions the option to become federally insured, several states have passed laws requiring state-chartered credit unions to become federally insured and many states require that they be insured by the federal government or a program approved by the state. As of year-end, 1980, 4,910 state credit unions were federally-insured. This number constituted 54 percent of the total number of state credit unions and 63 percent of the savings of all state credit unions.

To date, the NCUA has exercised its statutory discretion to forego examinations of state credit unions by NCUA and to accept the examination reports of the state supervisory authority. Thus, state-chartered, federally insured credit unions are spared the burden of double examinations such as insured state banks must endure. NCUA also uses the authority of the Intergovernmental Personnel Act of 1970 to conduct intergovernmental conferences of supervisors and examiners and for the exchange of personnel from state agencies to

NCUA and from NCUA to state agencies. In this manner, reasonable standards of quality are upheld.

State credit unions that have become federally insured have, in some respects, fared much better than the federal credit unions. Several states were quicker to permit state credit unions to offer certificates and other innovative savings deposits than was the NCUA. Of course, federally-insured, state credit unions are subject to the same termination of insurance, officer and director suspension or removal proceedings and cease and desist orders by the Board as federally chartered credit unions.

The Share Insurance Fund is financed with the premiums paid by the insured credit unions. The statutory maximum premium is 1/12th of 1 percent per year of the total amount of savings in insured accounts. Premiums received from credit unions in 1980 amounted to some $12.7 million. As of September 1980, the Share Insurance Fund had total assets of approximately $217 million. Most of these assets are invested in U. S. Government securities. The Fund is also authorized to borrow up to $100 million from the U. S. Treasury. Share accounts of individuals and other members are currently insured up to $100,000.

OTHER FORMS OF REGULATION

Traditionally, most financial institution laws and regulations were designed to reduce risk and to prevent destabilizing competition. Risk reduction has been accomplished by asset, liability and product restrictions, examinations, reserves and deposit insurance. Competition has been limited by such mechanisms as entry permitting, interest ceilings and geographic restrictions, among others.

The expansion of government regulation that has occurred in recent decades has expanded the traditional avenues of control and added many new ones. Again, credit unions have felt the impact of these regulations—perhaps to a greater extent than competing depository financial institutions since credit unions often have more limited resources with which to cope with the regulatory burden. A substantial portion of the recently added regulatory burden borne by credit unions grew out of the consumerism movement. Beginning with the Consumer Credit Protection Act, credit unions and other consumer credit grantors have been beset by a tide of regulations. The Civil Rights Act, the Fair Credit Reporting Act, the Equal Credit Opportunity Act, the Real Estate Settlement Procedures Act, Home Mortgage Disclosure Act and the Community Reinvestment Act have been enacted since then. Moreover, the Magnuson-Moss Warranty and Federal Trade Commission Improvements Act have subjected federal and state credit unions to the jurisdiction of the Federal Trade Commission.

The potential burden of increased govenrment regulation is difficult to estimate given the sparse empirical evidence, but surely the smaller credit unions operating with volunteer or part-time help find compliance difficult. Almost certainly, the increased complexity of operating a credit union coupled with the possibility of personal liability have decreased the numbers of people willing to serve on the board of directors. Definitely, the costs of operating a credit union have increased.

The cost factor is critical because it is difficult for most credit unions to pass the cost on in the form of higher prices or lower rates. A cost/benefit analysis of the Equal Credit Opportunity Act of 1974 made by the Federal Reserve Board concluded that the act costs credit unions $11.9 million in non-recurring costs and $8.4 million in recurring costs in 1975.[2]

Probably more dismaying than the cost of regulation is the effect that this burden is having on credit union managers, officers and directors. As will be seen in the discussion of the cooperative principles in Chapter 5, education of the members was mentioned as one of the main principles. Many observers now fear that due to the growing resentment with consumer legislation and regulation, a chasm between officers of credit unions and consumer advocates is developing. The anti-consumer tone of some recent meetings of credit union leaders is no different from what might be observed at any business conference. This may partially explain some of the current impetus for reform.

The Deregulation Trend

On March 31, 1980, the President of the United States signed a bill (H. R. 4986) that is revolutionizing the ways financial services are

[2] Federal Reserve Board, *Staff Papers, 1976.*

provided to corporations, business firms, consumers and others in the United States.[3] The Depository Institutions Deregulation and Monetary Control Act of 1980 calls for changes which are fundamental and will alter the ways of doing business for all regulated depository institutions including commercial banks, mutual savings banks, savings banks, and savings and loan associations as well as credit unions.

Recent Legislative History

The evolution of laws and regulations governing financial institutions in the United States is a story of recurring changes in response to economic, political and social forces. Change has been sporadic; relatively short periods of rapid change have been followed by fairly long intervals of slow evolutionary growth. During recent years trends have emerged that will significantly influence the structure of the financial system during the remaining years of the twentieth century. While there have been several indicators of change, the most important are the profound change in regulatory philosophy, technological developments in data processing and communications, innovative responses to regulatory actions and competitive forces by imaginative financial executives and an increase in international financial marketing activities and movement of funds across national boundaries.

The attitude and philosophy of federal regulatory agencies until quite recently evolved from developments during the early years of this century.[4] The essence of the recommendations contained in special studies was to remove all restrictions on regulated institutions that restrain competition among depository institutions including interest rate ceilings and limitations on the types of loan and investment powers open to banks and thrift institutions. Congress did not act immediately on the Hunt Commission's suggestions or those of other study groups. However, the culmination of years of study and congressional reluctance to act decisively, and rising public interest was enactment of perhaps the most revolutionary financial regulatory bill ever passed by Congress and signed by a President of the United

---

[3] Public Law 96-221, March 31, 1980.

[4] See Aubrey N. Snellings, "The Financial Services Industry: Recent Trends and Future Prospects," *Economic Review,* Federal Reserve Bank of Richmond, January/February 1980 for an expansion of this view.

States, the Depository Institutions Deregulation and Monetary Control Act of 1980. The most important features of the Act with respect to credit unions are summarized below.

The Depository Institutions Deregulation and Monetary Control Act of 1980

The essential features of the Act are contained in seven descriptive titles. Some parts of the law were effective immediately while others involving interest rate ceilings and reserve requirements will be implemented in stages during the next six to eight years. By October 1, 1988, all sections of the law will be in force. A summary of each title relevant to credit unions follows.

Title I—Monetary Control Act of 1980

Reserve requirements are imposed on all depository institutions including commercial banks, mutual savings banks, savings banks, and savings and loan associations along with credit unions.

Reserve requirements are applied to all transaction accounts in the depository institutions. Included are all accounts on which the account holder is permitted to make withdrawals, specifically demand deposits, negotiable order of withdrawal accounts, savings deposits subject to automatic transfers, and share draft accounts.

Reserve requirements are placed on 3 percent of the first $25 million in transaction accounts, 12 percent of the amount above $25 million with discretion to vary from 8 percent to 14 percent the requirement for amounts above $25 million. Also, 3 percent of all non-personal time deposits are subject to the reserve requirement with authority to vary this requirement from zero to 9 percent for the purpose of implementing monetary policy. All reserve requirements shall be applied uniformly to all transaction accounts at all depository institutions.

Supplemental reserves also may be imposed for up to 180 days on up to 4 percent of transactions accounts. The supplemental reserve could be extended for further periods not exceeding 180 days and would bear interest at the earning rate of the Fed portfolio during the previous calendar quarter.

Any depository institution in which transaction accounts or non-personal time deposits are held is entitled to the same discount and borrowing privileges from the Fed as member banks.

The reserve requirements allow for a four-year period for member banks of the Federal Reserve System to phase into the new reserve requirement structure. Nonmember institutions such as credit unions will be given eight years to adjust fully to the reserve requirements.

Title II—Depository Institutions Deregulation

The purpose of this title of the Act is to provide for the orderly phase-out and ultimate elimination of the limitations on the maximum rates of interest and dividends which may be paid on deposits and accounts by financial institutions. The period of time during which the phase-out will be completed is six years. However, credit unions are not directly governed by the Act as NCUA retained independent authority.

Authority to carry out this policy is vested in a Depository Institutions Deregulation Committee that consists of the Secretary of the Treasury, Chairman of the Board of Governors of the Federal Reserve System, Chairman of the Board of Directors of the Federal Deposit Insurance Corporation, Chairman of the Home Loan Bank Board, and Chairman of the National Credit Union Administration Board as voting members and the Comptroller of the Currency as a nonvoting member. The Deregulation Committee is expected to gradually increase the limitations on payment of interest on all transaction accounts and provide depositors with a market rate of return on their savings while showing due regard for the safety and soundness of depository institutions.

Title III—Consumer Checking Account Equity Act of 1980

This title provides for automatic transfer of funds, withdrawal of funds from accounts on which interest or dividends are paid (negotiated orders of withdrawals), and authorizes establishment of remote service units by Savings and Loan Associations. Insurance of Deposits in all depository institutions including credit unions is increased to $100,000 from the $40,000 limit that previously existed. Also, the ceiling on loans made by credit unions was increased to 15 percent inclusive of all finance charges. Provision is made for increasing the credit union ceiling as money market conditions dictate for periods up to 18 months.

Title IV—Powers of Thrift Institutions And Miscellaneous Provisions

Thrift Institutions, not including credit unions, are authorized to invest in a variety of investment instruments that heretofore had not been available to them. Included in the list are secured and unsecured consumer loans, commercial paper, corporate debt securities, education loans, mutual capital certificates, community development investments, unsecured construction loans, and certain nonconforming loans (second mortgages) on real property used for residential or farm purposes.

Title V—State Usury Laws

State interest rate ceilings on rates of interest permitted on mortgage loans (usury ceilings) are overridden permanently unless the state's bylaw or constitutional amendment take action to limit interest rates before April 1, 1983. Also state usury ceilings on agriculture and business loans larger than $25,000 are preempted for three years.

Title VI—Truth in Lending Simplification

A list of 100 changes in existing Truth in Lending Law are included in the act. They are designed to make compliance less complicated, less costly and more understandable for lenders and consumers. The Federal Reserve System (FED) is required to issue a revised Regulation Z to carry out the purposes of this title.

Title VII—Regulatory Simplification

Under this title the federal financial regulatory agencies are ordered to review all regulations for the purpose of eliminating costly, duplicative and unnecessary burdens on financial institutions and consumers. All regulations shall insure that a need exists, meaningful alternatives to the regulation are considered and compliance costs, paperwork and other burdens on financial institutions, consumers and the public are held to a minimum. Furthermore, the regulatory agencies are required to establish a program which assures periodic review of existing regulations to determine whether they are achieving stated objectives.

Implications of the Law

The new law contains provisions that have significant implications for all regulated financial institutions and the customers they serve. Review and reflection on the provisions included in the seven separate but related titles of the Act clearly suggests that during the 1980's there will be several changes in the ways financial institutions function in obtaining funds, making loans and investments and, hopefully earning reasonable profits. Among the more important changes that will occur during the decade are a sharp reduction in the scope and number of regulations on financial institutions' activities, an accompanying increased reliance on competitive free market forces, an increase in competition among all types of financial institutions, an increase in use of innovative techniques and technological changes, and more affirmative control over the major components of the money supply by the Federal Reserve.

Less Regulation—More Reliance on Free Markets

Probably the most significant implication embodied in the new law is the sharp change in the philosophy underlining the action taken by Congress. Although we have lived for nearly half a century in a regulatory environment that has been protective, prohibitive and highly restrictive, the new name of the game is freedom of initiative and choice based on free market forces and profit-making incentives. It appears to be abundantly clear that this change in attitude is one of the strongest intents of the Congress.

Such a drastic change in direction of national policy will require much patience, understanding and fortitude on the part of all agencies and institutions involved. On one hand the regulatory agencies will need to adjust their attitudes and policy directives to conform to the spirit as well as the substance of the law. For some, this adjustment undoubtedly will be difficult. At the same time, some of the regulated institutions will find the adjustment to more openness and competitive forces painful if not traumatic. For some of the institutions regulation has included a substantial amount of protection from competition and special treatment of their perceived special needs.

The impact on the general public, especially depositors, and borrowers, will be somewhat mixed. Depositors will be pleased with the increased interest income they will earn on their investments in the regulated institutions and the new services that will be available to them. Borrowers, however, can expect to see more volatility in the price of financial services they need as interest rates, fees and other credit service charges are adjusted to anticipated changes in the cost of funds to lenders.

Increasing reliance on free market forces will encourage institutions to develop innovative techniques and services that in the past have been restricted by regulation. Since regulation is in essence a tax, the removal of regulations eliminates one hidden cost of doing business for the depository institutions.[5] At the same time the institutions will be free to allocate their energies and creative talents in developing new services of all types for their customers. In the past innovation has been limited to finding ways to legally circumvent or avoid regulatory restraints. The result should be to see in the future a wide variety of new and improved services to the public that have not been available before.

On balance, as the law becomes fully effective, borrowers should expect to see fewer restrictions in loan terms, a wider variety of financial contracts to choose from, new and expanded financial services, wider use of technological innovations and special services for market segments that do not exist today. Eventually, although not specifically included in the act, barriers to branching across state lines will likely be removed permitting multi-state-offering of financial services.

Fed Control Over the Money Supply

One section of the Deregulation and Money Control Act that has received relatively little attention by the press and public is Title I which

---

[5] See Posner, Richard A., "Taxation by Regulation," *The Bell Journal of Economics and Management Science*, 2 (Spring 1971), for an expansion of this view.

requires all depository institutions to maintain reserves with the Fed on all transaction accounts. This action when fully implemented in 1988 gives the Fed full control over all deposits that make up the money base, currency and bank reserves, which is the "raw material" from which the money supply is made. In the past Fed control over the money supply has been limited to banks that are members of the Federal Reserve System.

In addition the law provides Fed control over the deposits of all commercial banks and the transaction accounts of all savings banks, savings and loan associations and credit unions. Transaction accounts include all types of deposits from which the depositor is permitted to make withdrawals by negotiable or transferable instrument, payment order, or telephone transfers to third persons or others. As a result, the Fed is now and in the future will be in a much stronger position to control the money supply for the purpose of implementing monetary policy to control inflation, support production of goods and services and maintain employment of the labor force.

SUMMARY

This chapter has reviewed government regulation of credit unions. The situation is not without irony. Over their history credit unions have enjoyed the active support of their regulators at both the state and federal level. More recently, however, the consumerism movement has fostered a spate of laws which have (1) resulted in a disproportionate compliance burden on credit unions and (2) driven a wedge between credit union management and the membership. The landmark Depository Institutions Deregulation and Monetary Control Act of 1980 and its many implications for credit unions was also reviewed. These developments portend both problems and opportunities for the industry in the future as well as the likelihood that credit unions will be substantially deregulated in the near future.

Credit Union Economics

INTRODUCTION

Having now looked at (1) the origins and the growth of credit unions from a rather disjointed movement to a relatively sophisticated industry and (2) the regulation of the industry, this chapter redirects the focus of the discussion to the uniqueness of credit unions. As we have seen, credit unions were established with certain goals in mind that set them apart from their competitors. This chapter addresses these characteristic features of credit unions and the economic implications thereof.

While some of the discussion will proceed along theoretical or conceptual lines, the purpose of this chapter is basically to examine the reality of credit unionism and the economic evolution of the industry. Only in this manner can a true appreciation of the forces determining the viability of credit unions be understood and appreciated. Poincare once said that there is nothing as practical as a good theory. This is true in the same sense that a good theory should provide useful insights into reality. That is, a theory should help answer the ultimate question—why?

Once an understanding of the internal dynamics of credit union operations is gained, challenges facing the credit union industry become more tractable.

CAPITAL FORMATION—THE ENGINE
OF ECONOMIC GROWTH

The primary source of funds available for investment at any time are the savings of individuals and households and the undistributed (saved) profits of business firms. Savings are determined by the level of income that is spent on current consumption. The amount of income spent is related to the spending habits (life style) of the household, expectations concerning future price levels and the rates of interest that can be earned by investing some fraction of current income in an earning asset.

The form of investment will be determined by the saver's attitudes and expectations. The ideal investment for many savers would be that security that yields a high rate of return, has good prospects for capital appreciation, entails a minimum amount of risk of capital loss and can readily be converted into cash. While very few investments meet most or all of these criteria, all forms of investment possess one or more.

Profits of business firms are determined by competitive forces in the economy that influence sales, costs of production and distribution, and the capital required to operate the business. Whether dividend payments are made to owners and the amount of dividend payments also determines the amount of funds available for future investment. Dividend payments made to individuals and households, of course, increase their incomes that are available for consumption or investment.

The users of funds accumulated through savings of individuals and earnings retained by business firms include the three major sectors of the economic system; business corporations, households, and governments. Business firms, primarily corporations but also including non-incorporated business enterprises, are one of the largest and most active seekers of credit in the financial system and they have played a dominant role in many of the swings in business cycles that have occurred during recent years. Household users of funds provided by the credit market borrow funds for current consumption as well as for investment in housing. During recent years households as borrowers have become increasingly important users of funds. As shown in Table 4-1, the total volume of outstanding household debt surpassed corporate borrowing by 1979.

As indicated in Table 4-1, governments including local, state, and

Table 4-1   The Debt Economy

Type	Debt Outstanding at Year End		
	1974	1976	1979
Corporate	$1,000 billion	$1,115 billion	$1,450 billion
Mortgage	600 billion	885 billion	1,200 billion
U.S. Government	500 billion	670 billion	920 billion
State and local government	200 billion	250 billion	310 billion
Consumer	200 billion	220 billion	380 billion
Total	$2,500 billion	$3,140 billion	$4,260 billion

Source: Federal Reserve Board, unpublished documents.

federal governmental units constitute the third major group of borrowers who seek funds through the financial markets. Since the spending programs of governmental agencies frequently exceed the income through taxes, fees and other sources, the agencies must seek funds in the financial markets. At the same time many governmental units collect and hold a number of financial assets in special purpose trust accounts. These funds together with household savings and business earnings become a source of funds in the financial system.

FINANCIAL INTERMEDIATION
AND DISINTERMEDIATION

Financial intermediation is the process through which financial resources are deposited in the major financial institutions for investment in securities, mortgages, loans, and other assets that earn income for the institution. The institutions acquire funds, i.e., savings, by offering holders a type of contract that will be more attractive than those offered by other forms of investment. Commercial banks, savings banks, savings and loan associations and credit unions, for example, offer checking accounts which pay interest on monthly balances, savings accounts and certificates that provide differential interest rates and maturities. Depending upon the extent to which the institution has limitations like Regulation Q placed on its freedom to offer terms sufficiently attractive to lure funds from its competitors, they will offer terms to savers that are attractive and commensurate with their capacity to invest such funds in investment assets that will yield a return high enough to cover costs of obtaining funds and of operating their business and also to provide a profit.

Funds obtained through the intermediation process are liabilities to the institution since they must be returned to the asset holders (savers) on terms stated in the deposit contract. These terms can be on immediate demand of the saver in the case of checking (including share drafts) and passbook (or share) savings accounts up to ten years or more in maturity. The majority of savers in the United States tend to have an interest in acquiring financial assets that contain special characteristics. In the first place, they desire safety of their capital in the form of deposit insurance or other acceptable safeguards. Safety is provided to investors in accounts in the regulated depository institutions, commercial banks, credit unions, mutual savings bonds, and savings and loan associations in the form of insurance of deposits up to $100,000 in the event of failure of the institution. Funds invested in other types of investment, including common stocks and money market mutual funds, are not insured.

Savers also desire convenience in dealing with the institutions with whom they entrust their savings. To provide convenience to customers the institutions have opened branches and remote service facilities in residential areas, shopping centers and major transportation interchanges. In addition, many institutions have made it possible for customers to transact much of their financial business over the telephone. For many savers liquidity and accessibility are important features of the savings contract. A financial asset is liquid if it can be converted into cash quickly with little or no loss in value. Checking accounts and passbook savings accounts at commercial banks, savings banks and savings and loan associations are highly liquid. Other types of contracts possess less liquidity although life insurance policies which carry cash surrender values are quite liquid. Savers also are interested in financial assets that are readily accessible, that is available in small denominations. Many financial securities including U. S. Treasury Bills and money market certificates, are only available in denominations of $10,000 or more which is beyond the reach of many savers.

Figure 4-1 illustrates graphically the nature of the financial intermediation process.

In contrast to intermediation, disintermediation describes the process through which funds are withdrawn from the financial inter-

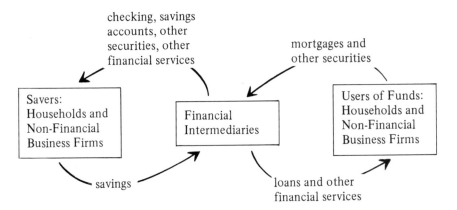

Figure 4-1   Financial Intermediation Process

mediaries and invested in other types of investment or spent on current consumption. Except for withdrawals of funds to meet current spending needs of households, disintermediation most frequently takes place when funds are withdrawn for the purpose of investing in securities sold on the open market especially common stocks, corporate and government bonds, and money market mutual funds. The occurrence of disintermediation usually takes place during periods of high and rising interest rates when the financial intermediaries have difficulty in adjusting the rates they offer savers quickly enough to match the increases in interest rates available in the open market. Problems associated with disintermediation have been somewhat ameliorated in recent years with the offering by financial intermediaries of floating rate (money market) savings certificates, passage of the Depository Institutions Deregulation and Monetary Control Act of 1980, and the arrival of the All-savers tax-exempt certificate in late 1981.

CONSUMER CREDIT

Not only are credit unions a vehicle for savings, they are also important sources of credit (note that we do not call them *savings* unions) for their membership and, thus, very much a part of the capital formation process. This is particularly true in those cases in which the credit is used for investment in human capital (say, a tuition loan) or productive equipment. The unique features of the consumer credit market and the characteristics which set credit unions apart from other financial intermediaries provide the focus for the balance of this chapter. Keep in mind that we are basically seeking answers to two questions: (a) How are credit unions and the markets they serve different and (b) Why are credit unions the way they are?

A UNIQUE AND UNDER-SUPPLIED MARKET

Consumer credit was a late-developing service at financial institutions. In fact, bankers traditionally resisted consumer lending on the theory that loans should be real-bills. That is, loans should be used for "productive" purposes—those generating the wherewithal to liquidate the loan. Consumer lending flies in the face of the real-bills theory, for consumer loans not only do not directly generate income, some (say, a loan for a Las Vegas vacation) can lead directly to financial stress making timely repayment even more of a problem. It took the competitive pressures of the Post-World War II era to cause consumer lending to be perceived as a "legitimate" banking service.

So, American households have demanded and received huge amounts of consumer credit. But why would a consumer want to borrow except for emergencies? After all borrowing adds (substantially these days) to the cost of the goods and services purchased plus the extra administrative costs involved. The answer lies in the consumer's positive time preference. This simply means that, other things being equal, most of us would prefer goods today to goods tomorrow. As with most things in life, the decision to borrow turns out to be a trade-off between the pleasure and convenience of having goods and services immediately and the cost of accessing this time utility—the interest rate.

Consumer credit is widely considered to be one of the more consistently under-supplied of the financial services. This is due to a number of factors. Some of these forces operate from the consumer's side of the market and others on the lender's.

THE COST OF LENDING.

A little understood aspect of the consumer finance field is the high (relative to the amount borrowed) cost of originating and servicing a consumer-oriented loan. First, there is the cost of collecting the underlying credit information. Also, processing the payments from the borrowers involves substantial handling costs. The sum of these processing and information costs constitutes the fixed costs of lending. The effect of these costs on small consumer loan interest rates (calculated Annual Percentage Rate as required by Regulation Z) is shown in Table 4-2.

When the variable cost such as interest on borrowed money, the cost of equity funds, and bad debt losses are added in, it soon becomes apparent that high interest rates are required to make consumer lending profitable. This is particularly true of the small principal, short maturity loans that typify this market. It is worth emphasizing that the risks associated with high default and loss rates in consumer lending has also put upward pressure on interest rates. Under such cost structures, it is easy to see how usury laws which put upper limits on interest rates could be counterproductive. If rates are held artifically low, lenders tend first to ration credit to large, longer maturity loans and may ultimately stop making loans at all if the interest rate does not allow a reasonable return. In fact, in 1979 and 1980 finance companies were able to improve their market share of consumer loans because credit union rate limits made loans unprofitable. Borrowers were turned away from credit unions and finance companies (with their higher usury limits) were able to pick up the slack.

Borrower's Costs

The cost of obtaining information is also high for the borrower in terms of time and money. (How many people do you know who actually shop for financing?) Thus, consumer loan demand has traditionally been quite interest inelastic.

Clearly, the consumer loan sector is plagued by institutional inefficiencies—particularly high fixed costs and poor information flows. These conditions tend to cause a consistent under supply of consumer

Table 4-2 Finance Charges and Corresponding APR's
Necessary to Recover Total Estimated Costs by Size of Loan

Amount Financed	Finance Charge	APR
$ 100	$ 56.06	91.36%
200	62.12	53.14
300	68.18	39.62
400	74.24	32.66
500	80.30	28.43
600	86.36	25.58
700	92.42	23.53
800	98.48	22.00
900	104.54	20.80
1,000	110.60	19.82
1,100	116.66	19.04
1,200	122.72	18.37
1,300	128.78	17.82
1,400	134.84	17.32
1,500	140.90	16.90
1,600	146.96	16.54
1.700	153.02	16.21
1,800	159.08	15.93
1,900	165.14	15.67
2,000	171.20	15.45
2,100	177.26	15.23
2,200	183.32	15.04
2,300	189.38	14.86
2.400	195.44	14.70
2,500	201.50	14.55
2,600	207.56	14.41
2,700	213.62	14.29
2,800	219.68	14.18
2,900	225.74	14.07
$3,000	$231.80	13.98%
Overall Average		22.38%

Source: *Report of the National Commission on Consumer Finance*, p. 144, U.S. Government Printing Office, 1975.

credit. This is the field upon which credit unions must play. However, as we shall see, many of the characteristics of credit unions give them a potential competitive edge in the consumer finance market.

COOPERATIVE CREDIT AND THE CHARACTERISTICS OF CREDIT UNIONS

Conceptually, the distinguishing features of credit unions are derived primarily from their cooperative nature. The most important of these distinguishing characteristics are:

1. Common bond
2. Reduced costs and subsidies
3. Convenience
4. Mutuality

The discussion that follows examines the impact of the cooperative nature of credit unions and these four specific features. It should be noted that these characteristics are not unrelated. For example, credit unions are often more convenient because employers provide (subsidize) offices at the workplace.

Credit Unions as Cooperatives

Credit union proponents rarely mention that credit unions are cooperatives. This is probably because they recognize that the word "cooperative" creates a communications barrier with the general public and partially because emphasis on the cooperative structure was believed to raise questions in the minds of potential sponsors, particularly during the early stages of credit union organization efforts. Instead, the industry promotes credit unions as member-owned or mutual institutions. But it is almost impossible to understand credit unions without recognizing that they are cooperatives. The organizational structure, the prohibition against paying directors and officers, and even the common bond feature are directly attributable to the cooperative form of economic enterprise. Indeed, the "philosophy" of credit unions that permeates credit union literature is mostly the philosophy of the cooperative.

The Cooperative Concept

A cooperative may be defined as an enterprise or organization owned by and operated for the benefit of those using its services. Certain well-known principles form the foundation for cooperatives. These are sometimes referred to as the Rochdalian Principles, derived from the Rochdale Society of Equitable Pioneers, a group of weavers who established the first cooperative in Rochdale, England in 1844. The principles include:

1. open membership,
2. democratic control with one vote per member,
3. distribution of earnings in proportion to patronage,
4. limited payments for the use of capital,
5. education of the members, and
6. volunteerism

A subsidiary principle is that the members should pool their labor as well as their capital and purchasing or producing power. Thus, the philosophy of unpaid, volunteer employees. As could be expected, however, many cooperatives have not strictly adhered to all of these principles, and through the years the principles have become more ideals than reality. Cooperatives have been traditionally formed to benefit either producers or consumers. In the credit union case, the members are usually both the suppliers and consumer of loanable funds.

Open Membership

The "open" membership precept is something of a misnomer. Actually membership is only open to those who are eligible to join. In credit unions, membership has always been restricted. Early credit unions restricted membership to those perceived to be willing and able to repay the loans. The members of a community knew each other so a person's reputation determined admission to the credit union. This practice is still reflected in the provisions of credit union law that require the board of directors to act on membership applications and that permit a member to be expelled by a vote of the membership.

Democratic Control

The principle of democratic control has been preserved in credit union laws. At the very least, the opportunity for member participation exists. However, credit unions (and most other organizations) are typically controlled by a small clique who have enough interest to take the time to participate actively. Frequently, this group acquires proprietary attitude, which can be helpful or not depending upon their abilities and aggressiveness. Member participation is one aspect of credit unions where there is considerable variation. In some credit unions, a substantial part of the membership votes and turns out for the annual meeting. Such credit unions are often as much social institutions as economic entities. On the other hand, there are other credit unions that have to go to some length to make sure that a quorum attends the annual meeting.

Limited Payment and Distribution of Earnings

The third and fourth of the Rochdalian Principles can be discussed together for they both involve returns to the members for participating either as a supplier or user of resources. The concept of distribution of earnings in proportion to patronage survives in credit unions in the form of dividends and interest refunds. Dividends are returned to the savers and interest refunds to the borrowers. The more one saves or borrows, the greater the dividends or interest refunds gained. However, there is an apparent contradiction in distributing earnings in proportion to patronage and then limiting payments for the use of capital. The limited payments principle gave rise to the now-rare credit union practice of paying a uniform percentage dividend to all members regardless of the amount of shares owned. A variation of this principle is still present in most credit union laws in a provision that allows the board of directors to place a cap on the number of shares any individual member can purchase. Doubtless, it was never anticipated that this concept would be used for limiting savings, but some boards of directors do place limits on shares when loan demand is weak.

Education of Members

Like member participation, the extent of member education programs varies considerably among credit unions. Those that belive in this principle provide personal financial counseling, self-study courses, and seminar extensive consumer information. Such credit unions provided the credit union industry its reputation for being consumer oriented.

Volunteerism

The idea of unpaid, volunteer employees died out in most cooperatives years ago. Typically, cooperatives learn quickly that full-time, paid management is essential to survival.

As of the end of 1980 there were full-time and part-time paid employees in credit unions. Additionally, several states now permit all officers to be paid and some state-chartered credit unions are even paying fees to directors. This trend is so well established the employee compensation is often the biggest expense item for credit unions.

This is not to deny the part that volunteers have played and continue to play in credit unions, for indeed volunteers have been a critical factor in the growth of the credit union industry. In the early years, these unions typically believed strongly in the need to provide a source of savings and credit to people denied such a source and manifested a missionary zeal for the cooperative form of enterprise. Their beliefs were a powerful catalytic force in the movement.

Common Bond

Bank Common Bonds

At one point in their history, commercial banks and savings and loan associations operated with a form of common bond. The first bank organized in the United States was founded by merchants for merchants. Other banks were formed to serve mechanics, farmers, and other occupational groups. Bank names such as "Farmers and Merchants Bank" and "Mechanics National Bank" reflect these origins. Savings and loan associations were frequently organized to serve groups with specific ethnic backgrounds or neighborhoods. This is all quite natural. People in the groups presumably knew each other and were familiar with each other's ways. This is precisely the reason the first credit unions had a common bond.

Origin of Common Bond

There is considerable misunderstanding regarding the common bond. The concept has its roots in Germany where the first credit unions were established within the boundaries of a village. Membership in the credit union was limited to those of good reputation and there were sound economic reasons for this limitation. Very often these early credit unions did not generate enough savings to meet the loan demand and were forced to borrow. When they did so, all the members of the credit union became jointly and severally liable for the loan. Consequently, the strict membership criteria was a method of limiting the liability of the members of the credit union. Everyone in the community could seek to join, but membership was limited to those who were judged to be of a character to repay their debts. In essence then, the credit union had a community charter and the "common bond" was membership in the credit union.

Desjardins established the first credit union in North America with a community base and the first credit union in the United States was community based. Moreover, the first credit union law, enacted in Massachusetts, permitted the organizers to specify in the charter the ". . . conditions of residence or occupation which qualify for membership."

The fixed costs of lending can be lowered if the credit union has access to special information that is not available to others. At a small credit union, one borrows through his peers on the Loan Committee—people who are likely to understand his job security and lifestyle. This was the essence of the movement's origin—neighbors lending to neighbors. However, this situation applies only slightly, if at all, to large credit unions for which the only common bond is residence in the same county or metropolitan area.

Some distinction can be drawn between occupational and non-occupational credit unions on the basis of payroll deduction plans. Payroll deductions which are alleged to lower the costs of collecting payments and receiving savings inflows, are not so readily available when the bond of association is non-occupational. It is also generally held that group membership induces borrowers to be more conscientious with respect to loan payments. Direct losses are thus reduced and lower delinquency rates, in turn, reduce collection costs.

Another benefit of the close associative bond and loyalty to a group is that the credit union is often able to attract volunteer labor. The officers of all credit unions are proscribed from accepting remuneration, and a volunteer clerical staff is crucial to the successful operation of every credit union. Salary costs as a percentage of income generally do increase with the age of a credit union and with its size. This may be symptomatic of the wavering effects of the common bond. However, such free labor is not a direct social saving as are the other cost reductions mentioned above. Rather, it serves to drive a wedge between the true social cost of consumer lending and the (private) costs that are incurred by credit unions. Credit allocation is thereby shifted in favor of the consumer sector. This can be considered a desirable result due to the chronic under-supply of such credit. Consequently, it can reasonably be expected that strong common bond will improve the supply of consumer credit in the economy by reducing information costs and creating a corrective distortion in capital markets.

Another impact of the circumscribed membership field of credit unions is on the supply of shareholdings and the demand for loans. In a competitive system, an "open" financial intermediary the size of most credit unions would face highly elastic (responsive to interest rate changes) supply and demand schedules (Figure 4-2). Actually depository intermediaries typically deal with sloped (less elastic) curves. Such a slope occurs to a great extent due to interest elasticity; but there are also nonpecuniary costs associated with borrowing and lending and these costs are dependent on an institution's physical location. The results is that household savings and borrowing markets can usually be represented by models of monopolistic competition. That is, supply and demand for consumer financial service depend on location and convenience (among others) as well as interest rates.

These phenomena apply to credit unions as well, but certain credit union characteristics result in a further modification of the situation. First, a limited field of membership means that a credit union will be able to attract less funds, *ceteris paribus,* than another savings institution located in the same area. Moreover, the elasticities of credit union schedules might be expected to result in lower interest elasticities than those of an open institution because of payroll deductions, loyalty to the common bond, etc. In sum, then, credit union demand schedules are likely to resemble $\overline{UU}$ and $\overline{U'U'}$ in Figures 4-3 in contrast to $\overline{BB}$ and $\overline{B'B'}$, which represent the schedules confronting a competitive open institution.[1]

Under the deregulated regime of the 1980s, it is likely that some-

---

[1] Mark J. Flannery. *An Economic Evaluation of Credit Unions in the United States* (Federal Reserve Bank of Boston), p. 74.

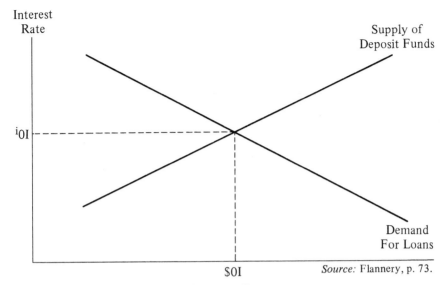

Figure 4-2   An "Open" Financial Intermediary

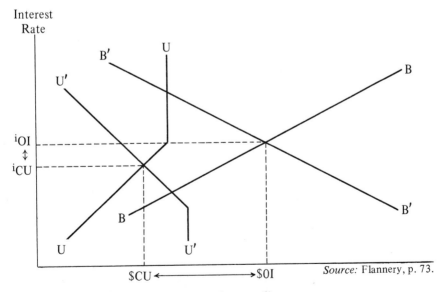

Figure 4-3   Credit Union Vs. An Open Intermediary

thing more akin to pure competition will prevail among depository intermediaries. Demand and supply schedules throughout the financial intermediary sector should accordingly become much more elastic. Credit unions, however, will continue to be constrained by their field of membership. In the case of smaller institutions, it is entirely possible that diseconomies of scale will outweigh the inherent information advantages of such credit unions. Small credit unions may find themselves unable to attract deposit funds. While this is not a possibility limited to credit unions, their characteristic membership limitations makes them particularly vulnerable in this regard.

Occupational Common Bond

The occupational common bond dominates in this country because it proved to be the easiest and simplest way to get credit unions organized. The general economic prosperity following World War I contributed to an era of corporate enlightenment and paternalism. However, some of these sponsors were suspicious of cooperatives, perceiving them to be contradictory to capitalism. It proved politic for credit union proponents to downplay the cooperative nature of credit unions. It may be that "common bond" became a substitute for "cooperative."

The common bond does connote working together for a common purpose while it also connotes a group of people who know each other by reputation. Such a group would of necessity be small. But then grocery stores, drug stores and many other businesses were once small enough for the proprietors to know their customers. The same economic and social developments that forced these businesses into mass marketing also have influenced credit unions.

Reduced Costs and Subsidies

As has been pointed out, common bond restrictions on credit union membership have been presumed to be effective in reducing the costs of operations when the common bond is such that the members know each other. The costs of gathering credit information are claimed to be low because the members themselves are the source of the information. Similarly, peer group pressure supposedly reduced bad debt losses and collection costs.

In the case of credit unions with occupational common bonds and a sponsor relationship, it is difficult to distinguish clearly whether the cost savings arise from the common bond or the sponsor relationship. The sponsor's willingness to supply income data may be an effective substitute for personal knowledge. The employee-employer relationship between the member and the sponsor may provide a subtle incentive for the repayment of loans. Moreover, the sponsor's furnishing of payroll deductions helps assure repayment.

Occupational and associational credit unions almost always have some kind of sponsor relationship and together they comprise 96 percent of all credit unions (with occupational bonds accounting for 80%). Thus, this section will deal primarily with employer-sponsors of occupational credit unions and the subsidies they provide.

A credit union is a legal entity separate and distinct from the sponsor and the relationship with the sponsor ranges from tolerance to a surprising degree of solicitude. In some credit unions, the sponsor's personnel manager or chief accountant and/or similar officers sit on the credit union's board of directors and, in effect, represents the management of the sponsoring organization. For other credit unions, management takes a completely hands-off attitude.

The sponsor relationship provides many advantages and some disadvantages. Often the sponsor furnishes the credit union with both capital and labor subsidies by providing some or all of the following:

1. paid "time-off" from regular employment for volunteer officials,
2. office space, furnishings and utilities,
3. accounting, bookkeeping and/or computer services,
4. supplies and purchasing assistance, and
5. payroll deductions.

Sponsor subsidies are particularly critical for new credit unions. Such support makes it possible to get started with a minimum of savings capital and frees the savings that are contributed to be used for loans rather than for expenses or fixed assets. Sometimes, as a credit union matures, subsidies are reduced either at the initiative of the sponsor or of the credit union. Frequently, larger credit unions move off the sponsor's premises and build their own building, but they usually try to retain payroll deduction privileges.

On the other hand, a disadvantage of sponsor subsidies is that they may dull competitive awareness. The subsidies and the captive membership may create an atmosphere of insularity that could easily be challenged by an aggressive competitor.

Other Subsidies

From their very beginnings in this century, credit unions have been heavily subsidized. Filene spent over $1.5 million of his own money to get credit unions off the ground. Sponsors provided labor and capital subsidies. And, as was seen in Chapter II, state credit union leagues and CUNA Mutual Insurance Society have been sources of subsidy.

In addition, there is an impressive menu of government subsidies made available to credit unions. They are exempt from federal income taxes and the subsidies furnished by sponsors are deductible business expenses for the sponsor. Credit unions serving government employees, a major factor in the industry, are granted free space and payroll deductions.

Many of the cooperative principles that have been codified in credit union laws amount to subsidies. Among these is the provision prohibiting compensation for officers and directors. This combination of subsidies from the private and public sectors has been absolutely essential to credit union development.[2]

Convenience

The sponsor relationship provides another great advantage to credit unions. That is convenience for the members. Not so much a location convenience, but the transaction convenience of payroll deductions. Approximately 90 percent of credit unions with occupational common bonds are provided with payroll deductions by their sponsors.

The supposed advantage of the location convenience tends to be overestimated by competitors. The effort by the American Bankers Association several years ago to promote in-plant banking as a means of competing with credit unions failed to recognize that the transac-

[2] Ronald J. Melvin, et al., *Credit Unions and the Credit Union Industry,* (New York Institute of Finance), pp. 44-46.

tion convenience was the key. With automatic teller machines and direct deposit of payrolls, the means are available to combat the transaction convenience.

However, Taylor and Flannery have demonstrated the particular significance of convenience and multiple service offerings (especially the availability of loans) in the case of credit unions. Apparently, convenience remains an important facet of the current "competitive balance" and must be considered along with any interest rate differentials that exists among financial institutions.

Along with convenience for the member, payroll deductions reduce expenses by cutting the cost of servicing savings accounts and loan accounts and by minimizing bad debts and their accompanying costs. Clearly, the direct deposit aspects of payroll deductions place credit unions in the vanguard of the electronic funds transfer system.

Mutuality

Potentially the most significant credit union characteristic of all is the mutual form of organization. Credit union advocates frequently make reference to the fact that credit unions operate differently from other financial institutions, because they are "owned by the members" and, thus, credit unions are alleged to be more member benefit oriented and less concerned with growth, profits, etc. This "concept that mutuality, like motherhood, is inherently desirable rests primarily on the belief that it is more noble to serve one's customers and depositors than, through the profit motive, one's stockholders."[3]

While the traditional cooperative (mutual) model provides important insights into certain features of mutual firms, it should not be applied directly to credit unions. The typical cooperative seeks to maximize the benefit of the members by extracting as much surplus as possible from the market, and the welfare of their customers (purchasers of their output) is thus of no concern. Such a model might be applied to mutual savings banks or mutual savings and loans because each might be said to maximize the return to savers at the expense of

[3] Elliott G. Carr, "Mutuality in Banking: Advantage or Disadvantage?" Unpublished document, Massachusetts Mutual Savings Bank Association, 1973.

borrowers. These mutual lenders (like their profit-seeking counterpart) have no incentive to cut borrowing rates below the market level.

On the other hand, credit unions have a duty to serve *all* their members, borrowers as well as savers, because they operate as a mutual on both sides of the market. Consequently, credit unions have been called the purest form of cooperative. This situation complicates the decision-making process markedly. Since membership and the attendant right to borrow requires but a single share, it is not necessary that there be a significant overlap between borrowers and savers. In fact, within each institution there tends to be two quite distinct groups—savers are middle-aged and have accumulated a relatively large amount of wealth, while the borrowing group is composed primarily of younger, lower income members.

It is debatable whether any firm or cooperative does in fact act in accordance with theoretical goals. Profit maximization, even by stock firms, has been questioned by many observers. However, given their relatively small size and closeness of bond, it seems that if any type of organization would likely seek to optimize the welfare of all members then credit unions should. Even without effective control, decisions are usually confined to a limited group and despite a regular turnover among the directors and loan committee, there is generally sufficient overlap to insure a continuous transmittal of their goals. Moreover, the typical credit union has a relatively small number of active leaders. This is particularly true after the credit union has grown to the point that a professional manager is hired.

Credit Unions vs Credit Unions

In preceding sections, credit unions have been treated as a group in order to contrast them with their competitors. Credit unions do, of course, have much in common with one another by virtue of their common purposes, cooperative nature and similar statutory environment. Nevertheless, it is important to note that credit unions can differ from one another in many ways. The level of dependence on free labor and space and the various forms of common bonds available result in a distinct segmentation of the industry.

The most extensive subsidization is enjoyed by the smaller, occupational credit unions. Larger credit unions generally have higher salary expenses and costs of office space and distinct cost discontinuities arise as a result of movement along the institutional life cycle— the credit union may purchase a new building of its own, hire a professional manager, and/or change from volunteer to paid clerical staff in order to handle increased deposit and loan activities. Several authorities have suggested scale discontinuities may develop in a credit union's cost curve due largely to the introduction of new, more efficient technology. Additionally, information costs are likely to increase as the credit union expands. In a small cooperative, personal knowledge and trust play an important role in lending, but as its membership grows, a credit union must retreat to more formal credit analysis methods. The credit union becomes more like other consumer lenders, and its costs and losses rise accordingly. Only if economies of scale offset this trend can larger credit unions maintain their cost advantage vis-a-vis the competition.

It should be noted that the value of the common bond in controlling losses and reducing lending costs is likely to vary considerably among types of bond. In particular, residential credit unions may derive little if any benefit from their common bonds. The original purpose of residential credit unions was to provide charters for groups within a *well-defined* neighborhood, community, or rural district. This philosophy has served as the basis for the hundreds of low income neighborhood credit unions that are sponsored and subsidized (primarily in inner city areas) by the Office of Economic Opportunity. These cooperatives were organized along distinct neighborhood lines—often in conjunction with other community action programs that were undertaken during the early and middle sixties. However, residential charters have also been granted to institutions that serve entire cities and counties. In such cases, the common bond has less impact and these credit unions are essentially able to offer their services to the same number of people in the community as any other financial institution. As deregulation progresses it may be particularly difficult to distinguish a residential credit union from other depositories.

The bond of association can also affect the activity level at credit unions. Occupational institutions tend to have a relatively stable and homogeneous membership and, therefore, the loan demand and savings supply may be highly correlated across individual shareholders. Associational and residential credit unions, on the other hand, suffer higher membership turnover but are not so likely to experience severe fluctuations in share and loan levels as a result the simultaneous demands to which occupational credit unions are subject. Moreover, since associational and residential cooperatives generally do not have payroll deduction plans, cost characteristics may potentially vary by type of bond.

SUMMARY

The goal of this chapter has been to provide a conceptual model or "ideal" of the credit union and the consumer market in which it has traditionally specialized. The provision of such a model is not an end itself but a means toward the end of understanding credit unions as they are today, and as they may become in the future. Thus, in describing the various unique characteristics of credit unions insight is developed into why credit unions operate as they do and why, in an ever more homogeneous market, credit unions remain and shall remain a distinctly different type of financial intermediary. It was also pointed out that there are many ways in which credit unions may differ from one another.

Credit Unions in the Financial Market Place

INTRODUCTION

As demonstrated in the previous chapters, credit unions have grown rapidly into a highly visible component of the consumer finance system. However, it is important to keep in mind that credit unions are also characterized by their small size. In fact, several individual commercial banks (Citibank, Bank of America, Chase Manhattan, etc.) in the United States have total assets which exceed those of the entire credit union industry.

This chapter explores the relationships between (1) credit unions and other intermediaries in the consumer finance market *and* (2) the consumer finance system and the broader money and capital markets . Clearly, the size factor prohibits credit unions from attaining great significance in the total financial sector. The question to be considered in this chapter is whether or not the credit union industry can achieve and sustain a rate of growth that will carry credit unions to a position of prominence (if not predominance) in the consumer finance market.

AN OVERVIEW OF THE FINANCIAL SYSTEM

Elements of the System

Consumer financial transactions occur in an environment that includes individuals, firms, institutions and agencies competing for the pool of funds available for investment at any given time. In order to fully understand and appreciate the problems associated with obtaining the funds required to finance purchases, it is necessary to place the consumer finance market in proper context with other financial markets and the overall financial system, because *to an ever increasing degree all financial markets are becoming interdependent.* The financial system is composed of those individuals, dealers, institutions and agencies that carry out the functions of allocating the monetary resources required to conduct the day-to-day activities of the economy. The system performs two essential functions through the financial markets. On the one hand, it provides the channels through which funds flow from suppliers to users. It is the interactions among the financial markets that direct the investment of funds into the consumer finance market, stocks, bonds, demand and time deposits and other types of financial instruments.

The flow of funds function allows for consumption and investment in the economy, provides for the accumulation of wealth through savings and earnings (profits) of business firms and distributes funds among the various sectors of society. The pricing mechanism assesses the risks associated with different types and maturities of securities and establishes the expected rates of return that they must offer if they are to be successful in attracting investors. This pricing process plays a dominant role in allocating capital (accumulated savings in this context) to the most productive (highest yield) forms of investment.

The financial system includes brokers and dealers who facilitate financial transactions by expediting transfers of funds from savers directly to users and to financial intermediaries which facilitate the transfer of funds more indirectly through the credit process. The major financial intermediaries in the United States include commercial banks, mutual savings banks, savings and loan associations, credit unions, life insurance companies, investment companies, money market funds, and finance companies. These institutions collect funds from the public in the form of deposits, savings accounts and other certificates, share accounts, policy premiums and related securities instruments and invest them in mortgages, securities and other assets.

Financial intermediaries provide the institutional framework through which the financial system functions. Intermediaries pool the funds of numerous savers and by assessing of risk and establishing prices for loans and securities, they provide a cost-effective method for channeling funds to users. By creating, maintaining and offering different types of assets and liabilities, they offer a variety of choices to savers and borrowers at prices that are more attractive and better tailored to needs of savers and borrowers than individuals would be able to offer.

Flow of Funds

An understanding and full appreciation of the nature and operation of the consumer market requires a look at other financial markets which function in the United States. Financial markets usually are classified on the basis of the length of maturity of securities traded in the marketplace. Markets where securities with maturities of less than one year are bought and sold usually are called money markets. Examples of money market financial instruments are commercial paper issued by business firms and U. S. Treasury Bills. Markets where securities carry maturities of more than one year are referred to as capital markets. Mortgages, stocks and bonds of corporations, and long-term bonds of state, local and federal governments are examples of capital market instruments. Investors frequently transfer their financial assets between short and long-term securities depending on their financial needs, motivations, expectations and their perceptions of risk.

A useful method for examining and improving knowledge of the relationship between money and capital markets is flow of funds analysis. This systematic analytical tool makes it possible to study both financial markets and track with precision the primary movement of funds from those who save to users of funds.

The most useful device for depicting the flow of funds through the money and capital markets in the United States is the statistical summary prepared by the Board of Governors of the Federal Reserve System and reported on a regular basis in the *Federal Reserve Bulletin* in the flow of funds accounts tables. The tables identify the funds raised in the credit markets by major category including consumer loans, mortgages, corporate stocks and bonds and borrowing by local, state and federal agencies. Annual comparisons of total amounts invested in each category clearly show changes that occur in the volume of funds invested each year in mortgages and other forms of investment. The changes that occur from year to year indicate the fact that competition for funds does take place constantly. Every claim that is created by a household, business firm or governmental agency includes an interest rate or dividend rate (expectation) which reflects the price the user is willing to pay for the use of money. The amounts invested in each type of security, then, represent the extent to which that security has been successful in meeting competition. Year-to-year comparisons of changes in funds can be made by examining Table 5-1 which portrays for selected years the funds raised by major users and advanced by the major institutions, government agencies, households, and business firms.

The lower part of Table 5-1 identifies the financial institutions and other private and governmental agencies that invest funds they have accumulated through deposits, sale of financial contracts or other means. Advances made by these intermediaries are made on a competitive basis and reflect the amounts directly advanced by households and business firms as well as those made by financial intermediaries. The volume of direct advances provides one indication of the extent to which funds are flowing away from the financial intermediaries which is one form of disintermediation as described above.

The federal government exerts influence on the financial markets primarily in two ways. On one hand when the government through implementation of fiscal policy incurs a budgetary surplus, the financial market generates a surplus, an event that has occurred only rarely during the past fifty years, the impact on financial markets is salutary. A balanced or surplus budget removes temporarily one source of demand on the pool of funds available for investment. This alleviation in demand has the tendency to ease interest rates.

When government, be it local, state or federal, incurs a deficit in its budget, that deficit must be financed in the same manner that a household or business firm finances its need for funds (deficit). It must borrow funds in the capital market by issuing financial securities in the form of short-term bills, notes or bonds. These notes are pur-

Table 5-1   Funds Raised and Advanced in Credit Markets,
Selected Years 1971-1980 (in billions $)

	1971	1975	1977	1979	1980
Total Funds Raised					
U. S. Government securities	25.5	85.8	57.6	38.8	79.2
State and local obligations	17.6	16.1	23.7	18.9	23.5
Corporate bonds	19.7	27.2	21.0	21.2	27.9
Home mortgages	26.1	39.5	96.4	109.1	81.8
Multi-family residential mortgages	8.8	NA	7.4	8.9	8.5
Other mortgages	12.0	15.6	27.2	41.9	36.4
U. S. Government-sponsored agencies	3.2	3.2	5.8	24.3	24.4
Mortgage pool securities	–	10.3	20.5	28.1	23.2
Consumer credit	11.2	9.7	40.6	44.2	2.3
All other funds raised	11.8	16.1	92.3	146.9	127.2
Total	135.9	223.5	392.5	482.3	434.4
Total Funds Advanced					
Households	12.3	27.1	30.5	70.8	22.5
U.S. Government-sponsored agencies	3.2	4.5	6.3	29.4	25.3
Mortgage pools	–	10.3	20.5	28.1	23.0
Commercial banking system	50.6	29.4	87.7	121.1	99.7
Thrift institutions*	41.4	53.7	82.3	56.2	56.1
Life insurance companies	13.5	18.8	28.6	33.8	34.1
Private pension funds	A	12.8	15.6	22.0	20.4
State and local retirement funds	A	11.7	15.4	15.5	24.4
All other funds advanced	4.9	55.2	105.6	105.4	128.9
Total	135.9	223.5	392.5	482.3	434.4

NA –Not available.
Source: Flow of Funds Accounts, Federal Reserve System, seasonally adjusted.
*Credit unions.
A –Combined with life insurance.

chased by households, business firms and financial intermediaries and compete with other users of funds for the supply of funds available for investment. Since 1965 a surplus has occurred only once, in 1969, while in other years deficits ranging from $2 billion to above $100 billion have been accumulated.

During those years that the federal government has incurred substantial deficits in its budget, considerable pressure is exerted on financial markets. Funds that otherwise would be available for investment in mortgages and other securities are diverted into government securities. This diversion places upward pressure on interest rates and drives some potential borrowers out of the market. This is referred to as "crowding out" some borrowers from borrowing because they cannot afford to pay the higher interest rate caused by the increase in borrowing by the federal government. This phenomenon occurs unless the Board of Governors of the Federal Reserve System takes action to increase the money supply to accommodate the increase in government borrowing. Such action by the Board of Governors is known as "monetizing" the debt and is discussed in the following section on the Federal Reserve System.

The other significant way the federal government influences financial markets is through monetary policy actions taken by the Federal Reserve System. In recent years, the FED has taken an active role in seeking, through monetary measures, to achieve broad economic objectives including full employment, price stability and economic growth. The Fed seeks to accomplish its objectives by controlling the supply of money available for spending in the economy.

AN OVERVIEW OF THE CONSUMER FINANCE MARKET

Credit union operations are generally limited to the consumer credit and savings segment of the financial services market. They are further contained by the common bond requirements which restrict credit union access to the general public. In their efforts to grow and prosper (in spite of these limitations) in the increasingly deregulated financial markets of the late 20th century, credit unions face a formidable array of competitors.

Figure 5-1 attempts to provide a simplified but graphic overview of the consumer finance system and the broader money and capital markets—the competitive environment in which credit unions must maneuver. Understanding the strengths and weaknesses of the competition is necessary if the credit union industry is to develop the strategic plans required to survive, much less grow and prosper.

In order to derive the maximum benefit from the subsequent discussion, a careful perusal of Figure 5-1 by the reader is necessary at this point. Using a simple "T-account" format (selected assets on the left side of the T and selected liabilities and equity on the right), the interactions which influence consumer credit availability and terms are detailed in the figure. The following comments will first address

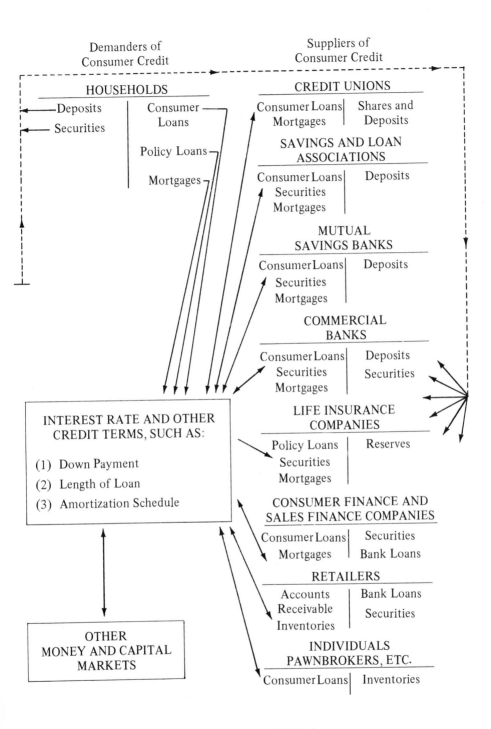

Figure 5-1   An Overview of the Consumer Credit Market

the credit union industry's competition and then credit unions themselves.

Commercial Banks

Despite their long-standing tradition of specializing in commercial and industrial lending, commercial banks have aggressively expanded into the consumer sector they once shunned. Commercial bank interest in the consumer finance market can be primarily attributed to cost pressures and a growing insight of the value of customer loyalty.

Cost pressures have forced commercial banks (and other depositories) to seek ever higher yields for the funds they invest. The wider spread between the costs of funds and yield provided by consumer loans was a major impetus for the banking industry's entry into the consumer loan market. These cost pressures resulted both from increasingly competitive money and capital markets and improved cash management on the part of corporate financial managers. Under these circumstances commercial banks were motivated to move more deeply into consumer loans where annual yields up to (and above) 18 percent could be earned.

In addition, in the post-World War II era, the banking industry began to gain an appreciaiton of full-service banking as a competitive device. Extensive postwar demand for consumer financing led commercial bankers to the realization that securing household (low cost) savings business required servicing of their borrowing needs.

Although commercial banks still hold only a relatively small proportion of consumer loans in their investment portfolios, such loans have been a rapidly growing segment of commercial bank assets since the 1950s. Because this growth has occurred during a period in which credit unions have been spreading their influence among middle and upper-middle income households, commercial bank-credit union competition has been intensifying continuously.

One avenue of commercial bank entry into what has traditionally been credit union turf is bank credit cards. The permanent, pre-authorized line of credit provided by bank credit cards have allowed commercial banks to extend medium and small consumer loans at competitive rates. This is true because with a permanent line of credit much of the high fixed costs of consumer lending are incurred but once. Therefore, credit cards have provided an important mechanism for markedly reducing the interest rate differential between their consumer loans and those offered by credit unions. Although credit unions may now issue bank credit cards (VISA and MASTERCARD predominantly), it is doubtful that much headway will be made against commercial banking's entrenched position in this market.

Finance Companies

Unlike commercial banks and other depositories, finance companies must borrow the bulk of the funds that they lend. Not having access to relatively low cost checking and savings deposits, finance companies have always been forced to seek out high yield consumer loans to obtain the spread needed for profitable operations. In fact, finance companies have usually had to specialize in the higher risk segment of the consumer lending market to earn sufficiently high yields. In most instances, this means that finance companies are something of a lender of last resort for consumers who for one reason or the other can not qualify for more favorable institutional financing or who find their lending institutions inhibited from lending due to usury ceiling differentials.

Rapid economic development and the aggressive growth of commercial banks and credit unions in the consumer finance sector have resulted in a general erosion of finance company market share (discussed in more detail later in this chapter). However, as deregulation forces depositories to pay savers rates more in line with those offered in the money and capital markets, finance companies have become more of a competitive factor.

The Other Thrift Institutions

Another major impact of deregulation will be the entry of savings and loan associations and mutual savings bank (which along with credit unions are often referred to collectively as thrift institutions) into consumer credit. As indicated in Figure 5-1, the thrifts have traditionally specialized in mortgage lending. This is particularly true of the savings and loans industry which has usually financed more than half the single-family mortgages originated in recent years.

As mortgage specialists, the thrifts have also suffered proportionately more adversity from disintermediation—the outflow of deposits from institutional savings accounts to money and capital market instruments. The thrift industry has been trying to deal with this disintermediation dilemma for nearly two decades. While generally very supportive of the Federal (Reg. Q and Stevens Act) regulations that limit the interest rates that depositories can pay on savings accounts, the thrifts have as a result of these ceilings experienced serious deposit hemorrhages in 1966, 1969-70, 1974-75, and 1980-81. The justification for keeping the interest rate ceilings has been the fact that the thrift's asset portfolios consisted primarily of fixed rate mortgages yielding much less than current market rates. Thus, it was argued, thrifts could not afford to pay rising short-term market rates.

While variable rate mortgages may be part of the ultimate answer to the thrifts disintermediation dilemma, the high interest rates (both short term and mortgages) experienced during 1980-81 proved to be more than most potential mortgage borrowers were willing and/or able to take on even in a variable rate context. Thus, many economists and thrift industry leaders argued for consumer lending powers on the basis that such logic would both improve thrift institutions' liquidity positions and markedly raise their average portfolio yield. Such powers were granted to thrifts by the Depository Institution Deregulation and Monetary Control Act of 1980.

At this juncture it is unclear to what extent the thrift industry will exercise their consumer loan options. If these financial intermediaries do eventually engage in a meaningful amount of consumer lending, they will form a new source of competition for credit unions, commercial banks, and the other established consumer lenders.

Retailers

Although their influence has been waning in recent years, retailers (including gasoline companies) still provided nearly 10 percent of the consumer credit outstanding as recently as 1980. In large part, the decreasing role of retailers can be attributed to consumer preference for bank cards (especially VISA and Mastercard). Most retail customers preferred the convenience of using one or two widely accepted cards and paying one or two bills to the alternative of carrying a card for nearly every store and facing an avalanche of monthly bills—however smaller in amount.

At this point, only the giant retailers (Sears, Penneys, Exxon, etc.) offer serious competition to bank credit cards, finance companies, and institutional lenders. It is by no means clear how long retailers can continue to successfully offer their own financing arrangements. Until that time, however, retailers cannot be overlooked as substantial sources of competition to credit unions.

Other Consumer Lenders

As also indicated in Figure 5-1, there are a number of other suppliers of consumer credit worthy of mention in this context. Although the extent of consumer lending done by individuals cannot be accurately measured there is reason to believe that it may be substantial—particularly during periods of tight money. The lack of data in this regard can be attributed to the fact this is an almost completely unregulated activity and much of this lending is intrafamily—parent to offspring (and vice versa) and sibling to sibling.

Another source of consumer financing is the cash value of life insurance policies. These so-called policy loans are often made available to life insurance purchasers at rates well below market norms. Therefore, there is a tendency for consumers to tap this source when money is tight. In many cases policy loan proceeds are likely reinvested at higher rates than the borrower is charged thus producing a profit. However, to the extent that policy loans are used as substitutes for other consumer loans, they represent a competitive challenge to credit unions.

The list of consumer lenders could, of course, be extended to include pawnbrokers and even unlicensed lenders. However, little if anything is known regarding the relative importance of these "underground" (if, in many areas, quite legal) credit sources.

COMPARATIVE FINANCIAL INSTITUTIONAL GROWTH

Although each type of financial institution's growth trend are interesting and remarkable in themselves, they need to be reviewed in perspective. Thus, a brief commentary of the comparable rates of change among the major competitive financial institutions seems in order at this point.

Commercial Bank Growth, 1950-1980

Commercial banking remains the mainstay of the financial intermediaries of the nation and the banking sector experienced marked growth throughout the period. Despite the very rapid growth experienced by credit unions and savings and loan associations, commercial banks remain in a dominant position. But through the years their degree of dominance, or the share of the market held by banks has declined.

In making direct comparisons of banks with credit unions over the past several decades, it may be more fruitful to look at total time and savings accounts held by banks since credit union savings shares have been considered as competitive with the "passbook" type savings account held by banks. Checking accounts, or demand deposits, are held in large measure for transactions purposes rather than household savings.

In Table 5-2 it may be seen that both demand and time deposits of banks have grown quite rapidly over the years, but that time deposits have outstripped demand deposits, particularly in more recent years. Between 1950 and 1960, demand deposits in the United States grew from $117 billion to $156 billion, or 33 percent, while time and savings deposits advanced from $37 billion to $73 billion, or 101 percent. Total deposits in the United States increased 49 percent during the 1950s.

Commercial bank changes in the 1960s were more significant than in the preceding decade. For the United States, total demand deposits grew from $155.7 billion to $247.2 billion, or 59 percent. But in the real growth area of banking in the 1960s, namely the time and savings deposit sector, deposits advanced from $73.3 billion to $235.3 billion, or 221 percent. Overall, total deposits in banks increased 111 percent during the decade.

Commercial banking continued its growth in the 1970s but at a pace below that of credit unions and savings and loan associations. Bank demand deposits rose from $247.2 billion in 1970 to $432.3 billion in 1980, or 75 percent. Time deposits advanced from $235.3 billion to $759.9 billion, or 223 percent. Total deposits held by banks grew 147 percent between 1970 and 1980.

Table 5-2   Demand, Time, and Total Deposits in All Insured
Commercial Banks in the United States, Year-End 1950-1980
(billions of dollars)

Year	Demand	Time	Total
1950	$117.0	$ 36.5	$ 153.5
1955	141.0	49.9	190.9
1960	155.7	73.3	228.9
1965	183.8	147.7	331.5
1966	191.7	161.1	352.8
1967	210.5	185.3	395.8
1968	228.7	205.9	434.7
1969	240.1	196.9	436.9
1970	247.2	235.3	482.5
1971	262.3	276.9	539.2
1972	296.4	320.5	616.9
1973	309.1	372.5	681.6
1974	314.4	432.0	746.4
1975	321.4	459.3	780.7
1976	333.9	496.9	830.9
1977	378.7	550.5	929.2
1978	400.3	616.4	1,016.4
1979	431.5	663.1	1,094.6
1980	$432.3	$759.9	$1,192.2

Source: Compiled from Federal Deposit Insurance Corporation,
Assets and Liabilities of Commercial and Mutual Savings Banks.

Growth in Savings and Loans and Mutual Savings Banks, 1950-1980

The growth aspect of the savings and loan industry which is more comparable to credit union growth is that of total savings held. This is particularly true since savings and loans have not been engaged traditionally in lending in the same area of credit as credit unions.

As shown in Table 5-3, savings and loans have experienced very rapid growth over most of the period under discussion. Rapidly growing housing markets and growth in institutional forms of savings have led to the growth in the industry. Inflation has also obviously been a major factor. Throughout the decade of the 1950s the annual rate of growth in savings in the industry ranged from 13 to 20 percent in the United States. For the period, savings dollars in savings and loans expanded 369 percent, growing from $12.8 billion to $60.3 billion.

Growth in the savings and loan industry continued throughout most of the 1960s although the rate of growth was somewhat diminished. Savings grew by only some 3 percent in 1966 and 1969 but at higher

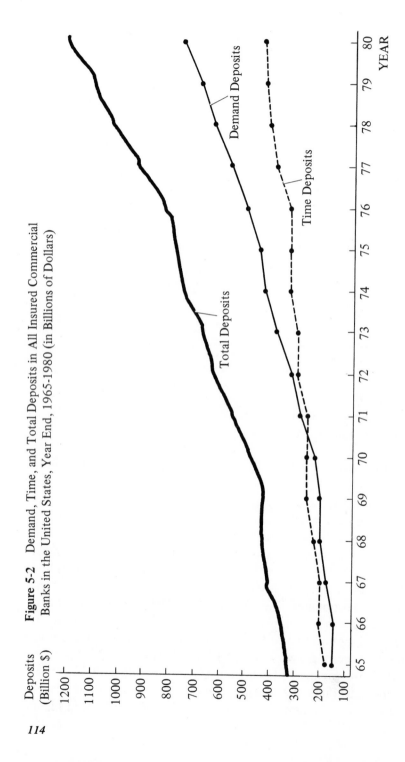

Figure 5-2 Demand, Time, and Total Deposits in All Insured Commercial Banks in the United States, Year End, 1965-1980 (in Billions of Dollars)

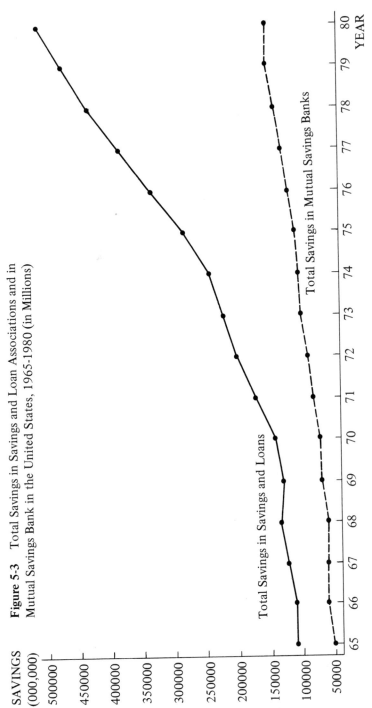

Figure 5-3 Total Savings in Savings and Loan Associations and in Mutual Savings Bank in the United States, 1965-1980 (in Millions)

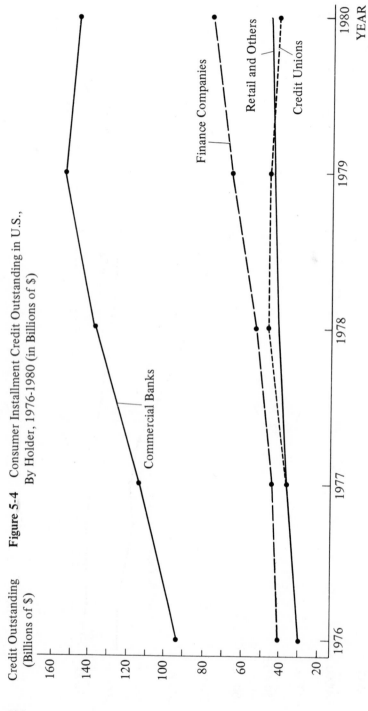

Figure 5-4   Consumer Installment Credit Outstanding in U.S.,
By Holder, 1976-1980 (in Billions of $)

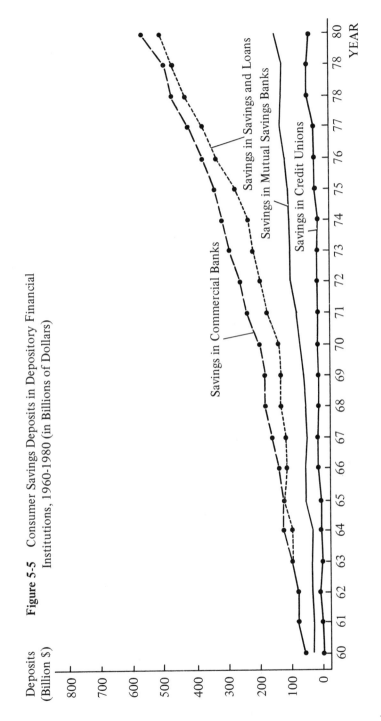

Figure 5-5 Consumer Savings Deposits in Depository Financial Institutions, 1960-1980 (in Billions of Dollars)

Savings in Savings and Loans

Savings in Mutual Savings Banks

Savings in Credit Unions

Savings in Commercial Banks

Deposits (Billion $)

800

700

600

500

400

300

200

100

0

60 61 62 63 64 65 66 67 68 69 70 71 72 73 74 75 76 77 78 78 80

YEAR

Table 5-3 Total Savings in Savings and Loan Associations
And in Mutual Savings Banks in the United States, 1950-1980

Year	Total Savings in Savings and Loans ($000,000)	Total Deposits in Mutual Savings Banks ($000,000)
1950	$ 12,861	$ 20,031
1955	30,813	28,187
1960	60,334	36,353
1965	108,703	52,761
1966	112,355	55,352
1967	122,769	60,497
1968	129,722	64,924
1969	132,739	67,540
1970	142,881	72,086
1971	169,035	81,978
1972	200,937	92,200
1973	220,443	97,200
1974	236,015	99,400
1975	277,674	109,873
1976	326,691	122,877
1977	377,302	134,017
1978	431,009	142,701
1979	470,004	146,006
1980	510,959	153,501

Source: Federal Home Loan Bank Board, *Statistical Abstract of the United States.*

rates during the other years. For the decade, the savings dollars of the industry expanded from $60.3 billion to $142.9 billion, or 137 percent. Savings and loan growth accelerated during most of the 1970-1980 period with annual growth rates ranging from 7 to 19 percent. The increase in savings dollars from $142.8 billion to $510.9 billion between 1970 and 1980 amounted to an increase of 258 percent.

Mutual savings banks compete in the savings markets with credit unions but their recent growth experiences have not been as favorable. While the mutual savings banks remain more than twice as large as credit unions, the growth trends in recent decades have not been favorable (Table 5-3). Mutual savings bank deposits expanded 81 percent in the 1950s, 98 percent in the 1960s, and 113 percent in the 1970-1980 period. Over the extended period 1950-1980, mutual savings bank deposits grew from $20.0 billion to $153.5 billion, or 667 percent. Except for the decade of the 1950s when mutual savings bank deposits grew more rapidly than commercial bank deposits, the growth rate in mutual savings banking lies considerably below that of any other depository institutional group.

Comparative Growth Rates, 1950-1980

Table 5-4 consolidates in the simplest manner the relative rates of change experienced by the four primary depository institutional groups in the nation. These data dramatize the rapid growth experienced by credit unions in recent decades. While the dollar amounts represented by the credit union industry remain relatively small, its underlying growth trend is most formidable. The $62 billion in credit union savings were but 4.3 percent of the combined time and savings of commercial banks, savings and loans, and mutual savings banks at year end 1980. But this amount is not an insignificant force in the market and will almost certainly grow both relatively and absolutely. In addition, the area of the strongest activity of credit unions, that is the field of consumer credit, demonstrates the trend of the industry even more tellingly.

ROLE IN CONSUMER CREDIT

Credit unions specialize in the extension of consumer loans and are the third largest consumer installment lender. Except for the unusual markets of 1979 and 1980, they have steadily taken over a larger share of the consumer credit market. The overall trends in consumer installment credit are shown in Table 5-5.

Total consumer installment credit expanded in the United States from $14.5 billion in 1950 to $313.4 billion in 1980. As demonstrated by the data of Table 5-5, commercial banks became dominant in the

Table 5-4 Comparative Growth Rates of Depository Institutions, 1950-1980

Percent Change	Commercial Banks		Savings and Loans	Mutual Savings Banks	Credit Unions
	Time Deposits	Total Deposits	Savings Dollars	Deposits	Savings Dollars
1950-60	101%	49%	369%	81%	485%
1960-70	221	111	137	98	211
1970-80	223	147	258	113	299
1950-80	1,981	677	3,872	666	7,164

Source: Calculated from previous tables.

Table 5-5   Consumer Installment Credit Outstanding in the United States,
By Holder, and Percent of Market, Selected Years, 1950-1980
(in billions of dollars)

Year	Total	(%)	Commercial Banks	(%)	Finance Companies	(%)	Credit Unions	(%)	Retail and Others	(%)
1950	$ 14.5	(100)	$ 5.8	(40)	$ 5.6	(39)	$ 0.6	(4)	$ 2.4	(16)
1960	42.6	(100)	16.7	(39)	14.8	(35)	3.9	(9)	7.1	(17)
1965	71.3	(100)	29.0	(41)	22.3	(32)	7.3	(10)	12.4	(17)
1970	105.5	(100)	48.7	(46)	27.6	(26)	13.0	(12)	16.3	(16)
1974	164.6	(100)	80.1	(49)	36.1	(22)	21.9	(13)	26.5	(16)
1976	194.0	(100)	93.7	(48)	38.9	(20)	31.1	(16)	30.1	(16)
1977	230.8	(100)	112.4	(49)	44.9	(20)	37.6	(16)	36.0	(15)
1978	275.8	(100)	136.2	(49)	54.3	(20)	45.9	(17)	39.2	(14)
1979	312.0	(100)	154.2	(49)	68.3	(22)	46.5	(15)	42.9	(14)
1980	313.4	(100)	145.8	(47)	76.8	(24)	44.0	(14)	46.8	(15)

Source: Derived from *Federal Reserve Bulletins;* and National Consumer Finance Association, *Finance Facts Yearbooks.*

field in the 1950s and 1960s and became even more significant in the 1970s. Since the early 1970s banks have held some 47 to 49 percent of total installment credit outstanding. Finance companies, both sales and consumer finance companies, lost market share throughout much of the period but recovered strongly in 1979 and 1980 as other lenders reduced their credits. Indeed, in 1950, finance companies held about 39 percent of total installment credit but their share has now declined to about the 20-24 percent of the market. Retailers and other lenders lost a small part of their market share over the years but the total change was not very great.

Credit unions stand out as the area in which the most remarkable growth in installment credit occurred over the 1950-1978 period. Starting from a position of some $600 million in 1950 their installment loans stood at $45.9 billion at year-end 1978. As a percentage of total installment credit in the nation, credit unions moved from a 4 percent level in 1950 to 10 percent in 1965, and to 17 percent in 1978, but did slip back in 1979-1980 to a level of some 15 percent. It would appear that the industry may achieve the finance company industry level in credit extensions and remain far ahead of the combined consumer credit extensions of retailers and miscellaneous lenders. Commercial banks will also face more and more competition from the credit union industry.

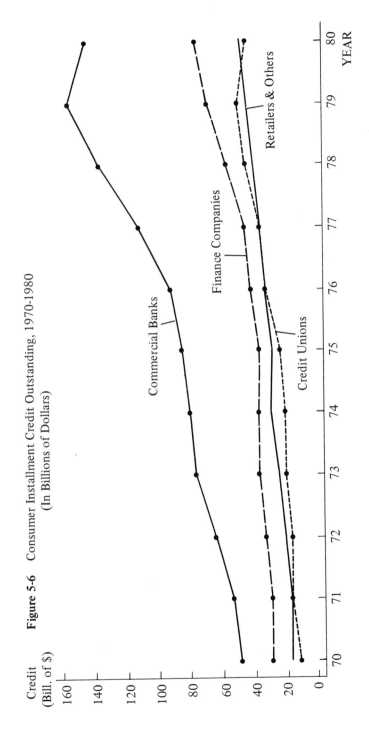

Figure 5-6 Consumer Installment Credit Outstanding, 1970-1980 (In Billions of Dollars)

Credit (Bill. of $)

Commercial Banks

Finance Companies

Retailers & Others

Credit Unions

YEAR

CREDIT UNIONS AND THE
CONSUMER FINANCE MARKETPLACE

Consumer Deposits

The rapid growth rate of the U.S. credit union industry since World War II, which was detailed earlier, must be interpreted with an understanding of the minor role of the industry in earlier years. As recently as 1950, credit union assets constituted only one-fifth of one percent of total financial assets of U. S. households. By 1978-1980, the credit union deposits accounted for 1.5 percent of total household financial assets (see Table 5-6). This is indeed remarkable growth in terms of the relative position of the credit union industry but its overall role in the marketplace must not be overstated. The credit union industry remains a relatively small part of the total financial market of the nation. It has been limited to doing business in the consumer credit and savings markets and restricted in growth to groups with some common bond of interest. One generally favorable factor for the credit union industry has been the overall growth and popularity of institutional savings deposits. As shown in Table 5-7 depository savings accounted for only 15 percent of household financial assets in 1950 but by 1980 had risen to about 30 percent. Credit unions outperformed other intermediaries during this period of rapid growth of savings.

Over the 1960-1980 period, total U. S. bank deposits increased at an annual rate of 8.6 percent, but there was a vast difference in the rates of growth of time and savings deposits and demand deposits. Demand deposits grew at an annual rate of 5.2 percent during this period while time and savings deposits enjoyed an annual growth rate of 12.4 percent. The savings capital of the savings and loan industry advanced at an annual rate of 11.1 percent over the 20-year period while mutual savings deposits grew at a much lower 7.5 percent rate. Credit union savings growth rates surpassed those of all other depository institutions at a level of 13.6 percent.

As portrayed by Table 5-7 deposit growth rates varied significantly from time to time but the overall competitiveness of the four depository institutional groupings persisted through the period. Savings and loans and credit unions did particularly well in a relative sense in the 1960-65 period but the savings and loan group slipped badly in the 1965-1970 period. Mutual savings bank growth rates remained rela-

Table 5-6 Financial Assets of Households, Selected Year-End Dates, In Dollar Amounts and Percentage Distribution

Asset Item	(Billions of Dollars)				(Percent of Total)			
	1950	1960	1970	1980	1950	1960	1970	1980
Demand deposits and currency	$ 56.1	$ 73.2	$ 117.8	$ 243.0	12.6	7.5	6.1	5.5
Savings accounts	66.9	164.8	426.7	1,307.2	15.0	16.9	22.1	29.7
Mutual savings banks	20.0	36.3	71.6	153.4	4.5	3.7	3.7	3.5
Commercial banks	32.1	62.8	195.4	583.6	7.1	6.4	10.1	13.2
Savings and loans	13.9	60.7	144.3	505.8	3.1	6.2	7.5	11.5
Credit unions	.9	5.0	15.5	64.4		0.5	0.8	1.5
Life insurance reserves	55.0	85.2	130.5	224.2	12.3	8.7	6.8	5.1
Pension fund reserves	24.3	90.8	239.4	729.1	5.4	9.3	12.4	16.5
Direct market instruments	217.1	510.2	916.9	1,660.8	48.6	52.4	47.7	37.6
U.S. government securities	68.2	74.0	107.2	292.6	15.2	7.6	5.6	6.6
State and local securities	9.2	30.8	46.0	69.7	2.0	3.2	2.4	1.6
Corporate and foreign bonds	6.0	10.0	34.3	80.0	1.3	1.0	1.8	1.8
Money market funds	—	—	—	74.4	—	—	—	1.7
Investment company shares	3.3	17.0	47.6	55.5	0.7	1.7	2.5	1.3
Other corporate stock	130.3	378.4	681.8	1,088.6	29.1	38.9	35.4	24.7
Other financial assets	27.5	49.6	95.3	248.3	6.1	5.1	4.9	5.6
Total financial assets	446.9	973.4	1,926.6	4,412.6	100.0	100.0	100.0	100.0

Source: National Association of Mutual Savings Banks, *1981 National Fact Book*, as derived from Federal Reserve Board data.

Table 5-7 Composition of Deposits, By Dollar Amounts and Growth Rates

	(Year-end data)					Annual Growth Rates			
	1960	1965	1970	1975	1980	1960-65	1965-70	1970-75	1975-80
Commercial Banks									
Total deposits	$229.0	$331.5	$482.5	$775.2	$1,187.4	7.7	7.8	9.9	8.9
Demand	155.7	183.8	247.2	319.8	432.2	3.4	6.1	5.3	6.2
Time and savings	73.3	147.7	235.3	455.5	755.1	15.0	9.8	14.1	10.6
Savings and Loans									
Savings capital	62.1	110.4	146.4	285.7	510.9	12.2	5.8	14.3	12.3
Mutual Savings Banks									
Total deposits	36.3	52.4	71.6	109.9	153.5	7.6	6.4	8.9	6.9
Credit Unions									
Member savings	5.0	9.2	15.5	33.0	64.4	13.0	11.0	16.3	14.3

Source: Federal Reserve Bank of St. Louis, *Review*, February 1981; and *Federal Reserve Bulletin*, July 1981.

tively low throughout the 20-year period. The 1970-75 period was one of great growth in savings and time deposits held by depository institutions; the annual growth rates of such accounts were above 14 percent in both the savings and loans and above 16 percent in credit unions. The rates of growth declined somewhat over the 1975-1980 period but remained above 10 percent in commercial banks and above 12 percent in savings and loans. Credit union savings growth was above 14 percent for the period.

For the total 1960-80 period, depository institution deposit growth was 419 percent for all deposits held by commercial banks, which breaks out as 178 percent increase in demand deposits and 930 percent in time and savings accounts. Savings and loans experienced a 723 percent increase in savings capital over the 20 years and mutual savings banks a 323 percent increase. Surpassing all other institutional growth experiences was the credit union industry's experience of a 1,188 percent growth for the period.

The details of the changes in depository growth are presented in a different way in Tables 5-8, 5-9, and 5-10. Consumer savings deposits are set forth for each year 1960-1980 in dollar terms. The commercial banks' savings figure approximate the individual, partnership and corporate data for time and savings deposits less the large certificates of deposits. The total growth percentage of bank savings on this basis and savings in savings and loan associations was approximately the same for the 20 years (731 percent versus 723 percent). The percentage growth in mutual savings and credit unions is as noted above.

The annual rates of change in consumer savings is reflected in Table 5-10 which shows the marked differences in growth rates from year to year as well as from one financial intermediary group to another. For the combined savings groups, years with savings growth about 12 percent include 1962, 1963, 1971, 1972, and 1975-1977. Years of general financial pressure in the economy, translating into significant disintermediation of deposits in 1966, 1969, 1974 and 1979, had overall savings deposit growth of 8 percent or less. Credit unions were impacted by the same market forces but the industry's underlying growth pattern enabled it to have more favorable growth rates than other depository institutions. Annual growth rates above 18 percent in credit unions occurred in 1971, 1972, and 1975-1977. The 7.5 percent credit union growth experienced in savings in 1979 was the lowest over the past 20 years.

Table 5-8   Consumer Savings Deposits in Depository Financial Institutions, 1960-1980
(in billions of dollars)

Year End	Commercial Banks	Savings and Loans	Mutual Savings	Credit Unions	Total
1960	$ 69.3	$ 62.1	$ 36.3	$ 5.0	$ 172.7
1961	76.6	70.9	38.3	5.6	191.4
1962	88.0	80.2	41.3	6.3	215.8
1963	99.2	91.3	44.6	7.2	242.3
1964	110.1	101.9	48.8	8.2	269.0
1965	126.1	110.4	52.4	9.2	298.1
1966	138.0	114.0	55.0	10.1	317.1
1967	155.9	124.5	60.1	11.1	351.6
1968	173.1	131.6	64.5	12.3	381.5
1969	176.3	135.5	67.1	13.7	392.6
1970	200.0	146.4	71.6	15.5	433.5
1971	231.9	174.2	81.4	18.3	505.8
1972	261.5	206.8	91.6	21.6	581.5
1973	291.0	227.0	96.5	24.7	639.2
1974	322.6	243.0	98.7	27.5	691.8
1975	347.2	285.7	109.9	33.0	775.8
1976	387.4	335.9	122.9	39.1	885.3
1977	427.6	386.8	134.0	46.5	994.9
1978	471.7	431.0	142.6	53.5	1,098.8
1979	505.5	470.2	146.0	57.5	1,179.2
1980	$576.0	$511.0	$153.5	$64.4	$1,304.9
Percentage Change					
1960-1980	731%	723%	323%	1188%	656%

Sources: Donald J. Melvin, Raymond Davis, and Gerald C. Fischer, *Credit Unions and the Credit Union Industry,* New York Institute of Finance, 1977, p. 179; and National Credit Union Administration "Statement of Mr. Connel to the Congress," July 14, 1981.

The rather marked variations in growth rates of savings flows noted above brought changes in the distribution of savings deposits among the four depository groups. Nevertheless, the changes in the proportions of savings held by the depository institutions was less than one might anticipate. The low base of credit union savings in 1960 ($5 billion) prevented the rapid growth of the industry from having a major effect upon the overall distribution of savings deposits. As shown in Table 5-10 in 1960 credit unions held 2.9 percent of consumer savings deposits which grew rapidly to a 4.9 percent share in 1978-1980. While this is a significant shift in market share, the total market impact may have been smaller than generally imagined by most observers.

The general story of shifts in depository holdings of consumer savings deposits is reflected by the steady decline in the market share of

Table 5-9 Rate of Change of Consumer Savings Deposits in Depository Institutions, 1961-1980
(Percent)

Year End	Commercial Banks	Savings and Loans	Mutual Savings	Credit Unions	All Institutions
1961	10.5%	14.2%	5.5%	12.5%	10.8%
1962	14.9	13.1	7.8	12.5	12.7
1963	12.7	13.8	8.0	14.3	12.2
1964	11.0	11.6	9.4	13.9	11.1
1965	14.5	8.3	7.4	12.2	10.8
1966	9.4	3.3	5.0	9.8	6.4
1967	13.0	9.2	9.3	9.9	10.9
1968	11.0	5.7	7.3	10.8	8.5
1969	1.8	3.0	4.0	11.4	2.9
1970	13.4	8.0	6.7	13.1	10.4
1971	16.0	19.0	13.7	18.1	16.7
1972	12.8	18.7	12.5	18.0	15.0
1973	11.3	9.8	5.3	14.4	9.9
1974	10.9	7.0	2.3	11.3	8.2
1975	7.6	17.6	11.3	20.0	12.1
1976	11.6	17.6	11.8	18.5	14.1
1977	10.4	15.2	9.0	18.9	12.4
1978	10.3	11.4	6.4	15.1	10.4
1979	7.2	9.1	2.4	7.5	7.3
1980	13.9%	8.7%	5.1%	12.0%	10.7%

Source: Computed from Table 5-8.

mutual savings banks (see Table 5-10). In 1960, mutual savings banks held 21.0 percent of the savings deposits of consumers; by 1980 the industry share stood at 11.8 percent. Much of the relative growth of the other depository groups was at the expense of the mutual savings banking industry which may be explained in part by the geographic location (Frostbelt) of the industry and its traditional role in the savings and capital markets. Other institutions were operating in more dynamic market sectors throughout the period.

Commercial banking's share of the consumer depository savings market remained around the 41 percent level in the early 1960s, rose to the 45 percent level in the latter 1960s and early 1970s and remained there through 1975. Some relative declines occurred in the 1976-1979 period but some recovery was achieved by 1980 when it stood at the 44.1 percent level. All in all, the bank market share of consumer savings remained remarkably stable throughout the period.

The savings and loan share of the depository consumer savings market was also rather stable except for relative declines in 1968-1970 and the rather significant increases in market share in 1976-

Table 5-10   Distribution of Consumer Savings Deposits Among Depository Institutions, 1960-1980 (Percent)

Year End	Commercial Banks	Savings and Loans	Mutual Savings	Credit Unions	Total
1960	40.1%	36.0%	21.0%	2.9%	100.0%
1961	40.0	37.1	20.0	2.9	100.0
1962	40.8	37.2	19.1	2.9	100.0
1963	40.9	37.7	18.4	3.0	100.0
1964	40.9	37.9	18.1	3.0	100.0
1965	42.3	37.0	17.6	3.1	100.0
1966	43.5	36.0	17.3	3.2	100.0
1967	44.3	35.4	17.1	3.2	100.0
1968	45.4	34.5	16.9	3.2	100.0
1969	44.9	34.5	17.1	3.5	100.0
1970	46.1	33.8	16.5	3.6	100.0
1971	45.8	34.4	16.1	3.6	100.0
1972	45.0	35.6	15.8	3.7	100.0
1973	45.5	35.5	15.1	3.9	100.0
1974	46.6	35.1	14.3	4.0	100.0
1975	44.8	36.8	14.2	4.3	100.0
1976	43.8	37.9	13.9	4.4	100.0
1977	43.0	38.9	13.4	4.7	100.0
1978	42.9	39.2	13.0	4.9	100.0
1979	42.9	39.9	12.4	4.9	100.0
1980	44.1%	39.2%	11.8%	4.9%	100.0%

Source: Calculated from Table 5-9.

1978. Mutual savings bank deposit losses were shared among the three other depository groups as mutual savings bank share declined from 21.0 percent of the market in 1960 to 11.8 percent in 1980 and credit unions rising from 2.9 percent to 4.9 percent, savings and loans from 36.0 to 39.2 percent, and commercial banks from 40.1 percent to 44.1 percent. These market share percentages summarize the effects of the competitive forces in a growing institutional savings market over a 20-year period. One of the dynamic market forces not represented by these shifts was the development of such nondepository competitive forces as the money market funds in the late 1970s.

Consumer Installment Credit

From the inception of the credit union movement, the general field of consumer credit has been the dominant avenue of its lending. Much credit union lending has not been on a scheduled installment payment basis but this has been the primary form of lending. In more recent years, the role of credit unions in the consumer credit markets of the United States has become more obvious. Comments in this section relate to credit unions as suppliers of installment credit. The relatively rapid growth of consumer savings in credit unions provided the funds for a rapid growth in installment lending by the industry.

Total consumer installment credit in the United States advanced from $14.5 billion in 1950 to $313.4 billion at year-end 1980, or some 2,000 percent. Installment credit extended by credit unions advanced from $0.6 billion in 1950 to $44.0 billion in 1980, or 7,200 percent (Table 5-11). Neither banks, finance companies nor retailers developed installment lending at such a pace. One of the best ways to detect the shifting patterns of depository institutions in the installment credit markets is to look at the relative market shares of the groups supplying total installment credit. Table 5-12 data demonstrates the changing patterns for the 1950-1980 period. In the 1950s and early 1960s commercial banks supplied about 40 percent of installment credit. Finance company share of the market declined from 38 percent in 1950 to 32 percent in 1965 while retailers and others maintained a fairly level share of the market. Credit unions raised their market position from 4 percent in 1950 to almost 10 percent in

Table 5-11   Consumer Installment Credit Outstanding, Selected Years, 1950-1980
(In billions of dollars)

Year End	Commercial Banks	Finance Companies	Retailers and Others	Credit Unions	Total
1950	$ 5.8	$ 5.6	$ 2.4	$ 0.6	$ 14.5
1955	10.6	11.8	4.4	1.7	28.5
1960	18.7	15.4	7.0	3.9	45.0
1965	31.8	23.9	10.9	7.3	73.9
1970	48.7	27.6	16.2	13.0	105.5
1971	51.6	29.2	16.4	14.8	112.0
1972	64.6	31.9	19.8	17.0	133.2
1973	75.9	35.4	24.2	19.6	155.1
1974	80.1	36.1	26.5	21.9	164.6
1975	82.9	36.0	27.8	25.7	172.4
1976	93.7	38.9	30.2	31.2	194.0
1977	112.4	44.9	35.9	37.6	230.8
1978	136.0	54.3	39.0	44.3	273.6
1979	154.2	68.3	42.9	46.5	312.0
1980	$145.8	$76.8	$46.8	$44.0	$313.4

Source: U. S. Department of Commerce, *Statistical Abstract of the United States, 1981;* Federal Reserve Board, *Federal Reserve Bulletins.*

Table 5-12   Relative Shares of Consumer Installment Credit Outstanding,
By Holders, Selected Years 1950-1980 (in percent)

Year End	Commercial Banks	Finance Companies	Retailers and Others	Credit Unions	Total
1950	40.0%	38.6%	16.5%	4.2%	100.0%
1955	37.2	41.4	15.4	5.9	100.0
1960	41.6	34.2	15.6	8.7	100.0
1965	43.0	32.3	14.7	9.9	100.0
1970	46.2	26.1	15.4	12.3	100.0
1971	46.1	26.1	14.6	13.2	100.0
1972	48.5	23.9	14.9	12.8	100.0
1973	48.9	22.8	15.6	12.6	100.0
1974	48.7	21.9	16.1	13.3	100.0
1975	48.1	20.9	16.1	14.9	100.0
1976	48.3	20.1	15.6	16.1	100.0
1977	48.7	19.5	15.6	16.3	100.0
1978	49.7	19.8	14.3	16.2	100.0
1979	49.4	21.9	13.8	14.9	100.0
1980	46.5%	24.5%	14.9%	14.1%	100.0%

Source: Calculated from data in Table 5-11.

1965. For the 1970-1980 period commercial bank share of installment credit rose somewhat, rising from 46 percent to almost 50 percent of the market in 1978. But by 1980, the bank share had slipped to the 46 percent level again. Finance company market share dropped throughout the 1970s, except for 1979-1980, and retailers and other suppliers share declined somewhat. Credit unions realized a significant growth in installment credits, especially in the 1974-1977 period. The generally unfavorable consumer credit markets in 1979-1980 impacted particularly hard on the credit union industry as its market share slipped to 14 percent of the national total.

Installment credit for automobile credit has grown as rapidly as total consumer installment credit throughout recent decades and constitutes the largest category of consumer credit. As detailed in Table 5-13, total automobile installment credit grew from $6 billion in 1950 to $116 billion in 1980. Credit unions held less than $1 billion in installment automobile paper in the first half of the 1950s and this grew to $22 billion by 1979. This market was dominated by banks and the finance companies during the 1950-1980 period. Banks held 41 percent of such credit in 1950 which grew to 61 percent of the market in 1970. The bank share remained near the 60 percent level throughout the 1970s but declined precipitously in 1980 to slightly

Table 5-13 Automobile Installment Credit Outstanding, By Holder, Selected Years 1950-1980 (in billions of dollars and percentages held)

Year End	Total	Finance Companies Amount	Percent	Credit Unions Amount	Percent	Commercial Banks Amount	Percent	Percent Total
1950	$ 6.1	$ 3.0	49.2%	$ 0.4	6.6%	$ 2.5	41.0%	96.8%
1955	13.5	6.9	51.1	0.7	5.2	5.3	39.3*	95.6
1960	17.7	7.5	42.4	1.7	9.6	8.1	45.8*	97.8
1965	28.4	9.2	32.4	3.0	10.6	15.9	56.0*	99.0
1970	36.3	9.0	24.8	5.0	13.8	22.3	61.4	100.0
1971	38.5	9.3	24.2	5.6	14.5	23.3	60.5	99.2
1972	44.1	9.9	22.5	6.4	14.5	27.3	61.9	98.9
1973	50.1	10.7	21.4	7.5	15.0	31.5	62.9	99.3
1974	52.9	10.6	20.0	10.9	20.6	31.0	58.6	99.2
1975	54.6	10.9	20.0	12.2	22.3	31.1	57.0	99.3
1976	67.7	12.8	18.9	15.2	22.5	39.6	58.5	99.9
1977	82.9	15.2	18.3	18.1	21.8	49.6	59.8	99.9
1978	101.6	19.9	19.6	21.2	20.9	60.5	59.5	100.0
1979	116.3	26.8	23.0	22.2	19.1	67.3	57.9	100.0
1980	$116.3	$34.2	29.4%	$21.2	18.1%	$61.0	52.5%	100.0%

*Credit unions and miscellaneous lenders combined as "other financial lenders" by Federal Reserve Board prior to 1970. Almost all of this credit was supplied by credit unions. Components may not add to totals.

Sources: Federal Reserve Board, *Banking and Monetary Statistics,* 1976; and *Federal Reserve Bulletin,* July 1981.

more than 52 percent. Finance company share dropped throughout most of the period, declining from near 50 percent in the 1950s to as low as 19 percent in 1976. Aggressive finance company lending in 1979-1980 brought their share back up to 29 percent at year-end 1980. Credit union participation in the automobile installment market, particularly in the 1965-1975 period when the credit union share rose from under 11 percent in 1965 to above 22 percent in 1975, proceeded at a more rapid pace than that of other institutions. Market share did, however, decline somewhat in the 1978-1980 period.

Tables 5-14 and 5-15 provide richer detail regarding the dynamics of the consumer credit market during the 1970s including the trends in market share outlined above. Table 5-16 focuses on the details of the 1979-80 period in which consumer loans generally showed little or no growth. It is worth noting that only finance companies registered any substantial increase in consumer credit outstanding during 1980.

Table 5-14   Consumer Installment Credit Outstanding, Extensions, Liquidations, and Net Change, by Holder, Selected Years, 1972-1980 (in billions of dollars)

	1972	1975	1977	1978	1979	1980
Outstanding at Year End–Total	$133.2	$172.0	$230.6	$273.6	$312.0	$313.4
Commercial banks	64.6	82.9	112.4	136.0	154.2	145.8
Finance companies	31.9	36.0	44.9	54.3	68.3	76.8
Credit unions	17.0	25.7	37.6	44.3	46.5	44.0
Retailers	15.0	18.2	23.5	26.0	28.1	29.4
Savings and loans	1.2	4.8	7.1	7.1	8.4	9.9
Gasoline companies	2.5	2.7	3.0	3.2	3.7	4.7
Mutual savings banks	1.1	1.7	2.2	2.7	2.7	2.8
Extensions During Year–Total	152.2	180.1	257.6	297.7	324.8	305.9
Commercial banks	63.9	80.8	117.9	142.4	154.7	133.6
Finance companies	35.7	31.2	42.0	50.5	61.5	60.8
Credit unions	16.0	24.1	34.0	38.1	34.9	29.6
Retailers	23.1	27.3	42.2	44.6	47.7	51.0
Savings and loans	0.7	2.8	5.0	3.7	5.9	6.6
Gasoline companies	11.8	12.5	14.6	16.0	18.0	22.4
Mutual savings banks	1.1	1.5	1.9	2.3	2.0	1.9
Liquidations During Year–Total	136.8	172.6	222.1	254.6	286.4	304.5
Commercial banks	54.3	77.9	99.3	118.8	136.6	142.0
Finance companies	33.1	31.3	36.0	41.1	47.5	52.4
Credit unions	13.8	20.3	27.6	31.4	32.7	32.1
Retailers	22.3	27.2	39.5	42.1	45.5	49.7
Savings and loans	0.6	2.3	3.7	3.7	4.6	5.1
Gasoline companies	11.8	12.4	14.5	15.8	17.5	21.4
Mutual savings banks	0.9	1.3	1.6	1.8	2.0	1.8
Net Change During Year–Total	15.4	7.4	35.5	43.1	38.4	1.4
Commercial banks	9.5	2.9	18.6	23.6	18.2	(–)8.4
Finance companies	2.7	(–)0.1	5.9	9.4	14.0	8.4
Credit unions	2.2	3.8	6.4	6.7	2.2	(–)2.5
Retailers	0.8	0.1	2.7	2.5	2.1	1.3
Savings and loans	0.1	0.5	1.3	–	1.3	1.5
Gasoline companies	(–)0.1	0.1	0.1	0.3	0.5	1.0
Mutual savings banks	0.2	0.2	0.3	0.5	–	0.1

Source: Federal Reserve Board
Note: Parts may not add to totals due to rounding.

CREDIT UNION VS OTHER INTERMEDIARIES

Earlier chapters have established the unique nature of credit unions. At this point, some discussion of how these characteristics impact on the competitive interface between credit unions and other components of the financial system is desirable.

Table 5-15 Consumer Installment Credit Outstanding at Year End and Net Change During Year, by Type and Holder, Selected Years, 1972-1980 (in billions of dollars)

	1972	1975	1977	1978	1979	1980
Outstanding at Year End—Total	$133.2	$172.0	$230.6	$273.6	$312.0	$313.4
Automobile	47.8	57.2	82.9	101.6	116.4	116.3
Commercial banks	28.9	33.3	49.6	60.5	67.4	61.0
Credit Unions	8.4	12.7	18.1	21.2	22.2	21.1
Finance companies	10.5	11.2	15.2	19.9	26.8	34.2
Revolving	9.7	15.0	39.3	48.3	56.9	59.9
Commercial banks	7.2	12.3	18.4	24.3	29.9	30.0
Retailers	NA	NA	17.9	20.7	23.3	25.1
Gasoline companies	2.5	2.7	3.0	3.2	3.7	4.7
Mobile Home	9.5	14.4	14.9	15.2	16.8	17.3
Commercial banks	6.4	8.7	9.1	9.5	10.6	10.4
Finance companies	2.9	3.4	3.1	3.2	3.4	3.7
Savings and loans	NA	2.1	2.3	2.1	2.3	2.7
Credit unions	0.2	0.3	0.4	0.5	0.5	0.5
Other	66.1	85.3	93.4	108.5	121.9	119.9
Commercial banks	22.0	28.7	35.3	41.6	46.3	44.4
Finance companies	18.5	21.3	26.6	31.2	38.2	38.8
Credit unions	8.4	12.7	19.1	22.7	23.8	22.5
Retailers	15.0	18.2	5.6	5.2	4.8	4.3
Savings and loans	1.2	2.8	4.7	5.0	6.1	7.2
Mutual savings banks	1.1	1.7	2.2	2.7	2.7	2.8
Net Change During Year—Total	15.4	7.4	35.5	43.1	38.4	1.4
Automobile	5.6	3.0	15.2	18.7	14.7	–
Commercial banks	4.2	0.5	10.0	10.9	6.9	(–)6.3
Credit unions	1.1	1.9	2.9	3.1	1.0	(–)1.2
Finance companies	0.4	0.6	2.4	4.7	6.8	7.5
Revolving	1.2	1.3	6.2	9.0	8.6	2.9
Commercial banks	1.2	1.2	4.0	6.0	5.5	0.1
Retailers	NA	NA	2.1	2.8	2.6	1.8
Gasoline companies	(–)0.1	0.1	0.1	0.3	0.5	1.0
Mobile Home	2.1	(–)0.2	0.4	0.4	1.6	0.5
Commercial banks	1.8	(–)0.3	0.4	0.4	1.1	(–)0.3
Finance companies	0.4	(–)0.1	(–)0.2	0.1	0.2	0.4
Savings and loans	NA	0.2	0.1	(–)0.3	0.2	0.4
Credit unions	–	–	0.1	0.1	–	–
Other	6.5	3.3	13.6	15.0	13.4	(–)2.0
Commercial banks	2.4	1.5	4.3	6.3	4.7	(–)1.9
Finance companies	2.0	(–)0.6	3.7	4.7	7.0	0.6
Credit unions	1.1	1.9	3.5	3.6	1.1	(–)1.3
Retailers	0.8	0.1	0.6	(–)0.3	(–)0.4	(–)0.5
Savings and loans	0.1	0.3	1.2	0.3	1.1	1.1
Mutual savings banks	0.2	0.2	0.3	0.5	–	0.1

Source: Federal Reserve Board.
Note: Parts may not add to totals due to rounding.
NA: Not available.

Table 5-16   Consumer Installment Credit Activity, By Type and Holder, 1980
(In millions of dollars)

	Outstanding Year-end 1979	Extensions 1980	Liquidations 1980	Outstanding Year-end 1980
Total Installment Credit	$312,024	$305,887	$304,477	$313,435
Commercial banks	154,177	133,605	142,017	145,765
Finance companies	68,318	60,801	52,363	76,756
Credit unions	46,517	29,594	32,069	44,041
Retailers	28,119	50,959	49,668	29,410
Savings and loans	8,424	6,621	5,136	9,911
Gasoline companies	3,729	22,402	21,414	4,717
Mutual savings banks	2,740	1,905	1,810	2,835
Automobile	116,362	83,002	83,037	116,327
Commercial banks	67,367	40,657	46,999	61,025
Credit unions	22,244	15,294	16,474	21,060
Finance companies	26,751	27,051	19,560	34,242
Revolving	56,937	129,580	126,655	59,862
Commercial banks	29,862	61,847	61,708	30,001
Retailers	23,346	45,331	43,533	25,144
Gasoline companies	3,729	22,402	21,414	4.717
Mobile Homes	16,838	5,098	4,609	17,327
Commercial banks	10,647	2,942	3,213	10,376
Finance companies	3,390	898	543	3,745
Savings and loans	2,307	1,146	716	2,737
Credit unions	494	113	138	469
Other	121,887	88,207	90,175	119,919
Commercial banks	46,301	28,159	30,097	44,363
Finance companies	38,177	32,852	32,260	38,769
Credit unions	23,779	14,187	15,453	22,512
Retailers	4,773	5,628	6,135	4,266
Savings and loans	6,117	5,476	4,420	7,174
Mutual savings banks	2,740	1,905	1,810	2,835

Source: Federal Reserve Board.
Note: Parts may not add to totals due to rounding.

Mutuality

Mutuality permits credit union net income to be returned to depositors (and borrowers) in the form of higher yield, (or lower rates)
than most other intermediaries can offer. Thus, credit unions theoretically should have a built-in advantage over all their competitors
except the mutual thrifts because stock institutions have an obligation

to their stockholders who may demand a return in excess of depositors. It should be noted that there is a strong movement afoot to facilitate savings and loan associations and mutual savings banks conversion to stock ownership. If this movement results in a number of conversions, credit unions may be left as the only mutuals in the market.

Common Bond and Subsidies

The common bond requirement should, at least theoretically, reduce the information costs and, thus, default rates compared with other lenders. These information costs constitute a considerable expense to other lenders who must depend mostly on external sources of credit data.

Additionally, there are several ways in which credit unions are routinely subsidized. Often credit unions are provided free office space, accounting, and computer services by the sponsoring firm or agency. Moreover, most of the officers of a typical credit union provide volunteer labor (often during work hours). Finally, the tax exemption of credit unions provides a possible, but debatable, advantage over non-mutual competitors. This tax exemption issue will be discussed in more detail in later chapters.

Payroll Deductions

Although CUNA's Research Department asserts that the availability of payroll deduction has been an important factor in credit union viability and growth, the evidence is mixed in this regard.[1] For example, Taylor found the payroll deduction factor to be an insignificant variable in attracting savings deposits and loan business to credit unions.[2] However, Taylor did conclude that payroll deductions were important as a device for lowering administrative costs. On the other hand, Flannery found that the payroll deductions feature was a significant factor in reducing credit union loan losses.[3]

On balance, then, it appears that having ready access to payroll de-

---

[1] "Report for the Commission of Financial Structure," CUNA, Inc., unpublished document, 1971, p. 25.

[2] Ryland A. Taylor, "The Demand for Credit Union Shares: A Cross Sectional Analysis," *Journal of Financial and Quantitative Analysis,* June 1972, p. 1749-56.

[3] Flannery, p. 104.

ductions has contributed meaningfully to credit union efficiency and growth. However, not every credit union has such access and the implications thereof could be a critical consideration in the case of residential charters. In addition, the development of EFT may bring the benefits of effective payroll deduction to many consumer lenders, thus diluting a traditional advantage enjoyed by credit unions.

Liquidation

To this point, the discussion has emphasized the relative strengths of credit union vis-a-vis their competition. On the liability side of the ledger there is at least one consideration that should be mentioned— the rate of credit union liquidiations. Flannery reported that between 1934 and 1970, 6,000 Federal credit unions were liquidated, representing a total of $135.3 million in assets.[4] Through the 1970s, state and Federal credit union liquidations averaged above 600 per year.

As might be expected, liquidations are concentrated among smaller, occupational credit unions, particularly in the manufacturing sector. Most liquidations usually involve the closing of a plant or firm. It should also be noted that most liquidations are voluntary in the sense that they are not ordered per se by the NCUA or state regulatory agency.

Due to cooperation between central credit unions, state leagues, and nearby credit unions, net losses to members of liquidated credit unions were limited to less than $2.0 million among all Federal credit unions prior to 1971. The availability of share insurance since that time has nearly eliminated liquidation loss risks at all Federal and most state credit unions. However, the inconvenience of reestablishing new financial services relationships may still be perceived as an unattractive possibility to many potential credit union customers.

As Flannery also notes, the high turnover rate among credit unions is indicative of some of their peculiar characteristics:

1. Small size—limits risks pooling and ability to absorb unanticipated stocks
2. Common bond—resulting in loan demand and deposit flow that are correlated, i.e., when loan demand is high (when lay-

---

[4] Flannery, p. 47.

offs are occurring) deposit in flow is also limited and vice versa.
3. Volunteer officers—especially at credit unions too small to hire professional management, volunteer officers may have neither the time nor the expertise required to effectively manage a financial institution.[5]

How Competitive Are Credit Unions?

The theoretical advantages outlined above not withstanding empirical research tends to indicate that credit unions do not enjoy the pronounced competitive edge they are widely alleged to have. It is generall assumed that credit union loan rates are lower and savings yields higher than the competition; but a study by NCUA discovered that:

> credit unions probably offer lower interest rates than other lenders on most loans, but that on new car loans credit unions rates may not have a marked advantage over rates charged by banks. Moreover, on loans completely secured by members' shares, credit unions may not be meeting the competition of savings and loan associations.[6]

This conclusion with respect to new auto loans has been contradicted by the National Commission on Consumer Finance. Their survey of 10 states indicates that credit union APRs are from 63 to 126 basis points above the average rate available at banks. (Finance company rates are, not surprisingly, even further above the credit unions.) For unsecured personal loans and loans for other consumer goods, however, the credit unions exhibited a distinct edge, in accordance with general expectations. In all of these cases it must be remembered that credit union loan rates are inclusive of all fees and charges, as well as borrowers' life insurance. This latter cost alone amounts to approximately 50 basis points in terms of APR.[7]

As far as savings yields are concerned it is usually true that the dividend ceiling on credit union shares is above passbook rates at other

---

[5] Flannery, pp. 47-48.

[6] Edwin J. Swindler, "Do Credit Unions Give the Best Loan Terms?" *NCUA Quarterly*, Spring 1973, p. 21.

[7] *Consumer Credit in the United States and Canada,* Report of the National Commission on Consumer Finance, Washington, D. C.: U. S. Government Printing Office, December 1972.

depository intermediaries. It seems likely that such high yields have in fact attracted funds into the movement.

Since the mid-sixties it has become increasingly obvious that it is the spread of rates offered by an institution, as well as the average level, that determines the choice of institution and/or medium. As recent events have indicated, and as emphasized in Figure 5-1, an ever more sophisticated populace is both willing and able to move their savings out of depositories into other components of the money and capital markets (money market funds, for example). While credit unions may enjoy at least limited loan and yield rate advantages over their immediate competition, the benefits thereof may be largely nullified if credit unions cannot compete with the broader markets. Whether or not credit unions can remain viable, much less grow substantially during the 1980s will depend on their ability to cope with a much wider range of competition than they heretofore have faced. At a minimum, energetic marketing of credit union services and the adoption of modern management practices (including those discussed in the subsequent chapter) will be necessary if credit unions are to meet the challenge of the 1980s.

THE COMPETITIVE IMAGE OF CREDIT UNIONS

To a large extent the competitiveness of credit unions will depend upon their ability to (1) create the impression among their clientele that they are satisfying the financial service needs of the membership at a fair (competitive) price and (2) read and respond to the moves of their competitors. The 1982 National Member Survey conducted by the Credit Union National Association reveals the current image of credit unions in the eyes of their members. A comparison of these results with those of the 1977 National Member Survey provides insight into the trends affecting the credit unions recent past as well as their future.

Traditionally credit unions have been institutions dedicated to providing savings and consumer loan services to their members. In the past 5-10 years other services have risen into prominence.

In the savings area, credit union performance did not match that of the banks between 1977 and 1982. In both 1977 and 1982, only 59 percent of members with savings viewed their share savings account as an active savings account. A large proportion apparently viewed their share savings account as a condition of membership allowing access to other services such as loans. In the same period, 1977-82, the percentage of credit union members with active savings accounts in banks increased from 62 to 70 percent.

In additon, in 1982 only 28 percent of credit union members considered their credit union share account to be their household's main savings account. This was a decline from 35 percent in 1977. The comparable figure for bank savings accounts increased from 37 percent in 1977 to 55 percent in 1982. The deterioration of the credit unions position as a primary provider of savings services for its members may well be due to the loss of its interest rate differential due to deregulation.

In the other traditional service area, loans, the picture is brighter. The credit union's share of personal loans outstanding to credit union members has increased dramatically from 33 percent in 1977 to 51 percent in 1982. Concurrently, the share of personal loans outstanding provided by banks to credit union members fell from 44 percent to 33 percent. Credit unions have become the number one choice of their members for personal loans.

No statistically significant changes have taken place in the auto loan market during the 1977-82 period. This is probably due to the low overall demand for autos and auto loans over this period.

Credit unions have moved swiftly to capitalize on the growing demand for IRA services. The 1982 survey reveals that 21 percent of credit union members with IRAs have them at credit unions, compared with 27 percent at banks and 17 percent with insurance companies.

Recent estimates are that 3.9 million share draft accounts serving 9.5 million adults are active at credit unions, yielding an expected market penetration of 25-30 percent of all adult members. As 36 percent of the members surveyed claimed to have a share draft account in their household, it would appear that there is some confusion between share drafts and share accounts.

By 1982 39 percent of all credit union members possessed an ATM card, with 59 percent of these members claiming they had used the card to transact business. This indicates that ATM usage has increased 23 percent for all members from the 1977 figure of 11 percent. However, the credit unions share in providing this service is small. Only 6 percent of the ATM cards possessed by credit union members were issued by credit unions, with 90 percent being issued by banks.

Officers' Perception of Credit Union Competitiveness

It is clear from the above survey data, that while credit unions have ventured into new service areas most customers view them as financial delicatessens rather than financial supermarkets. A key question is whether credit union officers view their movement as one of financial delicatessens or budding financial supermarkets. William Cox of the Federal Reserve Bank of Atlanta surveyed the managers of 23 large credit unions in Georgia and Alabama to clarify this question. These credit unions were represented at a conference, "Directions '83," arranged by the credit union centrals in the two states.

Two thirds of the institutions indicated that they wanted to move toward full-service orientation, if necessary at the expense of the close personal contact with customers traditional with credit unions. One-third wished to stay in the "delicatessen" niche.

Cox also asked which of several services the credit unions now offer or are seriously considering. The following results were obtained:

	Now Offer	Seriously Interested	Not Seriously Considering
Share drafts	23	0	0
Mortgage loans	13	5	5
Preauthorized transfers	13	5	5
Credit cards	4	9	10
ATMs	6	5	12
Debit cards	2	8	12
Telephone bill payments	1	16	6

The above statistics clearly show a move toward becoming financial supermarkets. Particularly interesting are the large number of credit unions offering or seriously considering the expensive ATM services.

Credit union managers feel they are doing well against their competitors. Only one of the credit unions replied that it had lost significant amounts to the new money market accounts or Super NOWs offered by banks and S&Ls.

Furthermore, the managers expect their credit unions to do well in the future. Twenty of the 23 credit unions expected their market share to grow between 1983 and 1990. The other three expected a stable market share. Sixteen of the credit unions expect their profitability to rise between 1983 and 1990. The other seven expect their profitability to hold steady.

Given the projections of a rosy future, it is interesting to note that only seven of the 23 credit unions had imposed monthly charges for checking services. This is a step most banks have taken to bolster profit margins in an era of high interest rates and interest payments on deposits.

Cox also conducted a telephone survey of 11 small Georgia credit unions. This was done to see if there were significant differences between the images held by large and small credit unions.

Six of the eleven said that they would be willing to give up some of their personal ties to move toward full service banking. Only seven of the eleven offer share drafts, but most say they are seriously considering adding ATMs, once again a surprise due to the high fixed cost. The associations were not seriously considering any other products.

SUMMARY

Following this overview of the financial system within which credit unions operate, the discussion focused on the competitive interface between credit unions and the other components of the consumer finance market *and* the overall money and capital markets. While it was determined that credit unions enjoy a limited competitive advantage over their competitors, the forces which could erode such an edge are currently gaining impetus.

Thus, the credit union industry faces a harrowing challenge in the years to come. If the industry is to emerge from the 20th century as a significant factor in the consumer finance sector, rather heroic efforts will be required by all its proponents.

Financial Management of Credit Unions

INTRODUCTION

The discussion to this point has concentrated on credit unions as cooperative financial institutions. This chapter will shift perspective somewhat to look at the credit union as a business firm. The analysis will focus on recent financial management practices and trends as the industry has matured during the 1970s.

Although the emphasis will be on financial management, successful enterprises of all types require skillful management across a broad spectrum of concerns. Adroit human asset management, for instance, may be as crucial (or even more) to the health and prosperity of a credit union as efficient financial management. That these other matters are outside the purview of this particular commentary should not diminish their importance.

This chapter will first analyze the balance sheet aspects of credit union financial management (including sources and uses of funds) and then proceed to a discussion of income statement factors (revenue and expenses). Finally, an attempt will be made to explain some of the basic techniques credit unions have (or should have) adopted to achieve the more efficient and effective financial management that their competitive situation will require in the future.

THE BALANCE SHEET

Assets may be viewed as those resources available to the credit union to generate income. Financial assets (funds) are financed and invested in a number of different ways by credit unions. In accordance with the fundamental tenets of double entry accounting, total assets must perforce equal the sum of the total liabilities and total capital. Table 6-1 records recent movements in the balance sheet accounts of the credit union industry. Balance sheets are often conceived of as "snap-shots" of the financial condition of a firm or industry at a particular point in time. The consolidated balance sheet of the credit union industry for the decade of the 1970s (Table 6-1) shows a threefold increase in the dollar value of loans outstanding during the period along with even greater growth rates in investments and other assets. Cash remained relatively stable indicating the increasing financial sophistication of the industry and the rising opportunity costs of holding cash during an era of high market interest rates. Member savings and reserves (particularly the undivided earnings component) accounted for nearly all the growth in liabilities and capital over the decade.

Table 6-2 summarizes the sources and uses of funds for the industry during the decade of the 1970s and, thus, provides an explanation for the balance sheet dynamics indicated in Table 6-1. Of note are the following

1. Steady growth in member deposits except for 1979 when significant disintermediation (outflow of funds from depositories to the broader money and capital markets) was experienced
2. Nearly constant increases in surpluses and revenues
3. Substantial (if relatively small) movement into home mortgage
4. Continued specialization and significant dollar volume growth (again, excepting 1979) in consumer credit
5. A marked jump in federal securities during 1980—evidence that the industry was quite liquid during a year in which other thrifts were experiencing real liquidity problems.

Tables 6-3 and 6-4 provide an insight into the sources and uses of funds for state and federal credit unions, respectively, over the same period. The two tables support the observations enumerated with

Table 6-1 Balance Sheet—All Credit Unions
Selected Years, 1971-1980
(Amounts in thousands)

	1971	Percentage of Total	1976	Percentage of Total	Percentage Change 1971-1976	1980	Percentage of Total	Percentage Change 1976-1980	Percentage Change 1971-1980
Assets:									
Amount of Loans Outstanding	$16,152,404	76.5%	$34,309,718	76.2%	112.4%	$48,983,231	66.9%	42.8%	203.3%
Cash	911,120	4.3	1,153,505	2.6	26.6	1,294,803	1.8	12.2	42.1
Total Investments	3,646,652	17.3	8,526,623	18.9	133.8	20,917,649	28.6	145.3	473.6
Other Assets	411,089	1.9	1,046,077	2.3	154.5	2,039,190	2.8	94.9	396.0
Total Assets	21,121,280		45,035,938		113.2	73,234,890		62.6	246.7
Liabilities and Capital									
Notes Payable	445,812	2.1	1,783,324	4.0	300.0	1,710,091	2.3	-4.1	283.6
Members Savings	18,358,341	86.9	39,098,255	86.8	113.0	65,743,056	89.8	68.1	258.1
Reserves	1,260,885	6.0	2,265,539	5.0	79.7	3,159,813	4.3	39.5	150.6
Undivided Earnings	795,573	3.8	589,007	1.3	-26.0	1,255,387	1.7	113.1	57.8
Other Liabilities	260,652	1.2%	1,299,794	2.9%	398.7	1,366,526	1.9%	5.1	424.3
Total Liabilities and Capital	$21,121,280		$45,035,938		113.2%	$73,234,090		62.6%	246.7%

Source: NCUA, Annual Reports.

Table 6-2 Sources and Uses of Funds—Credit Unions, 1971-1982
($ Billions)

	1971	1973	1975	1977	1978	1979	1980	1982 (estimated)
Sources of Funds								
Share Capital and Deposits	$2.9	$2.9	$5.5	$7.4	$7.0	$3.9	$ 8.3	$3.9
Surplus and Reserves	.2	.3	.4	.3	.6	.4	.2	.4
Total	3.1	3.2	5.9	7.7	7.6	4.4	8.5	3.9
Uses of Funds								
Home Mortgages	.5	.5	.1	2.0	2.1	.1	-1.6	—
Consumer Credit	1.8	2.7	3.8	6.4	6.7	2.2	-2.5	3.0
U.S. Government and Agency Securities								
U.S. Government Securities	-.1	.3	.8	-.5	-.5	.3	.6	.3
Federal Agency Securities	.4	.2	.4	.5	—	-.6	—	—
Total	.3	.5	1.1	.1	-.5	-.3	.7	.3
Total Funds	2.5	3.7	5.0	8.4	8.3	1.9	-3.4	3.3
Other Sources and Uses (Net)	.6	-.5	.9	-.7	-.7	2.4	11.9	.6
Total	$3.1	$3.2	$5.9	$7.7	$7.6	$4.4	$ 8.5	$3.9

Source: Bankers Trust Company, *Credit and Capital Markets*, New York, Annual.

Table 6-3 Percentage Distribution of Sources and Uses of Funds in
State-Chartered Credit Unions, Selected Years, 1971, 1976, 1980

Item	1971	1976	1980
Sources, Total	100.0%	100.0%	100.0%
Members' savings	86.7	87.1	88.9
Reserves and undivided earnings	9.9	6.7	6.7
Notes and certificates payable	1.9	3.3	2.6
Other sources	1.5	2.9	1.8
Uses, Total	100.0	100.0	100.0
Cash	4.0	1.7	1.8
Loans to members	76.5	77.5	68.3
Investments	17.1	18.1	26.9
Other assets	2.5%	2.7%	3.0%

Source: NCUA, *Annual Reports of State Chartered Credit Unions.*

respect to Tables 6-1 and 6-2 and demonstrate that there is a notable consistency in funds flows in both types of credit unions. These tables also indicate that member deposits are by far the predominant source of credit union funds. Table 6-5 documents the dynamics of deposit growth during the 1970s. Although some volatility in deposit growth rates can be observed from year to year, the credit union industry

Table 6-4 Percentage Distribution of Sources and Uses of Funds in Federal Credit Unions,
Selected Years, 1971, 1976, 1980

Item	1971	1976	1980
Sources Total	100.0%	100.0%	100.0%
Members' savings	87.1	86.6	90.4
Reserves and undivided earnings	9.6	6.0	5.5
Notes and certificates payable	2.3	4.6	2.1
Other Sources	1.0	2.8	2.0
Uses, Total	100.0	100.0	100.0
Cash	4.6	3.3	1.7
Loans to members	76.5	75.1	65.7
Loans to other credit unions	0.9	0.6	—
Liquid assets, total	13.2	14.5	27.2
U.S. Government Obligations Shares, deposits in S/L's, banks, and other credit unions	6.4	5.3	19.5
Federal Agency Securities	5.3	7.7	6.4
Other Uses	4.8%	6.5%	5.4%

Source: NCUA, *Annual Reports.*

Table 6-5 Percentage Increase of Total Shares Over Prior Year

Year	State Members' Savings	Percentage Increase	Federal Members' Savings	Percentage Increase	Total Members' Savings	Percentage Increase
1971	$ 9,167,159	16.7%	$ 9,191,182	20.5%	$18,358,341	18.5%
1972	10,669,759	16.4	10,956,007	19.2	21,625,766	18.0
1973	11,913,900	11.7	12,597,607	15.0	24,511,507	13.3
1974	13,147,717	10.4	14,370,744	14.1	27,518,461	12.3
1975	15,521,520	18.1	17,529,823	22.0	33,051,343	20.1
1976	17,967,962	15.8	21,130,293	20.5	39,098,255	18.3
1977	20,939,971	16.5	25,576,017	21.0	46,515,988	19.0
1978	23,715,491	13.5	19,802,504	16.5	53,517,995	15.1
1979	25,627,972	8.1	31,831,400	6.8	53,559,436	5.2
1980	$29,479,713	15.0%	$36,263,343	13.9%	$60,416,506	12.8%

Source: NCUA, *Annual Reports of State Chartered Credit Unions.*

recorded an influx of funds each year. On the other hand, competing depositories (particulary the other thrifts) endured net outflows of deposits during periods of disintermediation experienced over the decade. Finally, Table 6-6 shows that member deposits maintained their dominance as the major source of credit unions funds during the 1970s.

Although loans slipped as a percentage of total credit union assets when measured from 1971 to 1980, this can hardly be regarded as a definite trend. Note in Table 6-7 that the loan-to-asset ratio grew steadily through 1978. At that point the combined forces of weak loan demand, prevailing usury ceilings, and the high yields available

Table 6-6 Total Shares Divided by Total Assets in State and Federal Insured Credit Unions, 1971-1980 (Percentages)

Year	Associational	Occupational	Residential	Total
1971	86.2%	87.2%	86.1%	87.1%
1972	87.0	87.6	82.9	87.6
1973	83.9	86.5	85.2	86.4
1974	84.9	86.1	83.2	86.0
1975	84.6	86.9	83.2	86.7
1976	84.8	86.7	83.6	86.5
1977	82.4	86.3	83.6	85.9
1978	82.9	86.1	85.6	85.8
1979	86.4	86.1	81.4	86.0
1980	91.8%	89.5%	89.8%	89.8%

Source: NCUA *Annual Reports.*

Table 6-7 Distribution of Assets of Federal Insured Credit Unions, 1971-1980

	Federal			State			Total		
Year	Loans to Members	Cash and Total Investments	Other Assets	Loans to Members	Cash and Total Investments	Other Assets	Loans to Members	Cash and Total Investments	Other Assets
1971	76.5%	22.1%	1.4%	78.2%	19.4%	2.4%	76.7%	21.7%	1.6%
1972	75.3	23.2	1.5	77.4	20.2	2.4	75.7	22.6	1.7
1973	76.3	22.1	1.6	79.4	18.1	2.5	77.0	21.2	1.8
1974	76.2	22.1	1.7	79.0	18.3	2.7	76.9	21.1	2.0
1975	73.6	24.6	1.8	76.7	21.1	2.2	74.5	23.5	2.0
1976	75.0	23.0	2.0	80.0	17.7	2.3	76.6	21.3	2.1
1977	76.5	21.4	2.1	81.5	15.8	2.7	78.1	19.6	2.3
1978	79.7	18.1	2.2	84.3	13.3	2.4	81.2	16.5	2.3
1979	78.3	19.3	2.4	82.3	15.0	2.7	79.7	17.8	2.5
1980	65.7%	31.6%	2.6%	69.9%	27.4%	2.7%	67.1%	30.2%	2.7%

Source: NCUA, *Annual Reports.*

on investments prompted a portfolio shift toward money market securities. This may be regarded as a temporary anomaly, however. Credit unions are by their very nature prone to lend rather than invest, and one can reasonably anticipate a return to lending as market forces and deregulation again make loans attractive to both members and management. Tables 6-8 and 6-9 document the dynamics of credit union lending over the decade for the industry as a whole and in both the state and federal sectors while Table 6-10 addresses the lending and investment record by type of common bond.

Credit unions make loans to members for a variety of purposes and on both a secured and unsecured basis as indicated in Table 6-11. These data reveal a significant decline in unsecured lending by credit unions during the 1970s and a concomitant increase in loans for durable goods, homes (purchases, repairs and modernization) and business purposes at the expense of personal and household loans.

The proportion of unsecured loans has declined in terms of both the amount (33% decline) and the number (13% decline). This has occurred despite the lifting in 1973 of a security requirement on all loans of $2,500 or more. Further, the average unsecured loan is only somewhat larger than it was in 1970 while the average secured loan is 144% of the 1970 average. Table 6-12 indicates relative stability in consumer lending in general and automobile lending in particular over the decade.

Historically, credit union interest rates (paid and charged) have been closely regulated. However, one of the problems with interest rates on loans is obtaining a yield that will allow credit unions to pay rates on savings accounts which are competitive with other financial institutions. Recently, credit unions have been allowed some changes which should help solve this problem. First, in 1980, the loan ceiling was raised from 12% (where it had been since 1934) to 15% and on a temporary basis to 21%. Furthermore, rates for consumer loans are now allowed to vary in conjunction with a measure agreed upon by the consumer and the credit union. Still, many credit unions feel this will eliminate one competitive advantage of credit unions—namely, credit unions have, traditionally, offered loans to members at rates lower than members could secure elsewhere.

As indicated above, all the other assets of credit unions may best be perceived as residuals. That is, after prudent liquidity requirements are met, credit unions tend to invest primarily in loans to members.

Table 6-8 Credit Union Loans Outstanding to Savings Ratios, 1971-1980

Year	State-Chartered			Federal			Total		
	Loans Outstanding ($ thousands)	Members' Savings ($ thousands)	Loans/ Savings (%)	Loans Outstanding ($ thousands)	Members' Savings ($ thousands)	Loans/ Savings (%)	Loans Outstanding ($ thousands)	Members' Savings ($ thousands)	Loans/ Savings (%)
1971	$ 8,081,203	$ 9,167,159	88.2%	$ 8,071,201	$ 9,191,182	87.8%	$16,152,404	$18,358,341	88.0%
1972	9,238,499	10,669,759	86.6	9,424,180	10,956,007	86.0	18,662,679	21,625,766	86.3
1973	10,649,756	11,913,900	89.4	11,109,015	12,597,607	88.2	21,758,771	24,511,507	88.8
1974	11,701,900	13,147,717	89.0	12,729,653	14,370,744	88.6	24,431,553	27,518,461	88.8
1975	13,299,465	15,521,520	85.7	14,868,840	17,529,823	84.8	28,168,305	33,051,343	85.2
1976	15,998,514	17,967,962	89.0	18,311,204	21,130,293	86.7	34,309,718	39,098,255	87.8
1977	19,211,432	20,939,971	91.7	22,633,860	25,576,017	88.5	41,845,292	46,515,988	90.0
1978	22,581,869	23,715,491	95.2	27,686,584	29,802,504	92.9	50,268,453	53,517,995	93.9
1979	23,676,907	25,627,972	92.4	28,547,097	31,831,400	89.7	52,224,004	57,459,372	90.9
1980	$22,632,954	$29,479,713	76.8%	$26,350,277	$36,263,343	72.7%	$48,983,231	$65,743,056	74.5%

Source: NCUA, State Chartered Annual Reports.

Table 6-9 Credit Union Loans Outstanding to Total Assets Ratios, 1969-1980

	State-Chartered			Federal-Chartered			Total All Credit Unions		
Year	Loans Outstanding ($ thousands)	Total Assets	Loans/ Assets (%)	Loans Outstanding ($ thousands)	Total Assets	Loans/ Assets (%)	Loans Outstanding ($ thousands)	Total Assets	Loans/ Assets (%)
1969	$ 6,629,839	$ 8,123,896	81.6%	$ 6,328,720	$ 7,793,573	81.2%	$12,958,559	$15,917,469	81.4%
1970	7,136,667	9,088,839	78.5	6,969,006	8,860,612	78.7	14,105,673	17,949,451	78.6
1971	8,081,203	10,568,540	76.5	8,071,201	10,552,740	76.5	16,152,404	21,121,280	76.5
1972	9,238,499	12,274,869	75.3	9,424,180	12,513,621	75.3	18,662,679	24,788,490	75.3
1973	10,649,756	13,806,158	77.1	11,109,015	14,568,736	76.3	21,758,771	28,374,894	76.7
1974	11,701,900	15,232,991	76.8	12,729,653	16,714,673	76.2	24,431,553	31,947,664	76.5
1975	13,299,465	17,804,271	74.7	14,868,840	20,208,536	73.6	28,168,305	38,012,807	74.1
1976	15,998,514	20,640,042	77.5	18,311,204	24,395,896	75.1	34,310,718	45,035,938	76.2
1977	19,211,432	24,191,139	79.4	22,633,860	29,563,681	76.6	41,845,292	53,754,820	77.8
1978	22,581,869	27,587,866	81.9	27,686,584	34,760,098	79.7	50,268,453	62,347,964	80.6
1979	23,676,907	29,523,832	80.2	28,547,097	36,467,850	78.3	52,224,004	65,991,682	79.1
1980	$22,632,954	$33,143,035	68.3%	$26,350,277	$40,091,855	65.7%	$48,983,231	$73,234,890	66.9%

Source: NCUA, *State Chartered Annual Reports.*

Table 6-10 Ratios of Members' Loans or Cash and Total Investment to Total Assets for All Insured Credit Unions, 1971-1980

Year	Loans to Members Divided by Total Assets				Cash and Total Investments Divided by Total Assets			
	Associational	Occupational	Residential	Total	Associational	Occupational	Residential	Total
1971	74.9%	76.9%	76.7%	76.8%	23.3%	21.6%	20.4%	21.7%
1972	71.4	76.0	76.0	76.5	26.6	22.3	21.1	22.6
1973	76.3	77.0	76.7	77.0	21.6	21.2	20.2	21.2
1974	78.0	76.0	78.1	76.2	20.1	22.4	18.5	22.1
1975	74.5	74.4	79.8	74.5	23.3	23.7	16.7	23.6
1976	76.1	76.5	80.0	76.6	21.4	21.5	16.4	21.3
1977	76.7	78.1	80.7	78.1	21.1	19.6	15.5	19.6
1978	79.3	81.3	82.7	81.2	18.6	16.4	13.7	16.5
1979	70.3	80.6	81.8	79.7	27.4	16.9	15.8	17.8
1980	43.9%	70.5%	68.8%	67.1%	53.7%	26.9%	27.7%	30.2%

Source: NCUA, State Chartered Annual Reports.

Table 6-11 Purpose and Security of Loans Extended by Sample of
Federal Credit Unions, Selected Years, 1970-1978
($ amounts in millions)

	1970	1975	1978
Security			
Unsecured Loans			
Percentage of Amount	28.2%	27.1%	19.0%
Percentage of Number	45.3%	44.5%	39.6%
Average Size	$ 893	$1,220	$ 971
Secured Loans			
Percentage of Amount	71.8%	72.9%	81.0%
Percentage of Number	54.7%	55.5%	60.4%
Average Size	$1,882	$2,630	$2,714
Purpose of Loans			
Durable Consumer Goods:			
Percentage of Amount	41.4%	45.0%	44.9%
Percentage of Number	33.9%	37.8%	37.9%
Average Size	$1,751	$2,386	$2,401
Personal and Household:			
Percentage of Amount	42.5%	34.9%	32.1%
Percentage of Number	54.4%	47.6%	47.0%
Average Size	$1,121	$1,479	$1,384
Repair and Modernization:			
Percentage of Amount	8.7%	10.5%	11.5%
Percentage of Number	7.9%	10.3%	11.0%
Average Size	$1,594	$2,055	$2,134
Real Estate:			
Percentage of Amount	4.7%	6.8%	7.6%
Percentage of Number	2.1%	2.8%	1.9%
Average Size	$3,151	$4,826	$7,992
Business:			
Percentage of Amount	2.7%	2.8%	3.8%
Percentage of Number	1.7%	1.9%	2.2%
Average Size	$2,242	$2,901	$3,459

Source: Derived from NCUA *Annual Reports.*

Only when loan demand is inadequate to absorb the available funds
at profitable rates (see section on spread analysis below) will these
funds be invested in other assets. Liquid assets include cash, accounts
receivable, common trust investment and shares, deposits and certificates in other credit unions and financial institutions.

Likewise, as has been shown, member deposits account for the
lion's share of credit union liabilities. The other liabilities are comprised primarily of notes and accounts payable for such items as
buildings, equipment, supplies and accrued salaries, interest and taxes.

The final balance sheet category, capital, represents the difference between total assets and total liabilities. Credit union capital is made up of reserves (for liquidity and loan losses) and accumulated net earnings which credit unions have reinvested in themselves rather than distributed as additional dividends or interest rebates. Capital provides a safety cushion against unexpectedly large levels of loan losses and/or withdrawals. Tables 6-13 through 6-18 demonstrate while the capital assets ratio (an index of the safety margin provided by capital) and other measures of capital adequacy deteriorated slightly over the decade the marked increase in liquid assets experienced during 1980 more than offset this slippage. This left the credit union industry on relatively solid financial ground at a time when other depositories were undergoing severe deteriorations in balance sheet conditions.

INCOME AND EXPENSES

Before delving into an analysis of credit union revenues and expenditures, it is important to reemphasize that a cooperative's "bottom line" has a distinctly different meaning from that of a typical profit-seeking firm. Once again this is because the goal of credit unions is not simply to maximize the return to the equity investors (credit union members) but to provide a range of services to the membership. The educational programs and financial counseling provided by a given credit

Table 6-12   Selected Data on Credit Union Loans and
Automobile Credit, 1975-1980

Year	Total Loans ($ millions)	Consumer Credit Outstanding as Percentage of Total Loans	Automobile Credit as Percent of Total Consumer Credit
1975	$28,168	91.1%	49.6%
1976	34,310	90.8	48.9
1977	41,845	89.9	48.1
1978	50,269	88.2	47.8
1979	52,224	89.1	47.8
1980	48,983	89.9	47.8

Source: NCUA, *1980 Annual Report.*

Table 6-13 Percentage Increase/Decrease of Reserves and Undivided Earnings Over the Prior Year, 1971-1980

Year	State Reserves and Undivided Earnings ($ thousands)	State Percentage Increase	Federal Reserves and Undivided Earnings ($ thousands)	Federal Percentage Increase	Total Reserves and Undivided Earnings ($ thousands)	Total Percentage Increase
1971	$1,043,942	11.3%	$1,012,516	11.0%	$2,056,458	11.1%
1972	1,191,258	14.1	1,146,021	13.2	2,337,279	13.7
1973	1,315,784	10.5	1,290,745	12.6	2,606,529	11.5
1974	1,459,544	10.9	1,452,089	12.5	2,911,633	11.7
1975	1,638,612	12.3	1,639,560	12.9	3,278,172	12.6
1976	1,389,200	(18.0)	1,465,346	(11.9)	2,854,546	(14.8)
1977	1,576,252	13.5	1,571,217	7.2	3,147,469	10.3
1978	1,920,893	21.9	1,850,481	17.8	3,771,374	19.8
1979	2,114,572	10.1	2,072,511	12.0	4,187,083	11.0
1980	$2,209,167	4.5%	$2,206,033	6.4%	$4,415,200	5.4%

Source: NCUA, State Chartered Annual Reports.

Table 6-14   Liquid Asset and Capital to Asset Ratios of
Federally-Insured Credit Unions, 1971-1980

Year	Liquid Assets^a as Percent of Total Liabilities^b	Total Capital as Percent of Total Assets^c
1971	14.9%	7.5%
1972	14.7	7.2
1973	12.8	7.0
1974	13.4	7.0
1975	14.7	6.6
1976	13.0	6.3
1977	10.6	6.0
1978	8.3	5.9
1979	19.1	6.3
1980	23.2%	6.1%

Source: Harold Black and Robert H. Dugger, "Credit Union Structure, Growth and Regulatory Problems," *The Journal of Finance*, Vol. XXXVI, No. 2, May 1981; and NCUA *Annual Report*, 1980.

[a]Liquid assets represent the total cash common trust investments, and shares, deposits, and certificates in other credit unions and financial institutions.

[b]Total liabilities represents total shares plus notes and accounts payable and all other liabilities.

[c]Total capital represents the total of reserves and retained earnings.

union may add more to costs than to revenues and thus result in a loss of profits in a strict accounting sense. For a typical business venture such services might be considered irrational. For the credit union they are an integral part of the program.

On the other hand, credit union management is charged with the responsibility of achieving the goals of the credit union as efficiently

Table 6-15   Reserves and Undivided Earnings Divided by Total Assets by
Percentage of State and Federal Insured Credit Unions, 1971-1980

Year	Associational	Occupational	Residential	Total
1971	9.8%	9.7%	9.8%	9.7%
1972	9.1	9.2	9.2	9.2
1973	9.1	8.9	9.3	9.0
1974	6.7	7.0	8.0	7.0
1975	6.4	6.6	7.6	6.6
1976	5.6	6.3	7.9	6.3
1977	5.2	6.1	6.7	6.1
1978	5.3	5.8	6.9	5.8
1979	5.0	5.9	7.2	5.8
1980	3.7%	6.4%	6.4%	6.1%

Source: Calculated from NCUA *Annual Reports.*

Table 6-16   Regular Reserves and Undivided Earnings State and
Federal Insured Credit Unions by Type of Common Bond, 1971-1980
($ thousand)

Year	Associational	Occupational	Residential	Total
1971	$ 71,357	$1,116,551	$ 20,551	$1,208,458
1972	88,916	1,345,066	24,931	1,458,912
1973	113,059	1,546,797	34,624	1,694,481
1974	107,429	1,445,789	38,518	1,591,737
1975	134,875	1,707,808	46,287	1,888,970
1976	150,011	1,991,763	68,408	2,210,181
1977	184,638	2,353,527	79,762	2,626,927
1978	232,285	2,657,270	102,301	2,991,857
1979	255,920	3,060,688	120,249	3,436,858
1980	$277,920	$3,271,939	$139,207	$3,689,067

Source: NCUA, *Annual Reports.*

as possible. Consequently, a review of the income and expense record of the industry is in order and Table 6-19 provides an overview thereof for the 1970s.

Far and away the most important income source for credit unions is the interest earned on loans to members. However, as Table 6-19 shows, both investment income (particularly) and other income grew proportionately more rapidly over the decade. More ominously, the total expenses of the industry rose slightly faster (102.8%) than total income 100.7%) during the inflationary 1970s.

Naturally, the biggest culprits in the expense column growth that occurred during the period were employee compensation, office occupancy (rent, maintenance, utilities, depreciation, etc.), and interest on borrowed money (not dividends and interest paid member depositors—see discussion below). On a brighter note, many expense items including the following

1. Travel and conferences (86.6%)
2. Association dues (74.9%)
3. Member insurance (29.3%)
4. Annual meeting (56.5%)

all increased at significantly lower rates than total expenses and the general inflation rate over the decade.

Table 6-17 Ratio of Credit Union Reserves and Undivided Earnings to Loans, 1971-1980

	State Chartered			Federal			Total		
Year	Reserves and Undivided Earnings ($ thousands)	Loans	(Reserves and Earnings)/ Loans	Reserves and Undivided Earnings ($ thousands)	Loans	(Reserves and Earnings)/ Loans	Reserves and Undivided Earnings ($ thousands)	Loans	(Reserves and Earnings)/ Loans
1971	$1,043,942	$ 8,081,203	12.9%	$1,012,516	$ 8,071,201	12.5%	$2,056,458	$16,152,404	13.7%
1972	1,191,258	9,238,499	12.9	1,146,021	9,424,180	12.2	2,337,279	18,662,679	12.5
1974	1,315,784	10,649,756	12.4	1,290,745	11,109,015	11.6	2,606,529	21,758,771	12.0
1974	1,459,544	11,701,900	12.5	1,452,089	12,729,553	11.4	2,911,633	24,431,553	11.9
1975	1,638,612	13,299,465	12.3	1,639,560	14,868,840	11.0	3,278,172	28,168,305	11.6
1976	1,389,200	15,998,514	8.7	1,465,346	13,311,204	8.0	2,854,546	34,310,718	8.3
1977	1,576,252	19,211,432	8.2	1,571,217	22,633,860	6.9	3,147,469	41,845,292	7.5
1978	1,920,843	22,581,869	8.5	1,850,481	27,686,584	6.7	3,771,374	50,268,453	7.5
1979	2,114,572	23,676,907	8.9	2,072,511	28,547,097	7.3	4,187,083	52,224,004	8.0
1980	$2,209,167	$22,632,954	9.8%	$2,206,033	$26,350,277	8.4%	$4,415,200	$48,983,231	9.0%

Source: NCUA, State Chartered Annual Reports.

Table 6-18 Credit Union Reserves and Undivided Earnings Divided by Members' Savings, 1971-1980

Year	State-Chartered Undivided Earnings and Reserves ($ thousands)	State-Chartered Members' Savings	State-Chartered (Reserves and Earnings)/Savings	Federal-Chartered Undivided Earnings and Reserves ($ thousands)	Federal-Chartered Members' Savings	Federal-Chartered (Reserves and Earnings)/Savings	Total–All Credit Unions Undivided Earnings and Reserves ($ thousands)	Total–All Credit Unions Members' Savings ($ thousands)	Total–All Credit Unions (Reserves and Earnings)/Savings
1971	$1,043,942	$ 9,167,159	11.4%	$1,012,516	$ 9,191,182	11.0%	$2,056,458	$18,358,341	11.2%
1972	1,191,258	10,669,759	11.2	1,146,021	10,956,007	10.5	2,337,279	21,625,766	10.8
1973	1,315,784	11,913,900	11.0	1,290,745	12,597,607	10.2	2,606,529	24,511,507	10.6
1974	1,459,544	13,147,717	11.1	1,452,089	14,370,744	10.1	2,911,633	27,518,461	10.6
1975	1,638,612	15,521,520	10.6	1,639,560	17,529,823	9.4	3,278,172	33,051,343	9.9
1976	1,389,200	17,967,962	7.7	1,465,346	21,130,293	6.9	2,854,546	39,098,255	7.3
1977	1,576,252	20,939,971	7.5	1,571,217	25,576,017	6.1	3,147,469	46,515,988	6.8
1978	1,920,893	23,715,491	8.1	1,850,481	29,802,504	6.2	3,771,374	53,517,995	7.1
1979	2,114,572	25,627,972	8.3	2,072,511	31,831,400	6.5	4,187,083	57,459,372	7.3
1980	$2,209,167	$29,479,713	7.5%	$2,206,033	$36,263,343	6.1%	$4,415,200	$65,743,056	6.7%

Source: NCUA, *Annual Reports of State Chartered Credit Unions.*

Table 6-19 Income Statement—Selected Years for Federal Credit Unions and State-Chartered Federally-Insured Credit Unions
(Amounts in thousands)

	1971	Percentage of Total	1976	Percentage of Total	Percentage Change 1971-1976	1980	Percentage of Total	Percentage Change 1976-1980	Percentage Change 1971-1980
Income:									
Interest on Loans	$ 914,006	87.1%	$2,564,116	83.2%	180.5%	$4,687,981	75.8%	82.8%	412.9%
Income from Investments	114,870	11.0	473,915	15.4	312.6	1,411,888	22.8	197.9	1,129.1
Other Income	20,075	1.9	44,134	1.4	119.8	86,416	1.4	95.8	330.5
Total Gross Income	1,048,958		3,082,175		193.8	6,186,294		100.7	489.8
Less: Total Expenses	394,399		1,118,754		183.7	2,268,663		102.8	475.2
Employee Compensation/ Benefits	149,950	38.0	373,914	33.4	149.4	858,100	37.8	129.5	472.3
Travel and Conferences	4,492	1.1	19,094	1.7	325.1	35,627	1.6	86.6	693.1
Association Dues	8,883	2.3	17,476	1.6	96.7	30,558	1.3	74.9	244.0
Office Occupancy	8,396	2.1	36,838	3.3	338.8	87,395	3.9	137.2	940.9
Educational and Promotional	8,231	2.1	25,346	2.3	207.9	50,610	2.2	99.7	514.9
Members Insurance	98,325	24.9	185,820	16.6	89.0	240,277	10.6	29.3	144.4
Interest on Borrowed Money	15,067	3.8	85,778	7.7	469.3	211,024	9.3	146.0	1,300.6
Annual Meeting Expense	3,988	1.0	9,761	.9	144.8	15,276	.7	56.5	283.0
Other Expenses	97,014	24.6%	364,665	32.6%	275.9	739,750	32.6%	102.9	662.5
Net Income	$ 654,559		$1,963,418		200.0%	$3,917,625		99.5%	498.5%

Source: NCUA, Annual Reports.

Tables 6-20 and 6-21 detail the relative importance of interest, investment and other income by asset size category for federal and federally insured credit unions, respectively. Perhaps the most notable phenomena in the tables are:

1. The dominance of interest from loans for all sizes of credit unions over each year observed
2. The close relationship between asset size and investment income—the larger the credit union, the greater the proportion of gross income accounted for by investments
3. The increasing importance of investment income within each size category over the decade
4. The tendency of credit unions of all sizes to rely relatively more on investment income during periods of slack loan demand (1975 and 1980).

Virtually the same income distribution trends can be identified when the data are analyzed by common bond type as presented in Table 6-22.

Table 6-20   Gross Income Percentages, Federal Credit Unions, Selected Years, 1971-1980

Year	Asset Size	Interest on Loans	Income from Investments	Office Income
1971	$ 250,000-$ 499,999	89.7%	8.7%	1.4%
	1,000,000-$1,999,999	87.7	10.7	1.6
	5,000,000-$9,999,999	86.2	11.9	1.9
	20,000,000 or more	81.3	15.0	3.7
1975	250,000-$ 499,999	87.2	11.0	1.8
	1,000,000-$1,999,999	85.3	13.3	1.4
	5,000,000-$9,999,999	83.0	15.8	1.2
	20,000,000 or more			
1979	250,000-$ 499,999	88.7	9.7	1.6
	1,000,000-$1,999,999	88.8	9.9	1.3
	5,000,000-$9,999,999	86.9	12.1	1.0
	20,000,000 or more	79.4	19.6	1.0
1980	250,000-$ 499,999	85.3	13.1	1.6
	1,000,000-$1,999,999	84.0	14.7	1.3
	5,000,000-$9,999,999	79.2	19.6	1.2
	$20,000,000 or more	67.5%	31.1%	1.4%

Source: NCUA, *Annual Reports.*

By far the most significant "expense" items for credit unions is the dividends and interest paid to members. The quotation marks around expense are to provide a reminder that, technically, dividends paid to shareholders are just that—a disbursement of residual (net) income after all the expenses of the credit union have been satisfied. In practice, the dichotomy between credit union dividends and the interest paid depositors at other financial institutions blurs almost to the point of being meaningless.

Table 6-23(a) records the recent history of credit union dividend rates by both asset size and common bond. Note that:

1. Rates climbed for all sizes and types of credit unions during the decade
2. Larger credit unions paid higher dividends almost without exception
3. Earlier in the decade residential credit unions tended to pay higher rates than similar size associational and occupational credit unions, but fell behind the other two groups later.

Table 6-21   Gross Income Percentages, Federally Insured State Credit Unions, Selected Years, 1971-1980

Year	Asset Size	Interest on Loans	Income from Investments	Office Income
1971	$ 250,000-$ 499,999	90.9%	8.3%	0.8%
	1,000,000-$1,999,999	87.1	11.4	1.5
	5,000,000-$9,999,999	91.2	7.9	0.9
	20,000,000 or more	86.0	12.4	1.6
1975	250,000-$ 499,999	89.2	9.7	1.1
	1,000,000-$1,999,999	87.7	11.2	1.1
	5,000,000-$9,999,999	86.2	12.8	1.0
	20,000,000 or more	79.8	19.0	1.2
1979	250,000-$ 499,999	90.2	8.5	1.3
	1,000,000-$1,999,999	90.3	8.2	1.5
	5,000,000-$9,999,999	89.8	8.9	1.3
	20,000,000 or more	86.2	12.4	1.4
1980	250,000-$ 499,999	86.2	12.5	1.3
	1,000,000-$1,999,999	85.2	13.1	1.7
	5,000,000-$9,999,999	82.5	16.1	1.4
	$20,000,000 or more	75.1%	23.2%	1.7%

Source: NCUA, *Annual Reports.*

Table 6-22 Federal Credit Union Income Distribution by Common Bond Type, 1971-1980

Year	Income from Interest on Loans Divided by Total Gross Income				Income from Investments and Other Income Divided by Total Gross Income			
	Occupational	Associational	Residential	All Credit Unions	Occupational	Associational	Residential	All Credit Unions
1971	87.2%	86.8%	85.4%	87.1%	12.8%	13.2%	14.6%	12.9%
1972	86.2	85.1	84.7	86.1	13.8	14.9	15.3	13.9
1973	84.7	85.5	83.7	84.8	15.3	14.5	16.3	15.2
1974	82.7	83.9	82.4	82.7	17.4	16.1	17.6	17.3
1975	82.3	82.1	85.0	82.3	17.7	17.9	15.0	17.7
1976	83.1	83.9	85.3	83.2	16.9	16.1	14.7	16.8
1977	84.6	84.0	87.0	84.6	15.4	16.0	13.0	15.4
1978	85.6	84.8	87.7	85.6	14.4	15.2	12.4	14.4
1979	85.9	77.9	87.0	85.2	14.1	22.1	13.0	14.8
1980	78.7%	53.9%	76.5%	75.8%	21.3%	46.1%	23.5%	24.2%

Source: NCUA, Annual Reports.

Table 6-23 Average Dividend Rate of Federal Credit Unions by Asset Size and Type of Membership, 1970 and 1975

Asset Size ($ thousands)	1970				1975			
	Total	Associational	Occupational	Residential	Total	Associational	Occupational	Residential
Less than $10	4.11%	3.99%	4.17%	4.23%	4.02%	4.02%	3.82%	4.05%
10-24.9	4.38	4.10	4.49	4.26	4.66	4.43	4.84	4.65
25-49.9	4.68	4.31	4.80	4.46	5.04	4.76	5.15	4.02
50-99.9	5.00	4.75	5.06	4.68	5.41	5.10	5.50	5.08
100-249.9	5.18	4.95	5.23	4.82	5.66	5.41	5.72	5.39
250-499.9	5.28	4.95	5.34	4.85	5.76	5.35	5.85	5.16
500-99.9	5.28	4.86	5.34	4.87	5.82	5.59	5.87	5.30
1,000-1,999.9	5.37	5.07	5.40	5.09	5.92	5.53	5.97	5.56
2,000-4,999.9	5.46	5.09	5.48	5.16	5.96	5.72	5.99	5.71
5,000-9,999.9	5.61*	5.03	5.63	5.40	6.15	5.83	6.17	5.81
10,000-19,999.9	N.A.	N.A.	N.A.	N.A.	6.26	5.54	6.25	6.20
20,000 or more	N.A.	N.A.	N.A.	N.A.	6.42	6.55	6.42	6.25
Total	5.44%	4.97%	5.48%	5.05%	6.15%	5.67%	6.18%	5.75%

Source: NCUA, Annual Reports.
*$5,000 or more in 1970.

Table 6-23(a) Average Dividend Rate of Federal Credit Unions by Asset Size and Type of Membership, 1978 and 1980

Asset Size	1978				1980			
($ thousands)	Total	Associational	Occupational	Residential	Total	Associational	Occupational	Residential
Less than $50	5.01%	4.75%	5.18%	4.89%	5.57%	5.44%	5.68%	5.11%
50-999	5.48	5.30	5.54	5.43	5.86	5.83	5.88	5.88
100-249.9	5.80	5.54	5.88	5.50	6.10	5.96	6.15	5.71
250-499.9	5.95	5.65	6.02	5.60	6.27	6.12	6.31	5.95
500-999.9	6.11	5.75	6.18	5.64	6.42	6.13	6.48	5.94
1,000-1,999.9	6.19	5.93	6.23	5.83	6.51	6.35	6.54	6.21
2,000-4,999.9	6.30	6.04	6.35	5.77	6.59	6.35	6.64	6.17
5,000-9,999.9	6.41	6.20	6.44	5.97	6.64	6.62	6.66	6.32
10,000-19,999.9	6.45	6.15	6.47	6.19	6.65	6.39	6.68	6.34
20,000-49,999.9	6.59	6.50	6.60	6.29	6.69	6.55	6.70	6.44
50,000-99,999.9	6.68	7.00	6.68	–	6.71	6.27	6.73	–
100,000 or more	6.73	6.69	6.74	–	6.83	6.91	6.82	6.25
Total	6.47%	6.24%	6.50%	5.98%	6.65%	6.55%	6.67%	6.28%

Source: NCUA, *Annual Reports.*

Although not indicated in the tables, credit union dividends were typically higher than the interest rates paid on passbook savings accounts by other depositories of similar size.

Table 6-23(b) demonstrates the dominant role of dividends and interest as a claim on credit union income compared to total expenses proper. The data show that, in fact, dividends become relatively more important over the decade, increasing their share of total income from 48.3% in 1971 to 61.4% in 1980 while the expense to income rates declined slightly from 37.7% to 36.1% over the same period. Clearly, the increased competition for the public's savings dollar has had a major impact on credit union finances. Tables 6-23(c), 6-24 and 6-25 present recent trends in selected credit union expense items as a percentage of total income 6-23(c) and total expenses (6-24 and 6-25) and provides further evidence of the expense dynamics noted above.

Focusing on some expense problem areas, Tables 6-26 and 6-27 document the fact that credit union employee compensation has stayed in line with both income (Table 6-26) and expense (Table 6-27) growth during the decade. Of the other expenses that might be considered controllable from management's standpoint (interest rates and office occupancy costs are generally considered market determined), loan losses probably deserve the most attention. Perusal of the data in Tables 6-31 discloses a steady accretion of both loan loss ratios (total debt written off as a percentage of the amount of loan since organization) and delinquency ratios (total delinquent loans over total loans). While this trend is itself unwholesome, even the most recent ratios are well within reasonable boundaries for consumer lending. In fact, many lending officials at other institutions would read Tables 6-28 and 6-29 with envy—a tribute to the combined forces of the common bond and the loan underwriting decisions of credit union management.

It is also interesting to note in Tables 6-28 and 6-29 that occupational credit unions with their strong common bond have much lower ratios than the other types. Surprisingly, the residential credit union loss ratios are more similar to those of the occupational group than to those of the associational credit unions. By inference, the strength of the common bond in community credit unions may be more robust than might have been expected.

Table 6-30 takes a look at loan loss ratios from the asset size per-

Table 6-23(b)   Credit Union Dividends and Interest Divided by Total Income, 1971-1980

	State			Federal			Total			Ratios of Expenses to Income		
Year	Dividends and Interest	Total Income	(Dividends + Interest)/ Income	Dividends and Interest	Total Income	(Dividends + Interest)/ Income	Dividends and Interest	Total Income	(Dividends + Interest)/ Income	State-Chartered	Federal	Total
1971	$ 422,857	$ 865,744	48.8%	$ 423,195	$ 886,412	47.7%	$ 846,052	$1,752,156	48.3%	37.7%	37.8%	37.7%
1972	497,378	1,006,516	49.4	516,194	1,045,535	49.4	1,013,572	2,052,051	49.4	37.1	36.8	36.9
1973	590,744	1,180,537	50.0	635,142	1,251,034	50.8	1,225,886	2,431,571	50.4	38.7	36.3	27.4
1974	694,862	1,360,554	51.1	761,609	1,503,656	50.7	1,456,471	2,864,210	50.9	38.7	36.4	37.5
1975	875,491	1,533,624	57.1	924,966	1,748,693	62.9	1,800,457	3,282,317	54.9	36.8	37.5	37.1
1976	962,323	1,801,268	53.4	1,129,686	2,123,981	53.2	2,092,009	3,925,249	53.3	35.1	37.2	36.2
1977	1,136,635	2,128,057	53.4	1,387,328	2,580,231	53.8	2,523,963	4,708,288	53.6	35.5	37.5	36.6
1978	1,339,222	2,504,446	53.5	1,705,800	2,300,992	53.3	3,045,022	5,705,438	53.4	35.6	37.9	39.9
1979	1,723,485	2,852,898	60.4	1,940,779	3,642,996	53.3	3,664,264	6,495,894	56.4	36.6	39.5	38.5
1980	$2,139,336	$3,324,742	64.4%	$2,386,948	$4,044,274	59.0%	$4,526,284	$7,308,746	61.4%	34.7%	37.3%	35.9%

Source: NCUA, *State Chartered Annual Reports.*

Table 6-23(c) Credit Union Total Expenses to Total Income Ratios, 1971-1980
(Dollar amounts in thousands)

Year	State-Chartered			Federal			Total		
	Total Expenses	Total Income	Expenses/ Income (%)	Total Expenses	Total Income	Expenses/ Income (%)	Total Expenses	Total Income	Expenses/ Income (%)
1971	$ 326,207	$ 865,744	37.7	$ 335,167	$ 886,412	37.8	$ 661,374	$1,752,156	37.7
1972	373,130	1,006,516	37.1	384,629	1,045,535	36.8	757,759	2,052,051	36.9
1973	456,815	1,180,537	38.7	453,643	1,251,034	36.3	910,358	2,431,571	37.4
1974	525,904	1,360,554	38.7	546,866	1,503,656	36.4	1,072,770	2,864,210	37.5
1975	563,871	1,533,624	36.8	655,442	1,748,693	37.5	1,219,313	3,282,317	37.1
1976	631,705	1,801,268	35.1	790,639	2,123,981	37.2	1,422,344	3,925,249	36.2
1977	754,816	2,128,057	35.5	967,942	2,580,231	37.5	1,722,758	4,708,288	36.6
1978	892,080	2,504,446	35.6	1,213,968	3,200,992	37.9	2,106,048	5,705,438	36.9
1979	1,043,043	2,582,898	36.6	1,439,856	3,642,996	39.5	2,482,899	6,495,894	38.2
1980	$1,153,422	$3,324,472	37.7%	$1,508,439	$4,044,274	37.3%	$2,661,861	$7,368,746	36.1%

Source: NCUA, *State Chartered Credit Unions Annual Reports.*

Table 6-24 Selected Expense Ratios of Federal-Chartered Credit Unions

Year	Asset Size	Total Salaries	Office Occupancy Expense	Interest on Borrowed Money	Members' Insurance
1971	$ 250,000-$ 499,999	38.3%	2.1%	3.3%	23.6%
	1,000,000-$1,999,999	39.2	1.8	3.1	26.8
	5,000,000-$9,999,999	37.1	1.8	3.1	23.0
	20,000,000 or more	41.6	2.3	3.1	16.4
1975	250,000-$ 499,999	35.2	2.8	3.3	22.5
	1,000,000-$1,999,999	36.7	2.4	4.0	22.5
	5,000,000-$9,999,999	33.8	3.2	7.5	17.7
	20,000,000 or more	32.8	3.1	11.9	12.7
1979	250,000-$ 499,999	33.7	2.9	5.4	19.1
	1,000,000-$1,999,999	37.1	2.2	6.5	17.6
	5,000,000-$9,999,999	36.8	3.3	9.6	13.1
	20,000,000 or more	33.2	3.5	21.3	8.4
1980	250,000-$ 499,999	34.0	3.0	3.0	17.5
	1,000,000-$1,999,999	38.3	2.2	3.5	15.8
	5,000,000-$9,999,999	38.6	3.6	5.4	11.5
	$20,000,000 or more	36.5%	4.0%	13.6%	8.0%

Source: NCUA, *Annual Reports.*

spective. Clearly, the larger credit unions have amassed a better record in this regard. This would tend to indicate that the better established credit unions with professional management do, in fact, achieve more efficient credit management. This leads to the question of what can credit unions do to improve the financial management practices in the years to come.

ACHIEVING EFFICIENCY AND EFFECTIVENESS

A survey such as this cannot adequately cover the many financial management procedures and techniques that credit unions must learn to use to remain competitive in a deregulated environment. Consequently, this section will only attempt to introduce in summary form some of the more important of these considerations and provide references to other sources where these topics are discussed in greater detail.

Table 6-25 Selected Expense Ratios of Credit Unions, 1975-1980

	Total Expenses ($ thousands)	Office Occupancy and Office Operations	Insurance Expense	Interest on Borrowed Money	Employee Compensation	All Other
1975–Total	$ 918,843	12.9%	18.0%	7.2%	34.4%	29.4%
Associational	75,530	14.8	18.8	9.8	30.6	27.6
Occupational	817,858	12.7	17.9	6.9	34.8	29.6
Residential	24,454	13.7	17.2	8.8	34.1	27.6
1976–Total	1,118,754	13.3	16.6	7.7	33.4	30.9
Associational	94,464	11.1	16.7	8.9	29.0	35.8
Occupational	990,754	13.1	16.6	7.2	33.9	31.1
Residential	33,537	14.1	15.8	9.1	32.1	30.4
1977–Total	1,384,795	13.7	15.3	9.0	32.6	31.6
Associational	120,256	14.5	14.7	15.7	28.2	28.7
Occupational	1,218,807	13.5	15.4	8.3	33.1	31.9
Residential	45,731	15.0	14.0	9.9	31.2	31.7
1978–Total	1,737,575	14.0	13.3	11.2	31.7	31.6
Associational	152,915	14.8	12.6	18.0	27.3	28.8
Occupational	1,525,600	13.8	13.4	10.5	32.1	32.0
Residential	59,060	15.6	12.4	10.6	31.1	31.7
1979–Total	2,100,115	14.4	11.9	13.3	36.0	24.4
Associational	180,230	15.3	11.6	17.5	32.1	23.5
Occupational	1,848,557	14.3	12.0	13.1	36.3	24.3
Residential	71,328	16.0	11.7	9.8	37.0	25.5
1980–Total	268,663	15.9	10.6	9.3	37.8	26.4
Associational	192,986	17.4	10.5	11.9	34.8	26.4
Occupational	1,991,943	15.6	10.6	9.2	38.1	26.5
Residential	$ 83,735	18.2%	9.9%	5.7%	39.6%	26.6%

Source: NCUA, *Annual Reports.*

Table 6-26 Credit Unions Employee Compensation and Benefits Divided by Total Income, 1971-1980

Year	State-Insured			Federal-Insured			Total-Insured		
	Employee Compensation/ Benefits ($ thousands)	Gross Total Income	Benefits/ Income	Employee Compensation/ Benefits ($ thousands)	Gross Total Income	Benefits/ Income	Employee Compensation/ Benefits ($ thousands)	Gross Total Income	Benefits/ Income
1971	$ 21,389	$ 162,546	13.2%	$128,562	$ 886,412	14.5%	$149,951	$ 186,394	14.3%
1972	35,443	277,764	12.8	145,118	1,045,535	13.9	180,561	1,323,299	13.6
1973	47,603	381,699	12.5	168,161	1,251,034	13.4	215,764	1,632,733	13.2
1974	69,356	553,721	12.5	196,410	1,503,656	13.1	265,766	2,057,377	12.9
1975	92,666	756,761	12.3	223,838	1,748,693	12.8	316,504	2,505,454	12.6
1976	113,438	958,194	11.8	260,476	2,123,981	12.3	373,914	3,082,175	12.1
1977	142,245	1,222,814	11.6	308,855	2,580,231	12.0	451,100	3,803,045	11.9
1978	178,217	1,550,244	11.5	371,842	3,200,992	11.6	550,059	4,751,236	11.6
1979	251,391	1,848,634	13.6	504,709	3,642,996	13.9	756,100	5,491,630	13.8
1980	$294,261	$2,142,020	13.7%	$563,839	$4,044,274	13.9%	$858,100	$6,186,294	13.9%

Source: NCUA, Annual Reports.

Table 6-27   Salaries Divided by Total Expenses (by Percentages),
State and Federal Insured Credit Unions, 1971-1980

Year	Associational	Occupational	Residential	Total
1971	33.6%	38.4%	36.1%	38.0%
1972	32.5	37.5	35.9	37.1
1973	31.9	36.8	36.2	36.4
1974	29.6	36.0	34.7	35.4
1975	30.6	34.8	34.1	34.4
1976	29.0	33.9	32.1	33.4
1977	28.2	33.1	31.2	32.6
1978	27.3	32.1	31.1	31.7
1979	32.1	36.4	37.0	36.0
1980	34.8%	38.1%	39.6%	37.8%

Source: NCUA, *Annual Reports.*

Strategic Planning

The decade of the 1980s portends many changes. In addition to decreased regulation of financial services, expected increased competition will force managers of financial institutions to weigh all activities (costs versus benefits and expected benefits) not only to select which activities will be performed and how but also to develop programs to insure long-run competitive viability. In other words, managers of financial institutions will have to become strategic planners. As with

Table 6-28   Loan-Loss Ratios of Federal Credit Unions, by Type of Membership,
Selected Years, 1971-1980
(Percent of loans made since organization)

	Associational	Occupational	Residential	Total
Through December:				
1971	.29%	.27%	.38%	.28%
1972	.43	.28	.36	.28
1973	.43	.28	.38	.29
1974	.46	.29	.41	.30
1975	.42	.32	.39	.32
1976	.42	.31	.41	.32
1977	.42	.31	.42	.32
1978	.63	.31	.38	.33
1979	NA	NA	NA	.36
1980	NA	NA	NA	.38%

Source: NCUA, *Annual Reports.*

Table 6-29 Credit Union Loan Delinquency Ratio* by Type of Consumer Bond, 1971-1980

Year	Associational	Occupational	Residential	Total	Associational	Occupational	Residential	Total
1971	5.75%	2.34%	4.67%	2.58%	3.40%	2.46%	1.89%	2.52%
1972	5.44	2.11	4.54	2.33	3.93	2.36	2.31	2.48
1973	5.07	2.07	4.75	2.29	4.19	2.42	4.74	2.13
1974	5.41	2.12	4.59	2.36	4.41	2.51	4.63	2.74
1975	5.53	2.25	5.04	2.51	4.25	2.66	5.01	2.88
1976	4.63	2.01	4.73	2.24	NA	NA	NA	2.42
1977	3.98	1.97	4.87	2.19	NA	NA	NA	2.51
1978	3.69	2.12	4.77	2.30	NA	NA	NA	2.43
1979	5.27	2.48	4.80	2.74	4.12	2.89	4.26	3.08
1980	7.61%	2.93%	5.71%	3.31%	5.16%	3.23%	4.14%	3.50%

Source: NCUA, Annual Reports.
*The loan delinquency ratio is calculated as (2 Month Delinquent/Total).

174

Table 6-30   Credit Union Loan Loss Ratios by Asset Size
Selected Years, 1971-1980

Year	Asset Size	Federally Insured Loss Ratio	State Insured Loss Ratio
1971	$ 250,000-$ 499,999	.34%	NA
	1,000,000-$1,999,999	.30	NA
	5,000,000-$9,999,999	.24	NA
	20,000,000 or more	.19	
1975	250,000-$ 499,999	.39	NA
	1,000,000-$1,999,999	.32	NA
	5,000,000-$9,999,999	.29	NA
	20,000,000 or more	.33	NA
1979	250,000-$ 499,999	.49	.45%
	1,000,000-$1,999,999	.32	.47
	5,000,000-$9,999,999	.33	.40
	20,000,000 or more*	.35	.36**
1980	250,000-$ 499,999	.53	.55
	1,000,000-$1,999,999	.44	.48
	5,000,000-$9,999,999	.37	.43
	$20,000,000 or more*	.38%	.39%**

Source: NCUA, *Annual Reports of State-Chartered Credit Unions.*

*For 1979—the loss ratios of credit unions $50 million to $100 million was .33 percent, and for over $100 million, .36 percent; for 1980, the loss ratios for these size groupings were 0.42 and 0.36 percent.

**For 1979—the loss ratio for credit unions $50 million to $100 million was .38 percent and for over $100 million was .44 percent. For 1980, the loss ratio of credit unions $50 million to $100 million was .47 percent and for over $1-0 million was .39 percent.

any strategic plan, the objective will be more efficient and effective use of available resources.[1]

Strategic planning for credit unions is no different. Table 6-31 gives selected figures which help identify the differences among credit unions by type of bond and by asset size. As is evident. large credit unions tend to have substantially larger loans outstanding but only somewhat larger average loans made than smaller credit unions. Similarly, larger credit unions tend to have larger savings per member than smaller credit unions. The ratio of loans to savings is larger for smaller credit unions than for larger credit unions. Also larger credit unions have elicited greater participation of potential members than have smaller credit unions.

[1] Kotler, P., "Corporate Strategy: A New Role for Marketers." *Marketing News,* June 30, 1976, p. 4.

Table 6-31 Various Ratios and Averages, by Asset Size and by Type of Bond, 1980

Asset Size (in millions) ($)	Average Loan Made	Average Loan Outstanding	Number of Loans Per Member	Number of Loans Outstanding Per Member	Savings Per Member ($)	Loans/ Savings (%)	Assets Per Member ($)	Credit Unions (%)	Members/ Potential Members (%)
<0.2	$ 932	$ 871	.31	.35	$ 373	82.70%	$ 420	25.08%	24%
0.2-0.5	1330	1346	.35	.41	620	89.22	701	20.92	36
0.5-1.0	1618	1650	.35	.43	795	89.26	896	15.66	41
1.0-2.0	602	1879	1.06	.45	969	87.51	1087	13.60	40
2.0-5.0	1886	2088	.36	.47	1175	83.65	1317	12.39	48
5.0-10.0	1929	2251	.37	.40	1343	81.31	1500	5.82	48
10.0-20.0	1810	2329	.40	.50	1474	79.71	1641	3.26	55
20.0-50.0	873	2457	.87	.54	1729	76.18	1918	2.25	46
50.0 or more	1914	2759	.41	.54	2059	72.21	2303	1.01	61
Type of Bond									
Associational	2280	2402	.22	.34	1156	69.96	1290	16.17	29
Occupational	1260	2242	.57	.52	1464	79.14	1635	79.54	56
Residential	2473	2836	.26	.38	1396	77.14	1549	4.29	19
Total	$1334	$2274	.52	.49	$1430	78.31%	$1597	100.00%	47%

Source: CUNA, *1980 Credit Union Operating Ratios and Spreads.*

Similar results can be seen when the credit unions are examined by type of bond. Specifically, occupational bond credit unions have the lowest position for average loan made but the intermediate position for average loan outstanding. In addition occupational bond credit unions tend to make more loans per member than credit unions of the other types of bond. Further, savings per member and assets per member are highest for the occupational bond credit union. Finally, occupational bond credit unions have been able to generate greater participation by potential members than credit unions of the other types of bond.

Although seemingly unrelated, these ratios and averages highlight a significant point—credit unions of differing types of bond or differing asset size also differ in many other respects. These differences require the management of a credit union to strategically plan the course the credit union will take through the economically turbulent eighties.

Spread Analysis

One item about which the credit union manager needs to be particularly concerned is the spread between "earnings and payout." In determining the "proper" rate for loans, credit unions must earn enough to cover the dividends and interest paid to members on savings accounts plus operating expenses and a security buffer. Traditionally, the larger the credit union (total assets) the smaller the spread achieved. Credit unions have not typically analyzed the costs which would be covered by the spread such as operating expenses, required reserve transfers, etc., but have simply established a rate, then made adjustments by rebates or bonuses.[2] Table 6-32 shows that, as noted above, credit unions of the largest asset size have the lowest net (or gross) spread. This is likely because the large asset credit unions have a somewhat lower yield on assets but substantially higher cost of funds than credit unions of smaller asset size. The increased operating expenses of large credit unions likely result from attempts to compete with other financial institutions. Typically, smaller credit unions

[2] See Von der Ohe, Robert, "Part 2: Pricing Loans," *Impact*, Fall and Winter, pp. 4-6, 1981.

Table 6-32 Credit Union Spreads by Asset Size and by Type of Bond, 1980

Asset Size (in millions) ($)	Yield on Assets[a] (%)	Cost of Funds[b] (%)	Gross Spread[c] (BP)[d]	Operating Expenses[e] (BP)[d]	Net Spread[f] (BP)[d]
<0.2	10.50%	4.30%	620	501	119
0.2-0.5	10.87	5.08	579	494	85
0.5-1.0	10.98	5.31	567	470	96
1.0-2.0	11.05	5.58	547	456	91
2.0-5.0	10.99	5.21	508	417	91
5.0-10.0	10.98	6.16	482	400	83
10.0-20.0	10.85	6.42	443	383	60
20.0-50.0	10.66	6.58	408	350	58
50.0 or more	10.40	7.12	328	294	34
Type of Bond					
Associational	10.99	6.49	450	370	81
Occupational	10.69	6.44	425	365	60
Residential	11.08	6.12	496	401	95
Total	10.73%	6.44%	429	367	63

Source: CUNA, *1980 Credit Union Operating Ratios and Spreads.*

[a]Represents *total* operating income *before* interest refund divided by average assets.

[b]Computed by dividing *total dividends and interest* by average assets.

[c]Computed by subtracting "Cost of Funds from "Yield on Assets" and expressed in basis points (percent × 100).

[d]BP = Basis Points.

[e]Computed by dividing operating expenses (excluding interest on borrowings) by average assets and converting to basis points (percent × 1000).

[f]Computed by subtracting "Operating Expenses"

assets and converting to basis points (percent × 1000).

[f]Computed by subtracting "Operating Expenses" from "Gross Spread."

recognizing their limitations do not attempt to compete with the other financial institutions. Although the differences are less distinct for types of bond, occupational bond credit unions have a lower spread than either the association or residential bond. These figures merely confirm the earlier comment that because credit unions differ by asset size and by type of bond, different managerial techniques must be applied to properly utilize the available resources. Obviously, one area of much attention will be spread analysis.

Forecasting

Credit unions also need some procedure whereby future events can be projected more accurately. While credit unions have relied on intuition in the past, there needs to be an increasing reliance on more formal techniques. One relatively simple technique is application of regression analyses to historical data to achieve straight line or exponential results. The biggest drawback with such techniques is the underlying assumption that events will continue in the future in the same pattern in which they have occurred in the past. In many years, this assumption will hold. However, during years when a turning point occurs, the use of regression analysis will yield particularly misleading results. Even when researchers rely on indices to signal when a turning point will occur, the magnitude of change is difficult to predict. Therefore, forecasting techniques provide useful information to credit unions but plans based upon forecasts should not be so inflexible that adaptations in response to changes in economic indicators cannot be made.[3]

Asset-Liability Management

The crux of the asset-liability management problem has been termed "matching." Matching is "the process of attempting to equate the maturity structure of the asset portion of the balance sheet with the maturity structure of the liability/equity portion." While the concept of matching is easy to understand, matching itself is difficult to accomplish. At the time when credit union loans were "short term," matching was easier to accomplish than now with loans of longer maturity. In a recent article, Robert Von der Ohe provided a rough estimate of the maturity structure of credit union assets and equity/liabilities.[4] He concluded that the weighted average maturity of credit union assets is 26 months and the weighted average maturity of credit union equity/liabilities is 12 months. These figures suggest that despite the variety of investment opportunities (and maturity structures), there is a serious mismatch in the maturity structure between the assets and the equity/liabilities of credit unions.

Clearly, the present mismatch cannot continue to exist without posing a threat to the soundness of credit unions. Thus, credit union management must find alternatives to ameliorate the mismatch. In essence, there are three alternatives open to credit union managers.

---

[3] Von der Ohe, Robert, "Part 2: Forecasting," *Impact,* Fall and Winter, pp. 4-6, 1981.
[4] Von der Ohe, Robert, "Matching," *Impact,* February and April, 1981.

One solution may be more short-term loans and longer term certificates. However, issuing longer term certificates may be difficult since 6-month and 30-month certificates seem to be the primary type of certificates that members want at this time.

Another option is to shorten the maturity of the investment portfolio. For credit unions currently holding long term securities, this option may be difficult because of the capital losses involved. In some situations credit unions are paying more for sources of funds to support a long-term investment that the the investment earns. Credit unions may exercise a final option of enlarging their capital base, which would provide a cushion for the reduced spread in the short run.

Of particular note is the problem presented by mortgages. If substantial mortgage loans are to be made without exacerbating the maturity mismatch, credit unions will have to rely on the secondary mortgage markets. By selling mortgages in the secondary market rather than holding them to maturity, credit unions can largely avert the maturity mismatch that has plagued the savings and loan sector.

Economies of Scale, Data Processing and Other Technology

The expense/income (E/I) ratio, which serves as a measure of efficiency, declines for credit unions as asset size increases. Among the benefits which appear to accrue to size of the credit unions are decreasing personnel costs, administration costs (through increased usage of more sophisticated data processing methods) and unit fixed cost reduction via a wider range of financial services.

Electronic data processing (EDP) is viewed as a major factor in increased efficiency. However, some research suggests that scale economies will be developed as asset size increases regardless of the type of data processing used. Thus, one may conclude that larger credit unions would be more efficient than small credit unions without consideration of the type of data processing used. Research also suggests that batch processing with a service bureau appears more efficient than other types of EDP, particularly on-line processing (either in-house or with a service bureau). A suggested reason for this is that typically institutions using on-line processing offer more services.

The added services may result in spuriously high E/I ratios thereby suggesting a less efficient operation.[5]

Whether larger credit unions use more EDP to manage the increased volume of data to be processed or shift to more EDP to more efficiently manage services and, thus, attract more members is not at issue. Simply to maintain the status quo, credit unions must become increasingly more competitive, and those credit unions not using EDP may be at a disadvantage in a highly competitive financial services market. In particular, as competition among financial institutions increases, credit unions may find it necessary to offer even more competitive services such as electronic funds transfer and automatic teller machines.

SUMMARY

This chapter has attempted to review and analyze the financial management performance of the credit union industry in recent years and point out some of the basic approaches available to improving their effectiveness in the future. By and large, the industry can take some pride in what has been accomplished to date. However, in the ever more deregulated environment in which the industry must operate concomitantly more effective and efficient management must be achieved if credit unions are to hold their own and have a chance to move ahead and prosper.

[5] See NCUA, "White Paper on Federal Reserve Interface" for a more in-depth discussion.

The Future of the Industry

INTRODUCTION

The overall growth and development of the credit union movement in the United States has been set forth in the preceding materials. From a movement bordering on being philanthropic in nature for the first 40 years of its history in the United States, credit union activities have taken on the operating characteristics of an established part of the financial services industry of the nation. Such a transition has neither occurred easily in many circles nor has it been completed. This chapter is designed to enumerate some of the forces which have brought about a relative maturation of the industry as well as establishing more clearly some of the directions which may be anticipated over the next 5 to 10 years.

THE CREDIT UNION FINANCIAL SYSTEM

The credit union movement has evolved to the point that one may begin to refer to a credit union financial system as a subset of the nation's savings and payment system. The many financial services provided through CUNA-related activities have contributed immeasurably to the growth and sophistication of the industry. The creation of the National Credit Union Administration and its subsequent expansion of services and authority provides much of the thrust toward centralization and standardization of services and activities. A few of these financial services are set forth in this chapter.

CORPORATE CENTRALS

Groups within the credit union industry have from time to time favored a national system of credit unions somewhat similar to that provided for the savings and loan industry. In the absence of specific legislation in this direction, there evolved an element of such a system through the corporate central credit union device. The initial impetus was through state leagues to establish officer central credit unions which could lend to officers of regular credit union associations. These were generally established at the state level and they began to take on other functions. Some central credit unions opened membership to the regular associations, provided a mechanism for liquidity or merging associations, provided a system of matching funds with surplus and deficit associations in terms of funds flow, and established service centers to member associations.

The number of central credit unions has varied a great deal over the years. In 1971, for example, there were 57 state central credit unions operating in 35 states. While most states had one central credit union, Illinois had 13 in that year. In 1980, there were 42 state central unions operating in 26 states, with 8 in Illinois. Since the mid-1970s, federal central credit unions have been available and some have shifted their charters. Most of the corporate centrals now belong to a U. S. Central Credit Union. Strictly comparable data for the central credit unions are not readily available. The data of Table 7-1 does give a good overview of the data but should not be taken as being definitive. Most of the state central credit unions have been converted to the corporate central form as the means for providing greater liquidity at the national level became more desirable in the 1970s. Most of the references today within the industry refer to the corporate central concept since there is little need for the original format to provide financial services to individuals or small groups not otherwise eligible for membership in local associations.

The data of Table 7-1 demonstrate that reporting state central credit union assets rose from $444 million in 1971 to $870 million in 1977, and $1,978 million at year-end 1980. Loans to individuals were $116 million in 1971, or 26.1% of total assets in 1977, loans to individuals were $229 million, or 26.3% of total assets; but by 1980 loans to individuals were $202 million, or 10.2% of total assets. Loans In recent years, the central credit unions have become a repository of funds from operating credit unions. In 1971, savings of member credit unions accounted for 62.3% of total assets; by 1980, credit union savings amounted to 78.9% of total central credit union assets. The increased level of central credit union holdings of savings from member credit unions, along with varying loan levels extended to operating credit unions give some evidence of the fact that state central credit union activity has moved in the direction of providing one aspect of a centralized pooling of funds for operating credit unions, as well as a source of funds for other units from time to time. The resources of

Table 7-1 Selected Data for State Central Credit Unions

Item	1971	1975	1977	1979	1980
Number of State Central Credit Unions Reporting	57	58	52	48	42
Total Assets	443.7	736.9	870.0	1,149.1	1,978.1
Assets					
Loans, total	215.6	290.3	554.0	425.4	276.2
To individuals	115.5	184.3	229.0	233.3	202.1
To credit unions	100.1	106.0	325.0	192.1	74.1
Investments, total	199.1	303.4	283.6	673.8	1,641.6
U.S. Government obligations	152.0	158.0	107.1	261.3	212.6
Other	47.1	145.4	176.5	412.5	1,429.0
Cash and other assets	29.0	143.2	32.4	49.9	60.3
Liabilities and Capital Accounts					
Savings, total	377.9	616.2	711.1	975.1	1,791.2
Of individuals	101.5	176.5	206.4	229.8	230.4
Of member credit unions	276.4	439.7	504.7	745.3	1,560.8
Notes Payable	41.7	91.6	115.5	128.7	139.3
Reserves	11.7	17.3	22.9	20.8	17.0
Undivided earnings and other liabilities	12.4	11.9	20.4	24.5	30.6
Liquid assets to short-term liabilities[1]	44.5%	42.5%	16.5%	31.2%	13.8%
Reserves to loans	5.4%	5.9%	4.1%	4.9%	6.1%
Total Expenses to Gross Income	43.4%	52.3%	46.1%	44.4%	28.2%

Source: Derived from NCUA, *Annual Reports for State Chartered Credit Unions.*
[1] U.S. Government obligations plus Savings and Loan Association shares plus cash as a percentage of total savings plus notes payable.

federal corporate central credit unions are not included in these comments so that the total financial impact of this movement is understated.

Credit unions have relied upon private sources of liquidity to a very large degree. Market credit from loans, repurchase agreements, certificates of deposit and similar measures have been used for a number of years. One of the basic reasons for the system of state central credit unions, now moving toward the corporate central concept, was to gather the excess liquidity held within the credit union system and funnel it to other units in an illiquid condition. This reached a high level with the formation in 1974 of U. S. Central, an arm of the Credit Union National Association, located in Kansas. As of early 1980, U. S. Central stood ready to make loans to 28 state and 15 federal corporate centrals that were members. In turn, these corporate centrals were in a position to lend to their 16,000 member operating credit unions.[1]

The 1982 NCUA *Annual Report* gives summary data on 30 corporate credit unions which have as their hub the $7 billion U. S. Central Credit Union. These corporate centrals have been active in providing short-term investment options to the credit union industry. Shares held in the federally insured corporate credit unions have grown to $5.6 billion (1982) and these corporate have returned up to 93 percent of their total income as dividends to the operating credit unions. These "wholesale" financial services have proven very popular in recent years.

One example of the mutual assistance program within the credit union industry may be found in the case of the Tennessee Central Credit Union encountering financial difficulties in 1979 resulting from forward contracts on government securities. In addition to assistance from operating credit unions in the state, U. S. Central encouraged other state central credit unions to provide financial aid as well as providing a line of credit to Tennessee Central.[2] Another aspect of U. S. Central may be seen from the announcement in 1981 that it was developing a package of services for credit unions, to include funds and securities transfer, collection services, settlement and clearing house operations, and similar financial services. Many of these

---

[1] U. S. House of Representatives, 96th Congress, 2nd Session, Committee on Banking Finance and Urban Affairs, "Report of Interagency Task Force on Thrift Institutions," Washington, June 30, 1980.

[2] *The American Banker*, November 23, 1979.

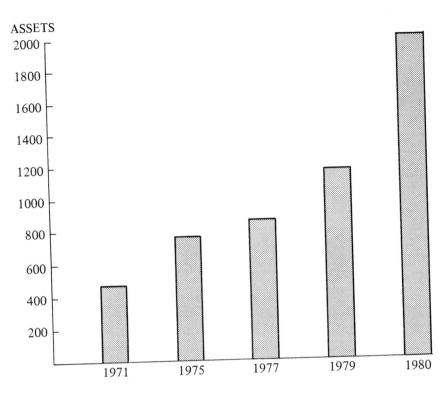

Figure 7-1   Total Assets of State Central Credit Unions, 1971-1980
(In Millions of Dollars)

services are designed to operate in a manner similar to those provided by the Federal Reserve and correspondent banks. The capability of U. S. Central to develop and provide such services is indicated by the fact that its assets as of late 1982 had grown to $7.8 billion.[3] U. S. Central is evolving into a central bank for the corporate centrals in an operating sense which in turn provides the equivalent of correspondent banking services to the member credit unions.

CENTRAL LIQUIDITY FACILITY

An additional source of liquidity for the credit union industry is the NCUA's Central Liquidity Facility established in 1978 which became

[3] NCUA, *Annual Report, 1982.*

operational in October 1979. A government-sponsored liquidity facility had been promoted for a number of years prior to its establishment as a means of adding to the safety of credits extending to borrowing associations as well as a means of obtaining additional funds from the money market. To a considerable degree, the CLF legislation was based upon many concepts underlying the Federal Reserve Act.

The CLF is a "mixed ownership Government Corporation" with membership open to all federal and state chartered credit unions. Member credit unions subscribe to CLF stock in the amount of ½ of 1 percent of the credit union's paid-in capital and surplus buy only ¼ of 1 percent of the paid-in capital and suplus must be invested in such stock, with the remainder being "on call" and kept in liquid form.[4] Individual credit unions may join on a voluntary basis, or they may join through their corporate centrals. Capital stock earns dividends but does not carry any voting privileges. In 1980, this effective dividend was 9.5% and in 1981 12.5%.

The CLF was designed to augment, rather than replace the traditional lines of credit union credit. CLF credit is intended to meet emergency liquidity needs, not provide permanent financing for credit unions. Three forms of liquidity assistance are available as "short-term adjustment" credit, "seasonal" credit, and "protracted adjustment" credit. During fiscal 1980 $115 million in short-term credits and $85 million as protracted adjustment credits were extended. In fiscal 1981, total loans of all types extended were $67 million. Some of the protracted adjustment credits are developed as joint ventures with the Share Insurance Fund as a means of reducing the risks of both funds by allowing basically sound credit unions to work out their problems over a period of rapid interest rate adjustments. Several of the protracted loan arrangements have gone into default.

The CLF obtains the bulk of its loanable funds through borrowing on the basis of its notes and debt securities from the Federal Financing Bank. Congress established the facility's borrowing authority for 1981 at $600 million. In addition, with Congressional approval, the facility may borrow $500 million from the Treasury in emergency circumstances. In fiscal 1981, CLF gross income was $21 million and expenses $12 million, for a net income of $9 million.

Credit requests from member credit unions are submitted to CLF and are scrutinized in terms of credit worthiness. Advances by the facility are secured by a general pledge of all assets of the borrowing

---

[4] National Credit Union Administration Central Liquidity Facility, *Annual Report for the Fiscal Year 1981*, Washington, December 1981.

credit unions. Loan rates must cover the full costs of all funds since it has no federal subsidy. In addition, the CLF has a policy of setting rates slightly above the rates charged by corporate centrals to their members to encourage credit unions to exhaust all other means of financing prior to applying to the CLF for emergency coverage. CLF rates tended to range between 10 and 19 percent over the 1980-81 period. Since the 1980 Monetary Control Act opens the Federal Reserve discount window to all institutions with transactions accounts, there may come a time when CLF loans would be available at rates significantly above the Federal Reserve rates. Some constraint on the availability of Federal Reserve funds will still make the CLF loans attractive to operating credit unions.

Membership in the CLF developed fairly slowly due to some misunderstanding of its plans and the basic costs of membership in the form of stock purchases. By November 1981, some 5,600 Federal and state chartered credit unions had joined the CLF either directly or through 13 corporate central members as agent members. These 5,600 CLF members represent 40% of all credit union assets.

The assets of CLF total $186 million in 1981 but this does not portray its potential role for the credit union industry. The fact that it is an integral part of the National Credit Union Administration, that it operates as a profit-making government corporation with its own borrowing capabilities, and that it can provide a source of emergency financing from outside the credit union industry are definite indicators of the long-term source of strength which the CLF provides. Together with the corporate central movement and U. S. Central activities and the NCUA Share Insurance Fund, the CLF provides a capstone for the modern credit union industry to handle more effectively its liquidity problems. It has become the central bank for the nation's credit unions.

CREDIT UNION MODERNIZATION ACT OF 1977 AND 1978

The Federal Credit Union Act was substantially revised in April 1977 (Public Law 95-22) bringing changes to the basic credit union lending and savings programs. Loan maturities were extended, real estate and home improvement loans were expanded, and self-replenishing credit lines to borrowers were authorized. Participation loans with other credit unions and other financial institutions and certain investment powers were standardized in the 1977 legislation. A two-tier reserve formula was also in this legislation which impacted the amount of gross income which has to be placed in reserve after credit unions attained a size of $500,000 or more and a reserve of 4% of loans and risk assets. Many other technical operating matters were addressed in the 1977 revisions which resulted in expanded lending and investment powers.

In 1978, Public Law 95-630 restructured the National Credit Union Administration, created the central liquidity facility, and set up a new administration board with increased supervisory functions. This Financial Institutions Reform Act replaced the Administrator of NCUA and its credit union board with a three-person board with specified terms of office. Board members are appointed by the President and are confirmed by the Senate. The NCUA does not receive any Federal appropriations but operates on funds received from Federal credit unions for services received. Prior to 1979 separate fees were assessed for examination, supervision, and chartering. In 1979 these fees were consolidated into a single operating fee. In 1982, operating income of NCUA was $22.5 million and operating expenses were $20.9 million. The NCUA also administers the National Credit Union Share Insurance Fund which was authorized in October 1970. The NCUSIF provides account insurance up to $100,000, provides standards for insured credit unions, and handles the liquidation of any insured insolvent credit unions.

THE DEPOSITORY INSTITUTIONS DEREGULATION AND MONETARY CONTROL ACT OF 1980 AND THE GARN-ST GERMAIN DEPOSITORY INSTITUTIONS ACT OF 1982

On March 31, 1980, the President signed the Depository Institutions Deregulation and Monetary Control Act of 1980, marking the culmination of many years of effort by the financial industry and the regulatory agencies to change some of the basic rules of the financial services industry. The Congress accepted the fact that many of the existing rules impacting upon banks and thrift institutions had grown obsolete by fundamental changes in markets, technology, and consumer desires. While the commercial banking industry and savings and loans are affected decidedly more by 1980 legislation, the credit union industry was also affected directly and indirectly. This omnibus legislation legalized share drafts and other interest bearing transactions accounts for all depository institutions, increased deposit insurance coverage, and increased loan rates for credit unions. In addition, the act requires the implementation of a uniform system of monetary reserves for depository institutions, provides for the phaseout of interest rate regulations, and preempts certain state usury laws.

Since credit unions were not as closely controlled in interest rates as other financial institutions and share drafts were already well underway in the industry, DIDMCA did not impact on credit unions as directly as banks and other savings institutions. Nevertheless, the effects of this Act will be major in the years ahead. Perhaps the principal effect will be the expansion and availability of financial services to consumers and a heightening of the competitive environment in the fields of consumer savings and consumer credit. The Garn-St Germain Act of October 1982 gave all depository institutions additional powers. The more direct effects upon credit unions included amendments which give credit unions more flexibility and broader authority to handle their own affairs. Investment powers were modified and greater freedom of activity in the mortgage markets added. Monetary reserve requirements for the first $2 million in reservable accounts were also suspended by the Act. This eliminated about 95% of all credit unions from monetary reserve requirements. Interpretations by the National Credit Union Administration in the past several years have also been directed toward returning more operating decisions to credit union managers and their boards.

A general broadening of asset powers and permissible activities of all thrift institutions has contributed to the competitive environment. It is within this new environment that the modern credit union industry exists today and to which it must adapt for future success.

COMPETITIVE POSITION OF CREDIT UNIONS

It is obvious that the competitive position of credit unions has been improved in recent years as a result of both legislative and regulatory changes. The industry has an expanded base for both assets and liabilities and it is empowered to diversify its activities on both sides of the balance sheet. It is relatively free of interest rate controls while maintaining the economic and political advantages of operating as not-for-profit cooperative associations. The industry's membership with a tradition of closeness to and participation in their local credit unions provides a strong base for future growth. The continuing willingness of regulatory and tax authorities to accept the industry as standing apart from other sectors of the financial services industry provides the credit union industry with many distinct advantages. These advantages do not always lead to stable operating conditions for the individual associations.

THE LIQUIDATION ISSUE

Data relating to the number of operating credit unions in the United States may give a somewhat incorrect impression of the institutional stability of credit union operations over the years. The industry has demonstrated a marked capacity for change in chartering and liquidations, while giving the impression of structural stability. Over the period of 1934-1982, federal credit unions chartered totaled 23,967, of which 11,925 were operating as federal institutions at the close of 1982.[5] There are shifts of charters back and forth from state to federal agencies but this does not explain away the fact that a high percentage of credit unions chartered do not continue over a long period of time. Earlier studies have indicated that the chances of financial survival for a new credit union are about 3 out of 5, a probability which would not be deemed favorable in chartering a bank or savings and loan association. Fortunately for all parties, the liquidation or cancellation of a credit union does not mean that there has necessarily been any financial losses to the participants. In some cases, there are losses, of course, but many credit union charters are canceled because of lack of potential for growth or lack of local leadership and many others are merged without any loss to the participants.

Table 7-2 illustrates the overall fluidity of the credit union structure in the United States. In 1965, for example, there were 330 state charters added and 246 canceled, while among federal associations, there were 584 chartered and 270 liquidated. In later years the proportions were reversed. In 1979, there were 383 state and federal charters issued and 602 cancellations. Most of the credit union cancellations or liquidations occurred among the small credit unions, many of which had never really gotten underway. In Table 7-3, it is shown that among federal credit unions cancellations of 3,302 over the 1970-1980 period, 1904, or 57.7% had shares of $25,000 or less, and another 919, or 27.8% had savings between $25,000 and $100,000. Only 13 out of 3,302 federal liquidations had share re-

[5] NCUA, *1982 Annual Report.*

Table 7-2 State and Federal Credit Union Charters Issued and Canceled,
Selected Years 1965-1982

Year	State Charters		Federal Charters		Total Charters	
	Added	Canceled	Added	Canceled	Added	Canceled
1965	330	246	584	270	914	516
1967	354	222	636	292	990	514
1969	222	268	705	323	927	591
1971	212	367	400	461	612	828
1973	208	295	364	523	572	818
1975	177	384	373	334	550	718
1977	134	333	337	315	471	648
1978	116	349	348	298	464	647
1979	97	266	286	336	383	602
1980	NA	NA	170	368	NA	NA
1981	NA	NA	119	554	NA	NA
1982	NA	NA	114	556	NA	NA

Source: Derived from National Credit Union Administration; *Annual Reports for State Chartered Credit Unions*; and *Annual Report*, 1982.

sources above $1 million. Put another way, only 14.5% of the federal liquidations over the 1970-1980 period had acquired savings capital of $100,000 or more. Thus, mergers, cancellations, and liquidations are not often major financial problems for the various supervisory bodies.

The basic reasons for Federal credit union cancellations in the 1970-1980 period included loss of field of membership, reductions in potential membership, and inability to obtain or maintain operating

Table 7-3 Federal Credit Union Charter Cancellations by Share Size

Year	Under $25,000	$25,000-100,000	$100,000-1,000,000	$1,000,000 and above	Total
1970	256	50	34	1	341
1971	275	68	38	2	383
1972	392	146	57	3	598
1973	249	143	62	1	455
1975	184	83	57	0	304
1975	108	57	26	0	191
1976	137	83	41	1	262
1977	89	70	30	1	193
1978	68	69	45	1	183
1979	82	73	40	1	196
1980	64	77	53	2	196
Total	1,904	919	466	13	3,302

Source: NCUA *Annual Reports.*

officials (Table 7-4). These reasons tended to decline in the late 1970s, as poor financial condition and mergers and conversions become much more important. In 1980, nonfinancial conditions and conversions and mergers accounted for almost 70% of the 368 Federal charter cancellations.

THE NATIONAL CREDIT UNION SHARE INSURANCE FUND

There have been plans for share insurance protection available through Credit Union National Association affiliates and private insurance firms for many years. Credit life insurance has been very prevalent as well. The result is that most participants in credit union transactions have a significant part of their savings accounts insured, as well as credit life insurance coverage for their indebtedness to credit unions. These programs continue to be very important to the industry but the passage of a standardized program of Federal insurance for all accounts in a way similar to FDIC coverage has greater long-term significance for the industry. Some 3,150 state chartered credit unions have share insurance with 16 private share insurers.[6] Some states now require Federal share insurance for all operating credit unions. By 1983, noninsured (either NCUA or state plan) credit unions will operate in only 9 states.[7] As shown in Table 7-5, the

Table 7-4   Distribution of Federal Credit Union Cancellations, by Major Reasons, 1971-1980

Year	Loss of Field Membership	Potential Membership Reduced	Poor Financial Condition	Merger and Conversion	Unable to Obtain Officials	All Other	Total Number
1971	21.5	7.8	20.2	12.5	22.1	15.9	461
1972	21.1	7.2	26.9	8.8	19.6	16.4	672
1973	23.5	7.8	26.5	12.1	18.1	12.0	523
1974	14.4	4.3	36.6	16.0	13.3	15.4	369
1975	14.7	5.4	23.4	39.5	7.2	9.8	334
1976	16.5	7.2	25.3	31.8	7.5	11.7	387
1977	10.8	9.5	25.9	36.8	5.7	11.3	315
1978	15.1	5.7	26.8	35.2	6.0	11.2	298
1979	16.1	4.8	21.7	39.6	5.4	12.4	336
1980	7.9	4.1	26.1	43.3	1.9	16.9	368

Source: NCUA *Annual Reports.*

[6] NCUA, *Annual Report 1982.*
[7] CUNA, *Credit Union Magazine,* September 1981.

Table 7-5   Growth in the Number of Federally-Insured Credit Unions and
Proportion of Insured Credit Unions, 1971-1982

Year	Number of Federally-Insured Credit Unions		Federally Insured Credit Unions as Percent of U.S. Total	Insured Savings as a Percent of U.S. Total Credit Union Savings
	Federally-Chartered	State-Chartered		
1971	12,717	793	58.1%	59.3%
1972	12,708	1,315	60.8	64.0
1973	12,688	1,656	62.7	66.6
1974	12,748	2,398	66.3	71.1
1975	12,737	3,040	69.8	75.6
1976	12,757	3,519	72.0	77.6
1977	12,750	3,882	74.1	80.2
1978	12,759	4,362	77.4	82.4
1979	12,738	4,769	80.5	82.9
1980	12,440	4,910	80.8	85.1
1981	11,969	4,994	80.3	85.4
1982	11,430	5,139	80.0	85.8

Source: NCUA, *1982 Annual Report.*

number of state chartered credit unions obtaining Federal share insurance has grown to 5,139 at the end of 1982. The result is that almost 80% of all operating credit unions are Federally insured and they represent 86% of total credit union savings in the United States.

The National Credit Union Share Insurance Fund (NCUSIF) was authorized in October 1970 to carry out a program of insurance for member accounts in both Federal and state-chartered credit unions. Account coverage is now at the $100,000 level. Account holders in credit unions becoming insolvent are paid promptly. In 1982, there were 160 insolvent credit unions resulting in payouts of $39 million in claims. Much of what is paid to share holders is recovered by NCUSIF in the process of liquidation of the assets of insolvent credit unions. At the close of fiscal 1982, the equity balance of NCUSIF was $177 million. Although 1980-1982 were unusually bad years in terms of share insurance losses, the NCUSIF balance remains as a source of protection for shareholders, and the fund is authorized to borrow up to $100 million from the U. S. Treasury. Insured credit unions are charged one-twelfth of one percent of total shares each year. Additional assessments of premiums were levied in 1981 and 1982.

The demonstrated performance of the NCUSIF and its close similarities to both the FDIC and FSLIC are proof of the overall success and widespread acceptance of its programs. At a time when there may be questions raised about the long term stability and solvency of some credit unions and in light of the large number which are canceled and liquidated each year, the existence of Federal share and account insurance does much to assure the public of the financial security of their relationships with the credit union industry.

SHARE DRAFTS

The demonstrated capability of mutual savings banks in New England to provide negotiable order of withdrawal (NOW) account services in the early 1970s led credit unions to begin experimenting with similar customer services in the late 1970s. The third-party payment instrument of the credit union industry is called a share draft and its usage prior to late 1979 created controversy and litigation by the commercial banking industry. Congress enacted temporary enabling legislation in December 1979 to permit share draft usage and the Depository Institutions Deregulation and Monetary Control Act of 1980 provided permanent authorization to the credit union industry. This is not to indicate that all of the industry provides such services. Many credit unions, particularly the smaller ones, do not offer share draft services as of 1982. Nevertheless, the growing popularity of NOW accounts among banks and other savings institutions is forcing credit union managements to give serious consideration to the development of such services.

Share drafts are not a low-cost service for credit unions and most credit unions do not now provide such services. The Credit Union National Association estimated that as of May 1981, some 2,500 credit unions had share draft accounts in the amount of some 3% of total credit union savings, and that some 3 million members have share draft accounts.[8] While these numbers are quite impressive in view of their short history of availability, it remains that such accounts are not used by the vast majority of credit union members. These accounts represent a chance for credit unions to expand member services and more and more associations will provide share drafts in the near future. Changes in accounting systems and computer service availability will make such services more practical for association managements to adopt. Share drafts are processed in many different ways, including CUNA, corporate centrals, regional and local banks, and service centers. As the credit union industry strives to become more of a full-service financial center the availability of share draft

[8] CUNA, *Impact*, May/June 1981.

services will grow rather rapidly. Credit unions may pay higher dividends on share draft accounts than other institutions may pay on NOW accounts, and truncation, or storage of share drafts by the credit union rather than returned to members, is required.

AUTOMATIC TELLER MACHINES

The development of automatic teller machine (ATM) services for credit union members follows the provision of share draft services. While ATM services are not prevalent at the moment in the credit union industry, they will become so over the near future. ATM services have become rather commonplace in the commercial banking industry, and to a lesser extent in the savings and loan and mutual savings banking industries. Since share draft services are not as prevalent among credit unions, it follows that ATM services are also less commonplace. No exact number of credit unions with ATM services is presently available but a CUNA publication estimates that there were 200 to 300 credit unions with ATM's in mid-1981, while there were more than 3,000 financial institutions with ATM's at that point in time.[9]

Consumer acceptance has long been considered one of the keys to a successful ATM program for any financial institution. Consumers must be marketed very skillfully and extensively in order to gain customer acceptance. This is one disadvantage facing credit unions in developing such a sophisticated service for members. The typical credit union has not been marketing oriented and it has not had the breadth of membership to permit an extensive media campaign. Nevertheless, credit unions should benefit from the continuing advertising campaigns of other financial institutions promoting ATM services since many members are also account holders in other institutions, as well as observers of the advertising efforts of competing financial institutions.

Prior to any commitment to provide ATM services credit union boards must engage in a serious cost-benefit analysis. The goals of an ATM program will generally involve supplementing or improving the efficiency of over-the-counter business, providing services for longer hours and in different locations, and attracting more deposits from present and potential members. There are many costs and many ben-

[9]CUNA, *Credit Union Executive,* Summer 1981, p. 28.

efits in the introduction of an ATM program. A shared network for the elaborate computer services required for such a program is probably the most viable option for credit unions, but even so the costs are quite significant. It has been estimated that for the large credit unions presently capable of providing ATM services that five years or longer will be required before they are likely to be considered as profitable.[10]

The basic barriers to ATM services by credit unions include lack of necessary funds, lack of expertise, and lack of a mechanism to provide such services in a cost-effective manner. Since ATM services are difficult to justify on a short-term cost basis, they remain the domain of the large credit unions. For example, in Wisconsin in 1981, 15 out of 600 credit unions provided these services, but the 15 held 75% of the credit union assets in the state. Other states with significant levels of ATM services include Florida, California, and Texas. At year-end 1981, the Credit Union National Association estimated that 500 credit unions were providing ATM services on some basis or other.[11] As consumers grow more comfortable with ATM's and as credit unions begin to understand the potential advantages for such services, more and more associations will provide these services. Nevertheless, the concept of share draft services and day-to-day accounting services for members must be more widely implemented before any dramatic expansion of ATM services can be anticipated.

ISSUES AND PROBLEMS CONFRONTING CREDIT UNIONS AS THEY COME OF AGE IN THE 1980s

It may be said that the U. S. credit union industry came of age with the passage of the Monetary Control Act of 1980. Despite stunning growth rates in the 1960s and 1970s, the credit union industry had not attracted much national attention from the standpoint of public policy until the late 1970s. It is true that the creation of the National Credit Union Administration and its program of account insurance in the early 1970s gave a tremendous boost to the industry, as did other legislation and regulatory rulings in the late 1970s. But it was the Monetary Control Act of 1980 which wrapped up the credit industry into a national structure of financial institutions with some uniformity of scope and purpose and with a certain level of uniformity in terms

---

[10] CUNA, *Credit Union Executive*, Autumn 1981, pp. 15-24.
[11] CUNA, *Credit Union Magazine*, December 1981, p. 34.

of regulations. Standardized services, such as NOW and share-draft accounts and standardized reserve requirements places the credit union industry in the mainstream of traditional depository institutions, along with the essence of central banking services through the Central Liquidity Facility and corporate central services.

At the beginning of the late 1970s credit unions were still regarded as small cooperative associations with few financial powers and with rather casual managements not attuned to the dynamics of a national money market. Credit unions matured greatly in the decade as they acquired greater strength on both the financial and political fronts. Overall growth in the economy and the financial marketplace aided this movement tremendously. The political debates over the introduction of share draft accounts by certain credit unions placed the entire industry in the mainstream of political controversy surrounding the need for reform of the financial services industry. Rising interest rates contributed to the pressures to provide relief to the credit union industry. Traditional rates on savings and loans made it impossible for the industry to exist without regulatory relief on rates. As credit unions entered the market with such instruments as money market certificates to obtain and retain consumer dollars, they were forced to charge far more than the traditional 12% on their loans. With the freeing up of state and federal interest rate levels and as credit union managements sought to remain competitive with other financial institutions in obtaining savings dollars, the credit union industry entered the mainstream of the depository institutional structure of the nation.

CREDIT UNIONS IN THE
NATIONAL FINANCIAL MARKETPLACE

While the Depository Institution Regulation and Monetary Control Act of 1980 has contributed to the maturation of the credit union industry, it also gave additional powers and freedom to market competitors which will test the capability of credit union management to operate in a more complex environment. Depository thrift institutions were given new asset and liability authorizations by the 1980 Act while providing for the phasing out of deposit rate controls. In a large measure many of the changes provided by the legislation were responses to innovations which were already taking place in the marketplace. Thus, the expansion of powers for various depository institutions strengthened the competitive forces in the marketplace within which credit unions operate.

The increased competition for savings funds from commercial banks, savings and loans, and mutual savings banks impacted very directly upon the credit union industry. Perhaps the most startling changes in the markets occurred as a result of alternative investment and other financial services provided through nonbanking institutions at relatively high rates of interest and with considerable degrees of liquidity. Uncertainty resulting from interest rate volatility and high rates of inflation impacted upon credit unions and all other depository institutions in an unfavorable manner, particularly in the 1979-81 period. Savers have responded to volatile market conditions by attempting to obtain market rates on investable funds adequate to offset the effects of inflation. In addition to these cost pressures upon depository institutions, there were many changes in technology in the field of financial service-delivery which lead to additional costs in the form of management skills and sophisticated equipment. Credit unions have not gone overboard in these adaptations up to the present but market forces will place more and more pressure upon the industry to provide many of these services.

In their search for consumer savings in the 1980s credit unions managements will have to confront all of the competitive forces from traditional financial institutions as well as the nontraditional, or banklike institutional arrangements. Money market funds provide the most dramatic form of competition for the public's funds. These money funds reached the $230 billion level after a relatively few years of operation. The recently authorized money market accounts for banks and all savings institutions brought a significant reduction in the money fund accounts. National credit card companies as well as brokerage firms, insurance companies, and national retailing firms now offer many financial services as well.

The injection of these new competitive forces in the marketplace for savings has many implications for credit union managment. There is now in fact a true national market for consumer savings of modest proportions. Local institutions can no longer presume that small local savers will continue to hold funds with them at below market-level rates. A wide range of financial services are now available in small towns as well as in metropolitan areas. Markets are no longer tightly segmented as was once thought to be the case and rates are extremely sensitive to national market conditions. It follows that credit unions can no longer expect to have a sheltered market for member savings. National market forces are to be reckoned with on both the demand and supply sides of the balance sheet.

INTEREST RATE CONSIDERATIONS

Credit unions have enjoyed a slight edge over other depository institutions in their ability to pay for consumer savings but the events of 1979-1981 have demonstrated that this advantage may not assure a growth of funds in the industry. The special characteristics of credit unions as cooperative associations serving a field of membership and organized with little capital have served the industry well in the past. These characteristics should also help the industry to maintain a competitive position in the future if managements will adapt to prevailing market conditions.

The savings share accounts which are typical of the credit union industry have tended to be smaller than the savings accounts in other savings institutions. To some degree this has sheltered the savings funds of credit unions since many of the savers did not have sufficient funds to enter the money market certificate arena or even many of the money market funds. In addition, the less frequent compounding of interest by credit unions has had the effect of imposing an interest penalty for early withdrawal.

Usury ceilings created many problems for credit unions in the late 1970s and early 1980s. Prior to 1979 the 12% usury ceiling for Federal credit unions was not particularly binding. But as market rates rose so rapidly, with the result that the marginal costs of funds began to exceed the legal loan rates available to most credit unions, lending activity declined markedly. During 1980, credit union loans outstanding actually declined as did asset growth rates. One additional impact was that since the 12% ceiling did not apply to many state chartered credit unions there was added activity in shifting certain charters from Federal to state to relieve some of the interest rate pressures. The Federal laws were changed in 1980 to permit Federal associations to charge 15% and then up to 21% on a temporary basis on consumer loans. This authorization has been continued in 1983.

Rate relief afforded credit unions has been given at the Federal level and by most states but many credit unions have been reluctant to raise rates to permissible rates because of the traditions of the industry which encourage maintaining loan rates below other market rates on consumer loans. Such reluctance demonstrates the dilemma confronting the industry as to whether savers should be compensated at competitive interest rates and borrowers charged accordingly, or whether borrowers should be favored by lower than market rates at the ultimate expense of member savings. All too often, credit union traditionalists find this a discomforting position to be in. Credit unions have the option of interest refunds to borrowers from time to time which makes interest rate adjustment easier than for other lenders.

Credit unions have been afforded more freedom in paying interest on savings than other depository institutions. Dividend rates on share accounts have generally been above passbook rates at banks and other thrift institutions. Under the Monetary Control Act of 1980, credit unions are not subject to the same interest rate controls (Regulation Q) as other depository institutions. In 1981, Federal credit unions were empowered to pay up to 12% on share account savings, rates on other types of accounts were liberalized, and all limits were removed entirely on individual retirement accounts. Despite the rising costs of funds, credit unions in 1980 managed to maintain close to a 4% spread between their costs of funds and their average yield on assets. The spread between a gross spread of 4.2% and operating expenses of 3.6% resulted in a net spread of about .6%. This may be more difficult to maintain in the future.[12]

The NCUA has deregulated rate ceilings on savings much more rapidly than the Depository Institutions Deregulation Committee. But as savings rate ceilings are lifted in the future, credit unions will not enjoy their present competitive advantage in attracting funds. This will place additional pressure upon credit unions as the competitive forces in the market are heightened and as small savers become even more aggressive in seeking market yields on their funds.

The aggressive posture of the NCUA in rate deregulation is indicated by an announcement by its Board on December 17, 1981, that Federal credit unions would be asked if they were prepared to take full responsibility for setting rates on share, share draft, and share certificate accounts. The comments were favorable, and the NCUA issued a rule incorporating these views and placed the responsibility for interest rate decisions on the boards of operating credit unions. A complete phaseout of rate ceilings has occurred with the result that much more freedom and flexibility has been given to credit unions in seeking funds. On the other side of the market, there is legislation under consideration (early 1982) which would eliminate state interest-rate limits on consumer loans. Federal preemption of interest rates is favored in many circles on the basis that usury ceilings distort credit markets and credit flows and do not reduce the overall costs of

---

[12] CUNA, *1980 Credit Union Operating Ratios and Spreads,* Madison, Wisconsin, January 1982.

credit to consumers. The Monetary Control Acts of 1980 began the process of Federal preemption of interest rate controls but states were given three years to override the provisions of the 1980 Act. Whatever the final outcome may be in this field, it is obvious that many changes are occurring in interest ceilings on savings instruments and usury limits on loans, all of which add to the competitive nature of the market.

RECENT CREDIT UNION DEVELOPMENTS

National economic and financial conditions have influenced the credit union industry throughout recent periods although not as severely as many other sectors of the financial services industry. The overall thrust of the industry during the 1981-1982 period was one of moderate growth in membership, savings, and loans in comparison with the rapid growth experienced in the 1960s and 1970s.

Credit union membership grew 3.3% during 1981, member savings continued its move toward consolidation. The number of credit unions continued to decline in 1982, and by April 1983, the total was below 20,000. Membership moved ahead, however. In 1981, total membership increased 1.5 million, reaching 45.3 million in 1981; this growth continues on into 1983, reaching above 47.4 million. Savings in 1982 and 1983 continued to grow reaching $87.0 billion in May 1983. Loans did not increase during the period, however, with the result that the loan-to-savings ratio declined to an extremely low level of 57.9% in May 1983.

Credit unions were able to raise their rates on loans during the period and to improve their operating margins in many cases. Portfolio turnover allowed the credit unions to raise their rates from a level of loan yields of 11.8% in 1980 to 12.6% in 1981. In the first part of 1983, loan yields were averaging almost 14%. These increases have strengthened the financial structure of the industry. Whereas some 30% of all credit unions had operating losses in 1980, only 15% operated at a loss in 1981. The average transfer to undivided earnings in 1981 was 0.62% of assets, far above the 0.18% of assets transferred in 1980.

Higher loan rates resulting from increased costs of funds, together with economic recession brought a reduced loan demand during the period. Nevertheless, credit union operating results are generally favorable. The gross spread between yield on assets and cost of funds rose from 4.29% in 1980 to 5.70% in 1982. Auto loan rates in 1982 were largely within the 12-15% range, with a significant number above 15%. Personal loan rates were largely in the 15-18% range even though credit unions were authorized to charge significantly higher rates.

Credit union savings climbed rapidly in both 1982 and 1983, at rates which ran ahead of those experienced by other financial institutions. In the face of such rapid growth in savings capital, loans did not grow sufficiently to absorb the influx of funds. The result was a loan to savings ratio of 72.6% in April 1982, and about a 60% level in much of 1983. Thus, in a period when many financial institutions experienced a serious liquidity problem the credit union industry became highly liquid.

The structure of member capital has continued to change during recent periods. In 1982, total savings were composed of 7.5% as share drafts, 38.0% as certificates, and 51.0% as regular share savings and 3.5% as money market accounts. A year earlier, share savings were 63.3% and certificates accounted for 30.0%. This trend away from the traditional share accounts will continue over the coming years. Indeed, the Credit Union National Association has predicted that by 1986 the traditional savings share account may supply only 25% of total savings to the industry. The inevitable result of such a major shift in funds sources will be a higher cost level of funds to the industry.

In late 1981, federal credit unions were empowered to raise their ceilings on share accounts from 7 to 12 %, but few were able to raise their interest on savings to such a degree. In 1982, credit unions were relieved of any rate restrictions so that the boards of each individual credit union are free to decide whether or not it can afford to pay any rate level. This freedom to raise rates on savings had maintained the savings growth of the industry and made it possible for the industry to have a favorable flow of funds during a period of general financial uncertainty. Previous forms of regulations, including usury laws and rate ceilings, had prohibited credit unions from competing aggressively against the new forms of financial services offering higher rates on savings. This is no longer the case. Indeed, the credit union industry has been given more freedom in rate making than any other depository institution. Usury laws were modified in 1980 and 1981. By the end of 1981 the NCUA was proposing the elimination of all rate controls and restrictions and this was implemented in 1982. The result is that the credit union industry is in a position to compete very effectively in the national marketplace for funds and in committing these funds to the market.

The decline in loan ratios at credit unions and the consequent rising liquidity ratios were very noteworthy events of the 1980-1983 period. Loans outstanding as a percent of savings stood at 90.9% at the end of 1979, 74.2% at year-end 1980, and 60% in early 1983. Relatively low loan demands for consumer credit in the nation and the higher rates being charged for credit brought about these very low ratios. In addition, the relatively favorable inflow of savings to the credit union industry is also an integral part of the downward shift in the loan to savings ratio. A marked increase in consumer financing by the finance companies since 1980 has also impacted upon credit union lending. But as consumer credit demand rises nationwide the loan to savings ratios will improve in the credit union industry.

REGULATORY AND GENERAL CHANGES IN 1981-1982

Deregulation has been the mainstay of the National Credit Union Administration in recent months. Chairman Edward F. Callahan successfully pushed for comprehensive deregulation in 1982, particularly on rates on both the demand and supply sides of funds for the industry. One result is to place much more responsibility upon individual credit unions to determine the needs of their membership and develop those tools or programs to meet these needs. In a period of heavy disintermediation in many savings institutions in 1981-1982 credit unions attracted savings and the liquidity of the industry was maintained. The fact that the industry is not bound by the decisions of the Depository Institutions Deregulation Committee has given the industry much more flexibility as competitors for funds in the national market. In addition, the Monetary Control Act of 1980 requirement that all depository institutions maintain some level of reserve with the Federal Reserve System has not been implemented for any institution with deposits under $2 million. This is likely to become a permanent exemption and it will prevent the vast majority of individual credit unions from having to maintain such reserves.

The National Credit Union Administration began a program of decentralization of its own structure in 1982. Regional directors were given more authority and the central staff was reduced in an effort to place more operating responsibility and decision making at the regional levels. Issues of supervision, merging, and chartering will presumably be resolved more readily as a result of the more streamlined administrative structure.

The number of credit unions had declined over the past several years through mergers and liquidations. Some mergers are initiated by individual credit union boards to improve their services to members, while other mergers result from an inability to remain self-supporting. Other credit unions are liquidated due to their inability to remain viable financial institutions. In certain mergers and liquidations financial assistance is rendered by the National Credit Union Share Insurance Fund.

Federally-insured mergers were 313 in 1980 and 333 in 1981. For the 1975-1981 period, federally-insured mergers totaled 1,620.[14] The number of federally-insured credit unions liquidated totaled 239 in 1980, and 251 in 1981. During fiscal 1981, the federal insurance expenses in mergers and liquidations totaled $39.7 million, the heaviest cost factor in history. Share insurance through NCUSIF continues to grow in both absolute and relative terms. In 1973, for example, 62.7% of total credit unions were insured; in 1981, the percentage had risen to 80.3%. The increase in total coverage results from state chartered credit unions electing or being legislatively required to obtain federal share insurance. Approximately 14.6 of credit unions in 1980 had insurance through state-chartered insurance corporations of one type or another. Very few credit unions now operate without share insurance.

The NCUSIF did have significantly greater losses in 1981 and 1982. In September 1981, the fund balance was $174.8 million to insure $58.2 billion in savings. This relatively small fund will be expanded in coming years through additional premiums to the insured associations. In 1982, the NCUA announced its intention to raise the insurance fund to a level of one percent of the total insured savings. The anticipated loss of some $20 million by some 150 credit unions holding jumbo certificates of Penn Square Bank of Oklahoma City in 1982 contributed to the move by the NCUA to increase its premiums to the insured credit unions.

Chairman Callahan of NCUA announced in May a drive to charter additional credit unions by bringing the benefits of credit union services to corporate managements. While the number of credit unions have been declining through mergers and liquidations, the industry is endeavoring to maintain its positive posture of growth and service. New charters are an essential part of such a posture, along with an accelerated effort to recruit as active members a larger proportion of the potential membership in existing credit unions. In 1981, NCUA

[13] CUNA, *Executive,* Spring, 1983.
[14] NCUSIF, *Annual Financial Report,* Fiscal year 1981, March 1982.

estimated that only 56.9% of potential membership were active members in federally-insured credit unions.

STRUCTURAL AND COMPETITIVE PROBLEMS

Comment has been made earlier in this study on the historical aspects of the credit union movement in the United States and how its structure and operations evolved through the years. Despite the many changes in structure which have occurred the basic doctrines of the cooperative movement remain today. Therein lies many of the strengths of the industry along with some of its problems as it looks to the future.

Credit unions have enjoyed the advantages of short term lending practices during the hectic period of interest rate volatility in 1979-1982. The traditional field of consumer credit has given the credit union industry the capability of adjusting the maturities of its loans over time as well as rate adjustments to the degree usury ceilings were raised or eliminated. In the 1979-1982 period credit unions felt put upon by the growth of money market funds in much the same way as other financial institutions have objected to credit unions in earlier periods. That is, the feeling that money market funds have had few restrictions placed upon their activities giving them specific advantages over the established depository institutions.

As a primary consumer savings and lending institution, the credit union is particularly vulnerable to the competitive effects of the operations of national retail and brokerage firms. To the extent that the public accepts the doctrine that credit unions do in fact best represent consumer interests the industry can withstand many of these competitive factors. The fact that the modern credit union industry can now provide regular savings, share draft programs, savings certificates, credit cards, direct deposit of funds, individual retirement accounts and other financial services places the industry in a position to remain highly competitive. The further advantages of payroll deduction and other financial services among the groups with occupational common bonding remains a major consideration. In addition, the fact that the industry is regulated by an agency (NCUA) charged with the responsibility to promote its interests is a valuable consideration.

The credit union industry cannot be considered as simply another depository institution because of its cooperative nature. The industry is based upon the broad concepts of mutuality, democracy, and a strong concern for members in financial education and counseling. Common bonding requirements makes start-up and survival of individual credit union associations more difficult but they do provide the basic rationale for the industry itself. If credit unions were like all other financial institutions, it would be impossible to defend such things as its tax exempt status. But their common bond requirements, their nonprofit nature, their employee relationships, and their relatively small size do set credit unions aside from other segments of the financial services industry. In terms of size, for example, more than 85% of the associations are under $5 million in assets. About 90% of the associatons are occupationally related in some way. Such factors taken together with the traditions of the credit union movement for generations suggest that credit union managements are facing many problems in adjusting to and surviving and growing in a complex national money market with a dynamism unknown in earlier periods. Therein lies the major challenge to credit union managment.

PROSPECTIVE STRUCTURAL CHANGES

The common bonding requirements through general interpretation have been liberalized through time. The mobility of the work force and the general population, the changing investment and productive patterns of industry, the rapid technological changes and transportation improvements impacting financial services, and the ready availability of these services in several forms to almost all segments of the population have led to less cohesiveness in the common bonding groups as visualized by the founders of the credit union movement in the United States. The promotional efforts of the credit union leadership through the years resulted in a very large number of credit unions being organized. Many of those founded were not financially feasible for one reason or another but the numbers remaining are quite large (some 20,000). Most of these are still very small in size and operate with a minimal amount of professional management. Organization along employment lines has always been far easier to accomplish and dominates the U. S. credit union industry but thought is being given to promoting associations on other bases.

Recent chairmen of the NCUA have promoted the concept of chartering credit unions on a community basis.[15] The issue revolved around the loss of sponsors as certain plants closed or were relocated. NCUA guidelines adopted in 1980 held that communities should gen-

[15] Lawrence Connell, *NCUA Review,* May 1981.

Table 7-6 Basic Changes in Credit Unions in the United States
January 1981-May 1982

	January 1981	December 1981	May 1982
Number of Operating Credit Unions	21,421	20,814	20,426
Federal	12,417	12,038	11,759
State	9,004	8,776	8,667
Number of Members (thousands)	43,881	45,333	45,931
Federal	24,608	25,514	25,873
State	12,273	19,819	20,058
Total Assets ($ millions)	$72,298	$77,682	$82,858
Federal	39,461	42,382	45,077
State	32,837	35,300	37,781
Loans Outstanding ($ millions)	$47,499	$50,449	$49,556
Federal	25,980	27,458	27,073
State	22,519	23,090	22,483
Savings ($ millions)	$65,285	$68,871	$73,602
Federal Shares	35,902	37,574	40,213
State Shares and Deposits	29,383	31,297	33,389
Average Savings Per Member	$ 1,488	$ 1,520	$ 1,602
Federal Shares	1,459	1,473	1,554
State Shares and Deposits	1,525	1,580	1,665
Loan-to-Share Ratio	74.3	73.3	67.3
Federal	74.2	73.1	67.3
State	76.7	73.5	67.3
Monthly Repayments as Percent of Loans Outstanding			
Federal	6.4	5.5	5.0
State	5.3	7.0	5.8

*As estimated by National Credit Union Administration.
Source: N.C.U.A., *Credit Union Statistics.*

erally fall within a population range of 1,000 to 25,000 and that credit unions might be permitted to convert to community charters if a strong common bond of interest can be shown. Many requests for conversion to community-based charters have been turned down although there is now far more receptivity to such requests than in the past.

The leadership thrust toward increasing the proportion of community based charters from the present 4% level to a significantly higher one is not without its critics both within and without the industry. Commercial banks have been the most vehement among the groups opposing community based credit unions because all persons residing within the prescribed geographic bounds are eligible to become members, both as savers as well as borrowers. Existing credit unions within a given community also become fearful of a loss of potential membership to the more broadly based community credit union. But perhaps the most general fear of credit union managements is that community chartering to any significant degree may open the door for general taxation of the industry.

Credit unions with a declining field of membership due to plant closings or relocations are the ones most likely to seek a conversion of charter from occupational to community-based associations. The expanded and more diversified field of membership resulting from such conversions appear to have many advantages to management but there are associated disadvantages as well. The occupational credit union converting to a community based charter will lose the advantages of payroll deductions as well as the physical facilities which may have been supplied by the sponsoring organization. Members may expect more financial services and more diversified borrowing opportunities since the community credit union will be competing directly with other financial institutions. Debt deliquencies may also rise as the sense of common bonding may be reduced and the concern of members for one another may be diminished. From such considerations one may conclude that community based credit unions is not likely to provide an effective alternative to many credit unions as long as the basic concepts and operating philosophy of the industry is maintained.

In a more general vein credit union structural changes which will continue to evolve at a rather rapid pace will include more involvement with corporate centrals and central associations as a means of providing more specialized services and liquidity management. The management of credit unions will become more specialized to provide more effective asset and liability management techniques and credit management procedures and decisions. As credit unions grow in size such changes become more feasible. It appears that such growth will occur both through the natural forces of growth of the industry as well as through consolidations and mergers of many of the smaller credit unions. The result will be a much larger credit union industry in terms of financial assets but with far fewer operating credit unions. The largest Federal credit union at the end of 1982—The Navy Federal Credit Union—had assets of $1,087 million; the largest state credit union in 1982—State Employees of North Carolina—had assets of $600 million. While credit unions may not be expected to attain the size levels of commercial banks and savings banks in the United States, it is obvious that the industry is proceeding to a point that large credit unions will not be unusual and that the average size of credit unions will be some multiple of present levels.

The credit union industry must implement those measures which will keep it competitive for the savings of an older membership with higher educational and income levels. Not only must the funds be made available but more members must be attracted through easy access to credit and for routine savings by the membership. Strong competitive factors will persist both on the supply of funds and the demand for loans. Structural changes and growth should make such adaptations by the industry more feasible.

CREDIT UNION INDUSTRY PROSPECTS

The inherent strengths of the cooperative credit union movement have been set forth in the preceding materials of this study. Rapid growth rates, growing levels of sophistication in management and financial services, expanded legal and regulatory empowerments, Federal insurance and liquidity measures, and a general thrust of households to utilize financial intermediaries for their savings and as a source of consumer credit all portend a bright future for the credit union industry. But the industry is not without its problems. The deregulation thrusts of the Monetary Control Act of 1980 and the Garn-St Germain Act of 1982 are reducing some of the competitive advantages of credit unions. As other institutions are freed from interest rate controls on savings instruments, the credit union industry will lose some of its rate advantages. Although these acts did expand the powers of credit unions, other depository institutions were also accorded expanded powers. These movements will result in more and more competitive pressures in the local and national markets to which credit unions must have effective responses. One area in which the industry may have particular problems responding is that of electronic technology due to the initial high costs of implementation.

The response of the credit union industry to the financial pressures of the national markets in 1979-1982 was generally favorable. Credit union growth rates slowed, lending declined, and industry liquidity increased. The fact that the industry did not have to buy a majority of its funds in the volatile certificate markets helped keep down its costs of funds. Gradual relief on usury ceilings allowed most credit unions to raise their lending rates, thereby permitting a favorable "spread" on funds used. The absence of a heavy commitment to long-term mortgages by the industry made possible a much more satisfactory adjustment to market rate variations. Credit union managements are now sensitized to the needs of careful "spread management" in funds committed in their markets and should be able to cope with similar conditions in the future.

More effective management may be anticipated within the industry. Growth in size and growth in full-time managers will contribute to this end. Educational programs and management assistance are becoming more and more available through state and national associations. Supervisory agencies are more capable of providing guidance and assistance to the individual associations. In the process, the credit decisions of the industry should be improved along with collection techniques and procedures. With careful attention to improvements in all operating procedures, with more effective cost controls, and with better collection procedures the overall required spread between the costs of funds and the rates earned thereon should be narrowed. All in all, the not-for-profit credit union industry must make its operating decisions on the same basis as organizations comprising the profit economy. Funds procurement and loan decisons must be on the same basis since credit unions operate in the same arena. This fact still represents a significant dilemma for many managements and members in the industry but it must be resolved in a positive manner for significant long-term growth to occur.

In spite of these and other problem areas confronting the credit union industry in the United States, the industry's future must be regarded as favorable. The many advantages of the credit union movement will not soon disappear. Member interest and loyalties will persist, sponsor interests and political support will continue, and the momentum gained by an industry with 47 million members assure a positive growth pattern for the future. Reduced restrictions and regulations should better enable the industry to adjust to the modern financial marketplace. As the industry improves and expands its member services, as it moves toward more effective pricing of its funds and develops more interest-rate sensitive assets and liabilities, the credit union industry will move ahead. In the absence of political and tax restraints in the future, the modern credit union industry will remain a true growth sector in the nation's financial markets. As a result the consumer services available from the thousands of credit union associations to their members will be even more available than at present as the role of the credit union industry becomes more prominent in the nation.

The industry is being propelled toward becoming more and more like a general food store rather than a specialized delicatessen. The smaller credit unions will endeavor to remain in their more traditional roles, but the larger ones have already decided to move into a more aggressive stance in the total financial marketplace. These conflicting objectives will no doubt provide many of the problems confronting the industry during the next decade.

REFERENCES

I. Books

1. Bergengren, Roy F. *Credit Union North America,* New York, Southern Printing, Inc., 1940.
2. Clements, Muriel. *By Their Bootstraps: A History of the CU Movement in Saskatchewan,* Toronto, Clarke, Irwin and Co., 1965.
3. Croteau, John T. *The Federal Credit Union,* New York, Harper and Bros., 1956.
4. ——. *The Economics of the Credit Union,* Detroit, Wayne State, University Press, 1963.
5. *Consumer Credit in the United States, Report of the National Commission on Consumer Finance,* Washington, U. S. Government Printing Office, 1972.
6. Dublin, Jack. *Credit Union: Theory and Practice,* 2nd ed., Detroit, Wayne State University, 1971.
7. Filene, Edward Albert. *Speaking of Change,* Kingsport, Tenn., Kingsport Press, 1939.
8. Flannery, Mark J. *An Analysis of Credit Unions,* Federal Reserve Bank of Boston, Research Report No. 54, 1974.
9. Melvin, Donald J., Davis, Raymond N. and Fischer, Gerald C. *Credit Unions and the Credit Union Industry: A Study of the Powers, Organization, Regulation and Competition,* New York, New York Institute of Finance, 1977.
10. Moody, J. Carroll and Fite, Gilbert C. *The Credit Union Movement: Origins and Development, 1850-1970,* Lincoln, University of Nebraska, 1971.
11. Shapiro, Eli. *Credit Union Development in Wisconsin,* New York, Columbia University Press, 1947.
12. Tucker, Donald S. *The Evolution of People's Banks,* New York, Columbia University Press, 1972.
13. Wilson, Charles Morrow. *Common Sense Credit: Credit Unions Come of Age,* Devin-Adair Co., 1962.

II. Articles

1. Black, Harold and Robert H. Dugger, "Credit Union Structure, Growth and Regulatory Problems," *Journal of Finance,* 36 (May 1981), pp. 529-538.
2. Brockschmidt, Peggy, "Credit Union Growth in Perspective," Federal Reserve Bank of Kansas City *Monthly Review,* February 1977, 3-13.
3. Burke, Jack, "Credit Unions: Past, Present, Future," *Banking,* 68: 42-44, September 1976.

4. Cargill, Thomas T., "Recent Research on Credit Unions: A Survey," *Papers in Business and Economics,* No. 76-3, University of Nevado, Reno, 1976.

5. Duke, R. A., Jr., "Lending to Lenders, A Look at Lending to Credit Unions," *Journal of Commercial Bank Lending,* 62:11-22, June 1980.

6. Edmonds, C. P. and R. B. Rogow, "Credit Unions Move Into the Home Mortgage Market," *Real Estate Review* 9 (Spring 1979), pp. 31-34.

7. Edwards, D. G. and Sweikanshas, C. D., "Credit Unions and S & L's, A Comparison," *Federal Home Loan Bank Board Journal,* 11:7-11, July 1978.

8. Fry, Clifford L., Charles P. Harper and Stanley R. Stansell, "An Analysis of Credit Union Costs: A New Approach to Analyzing Costs of Financial Institutions," *Journal of Bank Research,* Winter 1982, pp. 239-249.

9. Kidwell, David S. and Petersen, Richard J., "A Close Look at Credit Unions," Boston, *Bankers Magazine,* 161:71-80, January 1978.

10. Koot, R. S., "On Economies of Scale in Credit Unions," *Journal of Finance,* 33:1087-94, September 1978.

11. Navratil, Frank J., "An Aggregate Model of the Credit Union Industry," *Journal of Finance,* 36 (May 1981), 539-549.

12. Polner, Walter, "Credit Unions in Wisconsin: Looking at the 1970s," *Marquette University Business Review,* Vol. 15, No. 3, Fall 1970, pp. 133-43.

13. Pugh, Olin S., "Credit Unions: From Consumer Movement to National Market Force," Boston, *Bankers Magazine,* 163:19-27, January 1980.

14. Taylor, Ryland A., "The Demand for Credit Union Shares," *Journal of Financial and Quantitative Analysis* (June 1972), 1749-1756.

15. Von der Ohe, Robert, "Forecasting and Matching," *Impact,* Credit Union National Association, Madison, Wisconsin, 1981.

16. Wolken, John D. and Frank J. Navratil, Economies of Scale in Credit Unions: Further Evidence," *Journal of Finance,* 35 (June 1980), 769-777.

17. Wolken, John D. and Frank J. Navratil, "The Economic Impact of the Federal Credit Union Usury Ceiling," *Journal of Finance,* 36 (December 1981), pp. 1157-1168.

III. Administrative and Associations

1. Credit Union National Association, Inc., *Comparative Digest of Credit Union Acts, 1981,* Robert W. Davis, editor, Madison, Wisconsin, 1981.

2. ———. *Legislative History of the Federal Credit Union Act,* Robert W. Davis, editor, Madison, Wisconsin, 1981.

3. ———. *The Credit Union Yearbook,* Madison, Wisconsin, various years.

4. ———. *Credit Union Magazine,* Madison, Wisconsin, various issues.

5. ———. *Credit Union Executive,* Madison, Wisconsin, various issues.

6. ———. *1977-1978 CUNA National Member Survey,* Madison, Wisconsin, June 1978.

7.   ——. *White Paper on Federal Reserve Interface*, Madison, Wisconsin, May 1980.

8.   ——. *1980 Credit Union Operating Ratios and Spreads*, Madison, Wisconsin, January 1982.

9.   National Credit Union Administration, *Annual Report of the NCUA*, Washington, various years.

10.   ——. *The Federal Credit Union Act*, Washington, 1980.

11.   ——. *Chartering and Organizing Manual for Federal Credit Unions*, Washington, 1980.

12.   ——. *State Chartered Credit Union Annual Report*, Washington, various years.

13.   ——. *The NCUA Review*, Washington, various issues.

14.   ——. *Central Liquidity Facility Annual Report for the Fiscal 1981*, Washington, December 1981.

15.   ——. *Regulatory Alert*. Washington, March 4, 1982.

Index